The Enemy's House Divided

THE ENEMY'S HOUSE DIVIDED

Charles de Gaulle

Translated, Annotated, and with an

Introduction by Robert Eden

THE UNIVERSITY OF NORTH CAROLINA PRESS

Chapel Hill and London

© 2002 The University of North Carolina Press
All rights reserved
Manufactured in the United States of America
Set in Charter and Bell Gothic
by Tseng Information Systems, Inc.
The paper in this book meets the guidelines for permanence
and durability of the Committee on Production Guidelines for
Book Longevity of the Council on Library Resources.

Ouvrage publié avec l'aide du Ministère français
chargé de la culture—Centre national du livre.
This work has been published with the assistance of
the French Ministry of Culture's National Book Center.

Library of Congress Cataloging-in-Publication Data
Gaulle, Charles de, 1890–1970.
[Discorde chez l'ennemi. English]
The enemy's house divided / by Charles de Gaulle; translated,
annotated, and with an introduction by Robert Eden.
    p. cm.
Includes bibliographical references and index.
ISBN 0-8078-2666-9 (cloth: alk. paper)
1. Germany. Heer—History—World War, 1914–1918.   2. World
War, 1914–1918—Germany.   3. Germany—Politics and
government—1871–1918.   4. Military art and science—
Germany—History—20th century.   5. Strategy—History—
20th century.   I. Eden, Robert.   II. Title.
D531 .G3313   2002
940.54'1343—dc21   2002005326
cloth   06 05 04 03 02   5 4 3 2 1

To the

firefighters and policemen

who died in New York City

on September 11, 2001

Contents

Figures

Acknowledgments

This translation has been a long conversation with de Gaulle, in which exceptional friends and colleagues have generously taken part. At the beginning, I would not have dared to hope for such a distinguished translating team. Doing justice to what each has contributed may not be possible, because the threads have become so thoroughly interwoven, over many revisions. My first purpose here is to give them the prominent place they deserve in this book. It is a tribute to de Gaulle's thought, that individuals of such quality were willing to give their best to make it available in English, with only the reader's gratitude and mine for reward.

Frederic Fransen completed his doctoral work at the University of Chicago's Committee on Social Thought in 1996, under the French historian François Furet. His principal field is nineteenth- and twentieth-century European political thought; his first book is *The Supranational Politics of Jean Monnet* (Westport, Conn.: Greenwood, 2001). Now a senior fellow at Liberty Fund, Inc., he is currently writing a comparative history of nineteenth-century European liberalism. His thorough critique of the translation saved it from numerous errors, and his judicious comments, particularly on ongoing controversies in World War I historiography, guided my judgment about points the annotations should clarify and issues the Introduction should address.

Some of the most intransigent difficulties were presented by technical terms. Insofar as the English of this translation conveys de Gaulle's military French correctly, it is due to Major David Lasalle, military attaché at the United States Embassy in Paris. In the course of his careful reading, he also came up with felicitous renderings for several of de Gaulle's subtler remarks on military-civilian relations and diplomacy. My friend Ken Masugi, Lasalle's colleague at the Air Force Academy, did me a great favor in seeking him out for the task.

De Gaulle's style in this work is for the most part direct and matter-of-fact. However, even in this less rhetorical, early book, the translator should be alert to de Gaulle's extraordinary ear for words that echo with older connotations. I was very fortunate to have two friends who were able to help me with this challenge, as well as with more common problems of translation. One was Herbert J. Izzo, professor emeritus of the University of Calgary, who received B.A., B.S., M.A., and Ph.D. degrees from the University of Michigan in historical linguistics and comparative Romance linguistics. He did additional studies in Mexico, New Mexico, and Italy, and has taught at the University of Arizona, San Jose State University, Stanford University, and the University of Michigan. The other was Olga F. Koutna-Izzo, who received her B.A. in French and Latin in Czechoslovakia, where she taught for several years. After moving to Canada, she earned her M.A. in linguistics and a Ph.D. in French and Romance linguistics at the University of Calgary. She has taught at the University of Calgary and Hillsdale College and is now on the faculty of Ave Maria College in Ypsilanti, Michigan.

A good colleague, Dr. Jerry Fallon, wisely urged me to show my first draft to a Hillsdale neighbor from France; this proved to be invaluable advice. Solange Roberts was raised in the Suez Canal Zone; her father directed the Canal Authority until the war over Suez in 1956, when the family returned to France. She has been associated with Hillsdale College since 1976. Her love of her native language and of good English have been a constant inspiration to me. She studied my draft in painstaking detail, comparing *La Discorde chez l'ennemi* line by line. She also brought it to the attention of her sister, Madame Patricia Percival, Minister for French Veterans of Foreign Wars Living Abroad, and a member of the Fondation de Gaulle, whose warm encouragement and timely support did much to advance the project. Madame Percival was decorated for the Legion of Honor, in Paris, on June 14, 2001. Together, these two cultivated Frenchwomen have been guardian angels to this edition. It owes a great deal to their lively admiration of de Gaulle, and I hope it meets their high standards.

Alexander Shtromas graduated from Moscow University Law School and was a prominent legal scholar in several Soviet research institutes before placing his expertise at the service of Andrei Sakharov's dissidence. Expelled from the Soviet Union in 1972, he taught at the University of Salford in Great Britain, the University of Chicago, Boston College, and Assumption College before joining the Department of History and Political Science at Hillsdale College in 1989. Famous throughout Eastern Europe as an indefatigable enemy of tyranny and a scholar of prodigious learning, Alex was also an amazing linguist. In 1997, he took time from more urgent and timely projects of his own to help me translate de Gaulle's French more precisely. Alex Shtromas died of cancer in 1998, leaving a place no one can fill.

I owe a special debt of gratitude to Daniel J. Mahoney, whose excellent work on de Gaulle persuaded me that I should study the *Mémoires de guerre* in depth, and thus launched the inquiry that led to this translation. I have drawn strength from his friendship throughout the project. It would not have been nearly so fruitful or so instructive without Dan's steady reinforcement: his common sense, his exemplary appropriation of the moral and political traditions of the West, his staunch defense of the most serious citizens of our time, and his constant attention to France.

In revising the Introduction, I benefited from the astute criticism of my Hillsdale colleagues Will Morrisey, Mickey Craig, and Marie-Claire Morellec; and my debt to Morrisey's books on de Gaulle and Malraux are also reflected in it. Robert K. Faulkner's thorough, exacting reading led to many stylistic improvements and to a general tightening; his enthusiasm for de Gaulle's book also refreshed me at a crucial time in writing the Introduction. Paul Rahe's suggestions on an early draft prompted major improvements. So did the valuable suggestions of Samuel Williamson. My wife Anne read draft after draft with great patience, and her powerful response to its story assured me, amidst a sea of troubles, that I was on the right course.

I am grateful to the staff of the Map Collection of Harvard University, who patiently helped to me to use their quite splendid computer equipment and maps, and taught me how to organize cartographic information for the maps that accompany Chapter 1. The staff of Allan Cartography of Medford, Oregon, is primarily responsible for the excellence of these panels. The founder of the company, Stuart Allan, gave the translation a careful reading to improve its English, and then undertook the map work. Since our friendship goes back to 1960, when we were freshmen at Reed College, working with Stuart on this has been especially satisfying, and rejuvenating. Curt Shaffer did the drafting and computer work, much of it on weekends; his fine craftsmanship has been a delight throughout our collaboration.

A research grant from the Earhart Foundation made it possible to bring this work to completion in a timely fashion. In 2000–2001, I was privileged to be a visiting scholar at Harvard University; my thanks to the Government Department, to the staff of Widener Library, and above all to Professor Harvey C. Mansfield, for putting the great resources of the university at my disposal.

Over the years, several summer research grants and a sabbatical grant from Hillsdale College have supported my work on de Gaulle. Thanks for special help along the way go to Robert Blackstock, provost of Hillsdale College; and to John Willson, Mickey Craig, and Thomas Conner, each of whom chaired my division during the work. Judy Leising did yeoman service in securing materials through interlibrary loan; and our secretaries, Carol Kratzer and Denise Nivison, were of great assistance.

Much of the credit for the quality of this edition is due to the referees for the University of North Carolina Press, whose critiques and suggestions I have adopted in their entirety. Thanks also to the staff of the press and to the member of their Board of Governors, fluent in French, whose detailed report helped improve the translation. I am especially grateful to Kathy Malin, who supervised me with unflappable professional poise through the final editing. Her excellent judgment and fine taste led to great improvement in my Introduction, to an elegant integration of the map-figures with the text in Chapter 1, and to the countless corrections in detail which make or break a book of this kind.

Finally, a word about marriage. No one who has not raised a child with severe disabilities can know the virtues it requires; films like *Lorenzo's Oil,* valuable as they are, give us only an inkling. Everything depends on the mother, especially when the father is preoccupied with teaching and scholarship, as I have been. My wife Anne has been my unfailing intellectual companion and moral anchor, while raising our son Joshua to health and maturity. She has pioneered successful methods for overcoming the obstacles that autism imposed on Joshua; while medical science could offer neither accurate diagnosis nor remedies, yet doctors persisted, to cover their ignorance, in the vile practice of blaming the mother. De Gaulle directed that the proceeds from his *War Memoirs* should go to the Fondation Anne de Gaulle. If this edition deserves any honor or appreciation, it should go to my Anne. She has earned it several times over.

Translator's Note

The first goal of this edition was to achieve an English rendition so accurate and so faithful that de Gaulle's *La Discorde chez l'ennemi* would not have to be translated again. In the very few instances where no adequate equivalent could be found, a translator's note on the French has been provided.

The second goal was to bring de Gaulle's book into the English-speaking world in a form that would reflect de Gaulle's intentions and his adherence to the very highest standards of excellence, as a scholar and teacher. In some measure this required that the book be issued as de Gaulle would have issued it today. A scholar of de Gaulle's seriousness, writing today, would give a citation for every passage he quoted and would provide more elaborate bibliographic references, so it seemed appropriate to supply these, if I possibly could. Many of the editor's notes are of this character. In a few instances, such citations have been added to de Gaulle's notes, in editorial brackets.

De Gaulle supplied footnotes wherever he thought his colleagues and contemporaries would need them for clarity. Since the events of the war were still fresh in memory, and kept alive by burning controversies, de Gaulle offered few notes. Readers today will need many more, just to follow his inquiry. Hence, this edition is annotated more elaborately than the original.

For kindred reasons, it seemed worthwhile to supply diagrams to help the lay reader follow the "technical" accounts of military events given in Chapter 1, where de Gaulle's bona fides as a professor of military history are most in evidence. There were no maps or diagrams in the original. However, one of de Gaulle's predecessors at St.-Cyr, the prolific Henri Bonnal, had published substantial studies of two German victories to which de Gaulle compares the German defeat at the Marne (in Chapter 1). Bonnal's maps correspond closely to de Gaulle's account; I strongly suspect that he deliberately built upon General Bonnal's work and meant French commanders to recall these maps. Figures 2a–c and 3a–d draw heavily on the information in Bonnal's maps to illustrate de

Gaulle's argument. Finding no such privileged source on the first Battle of the Marne, I based Figures 4a–e on plates in a wide variety of studies published during or just after the Great War. The sources are cited where the figures appear. It is my hope that de Gaulle will forgive my presumption in making these additions; and that they will make the book welcome to serious readers wherever English is spoken.

The French edition on which the translation is based is Charles de Gaulle, *La Discorde chez l'ennemi* (Paris: Plon, 1924). Because the work circulated in this version for much of de Gaulle's lifetime, from its publication in 1924 until his death in 1970, it is widely accepted by de Gaulle scholars as satisfactory to his own high standards. I have not, therefore, gone behind it in quest of manuscript versions.

Introduction

The reader who opens this slender book may be surprised to find so much high-caliber historical scholarship, political science, and practical good sense concentrated between its covers. The discovery may also make one wonder how many such treasures we have lost. For de Gaulle's study of the First World War has been hidden from our view for most of the twentieth century. Buried by an avalanche of political and civilizational catastrophes, which kept de Gaulle and his potential readers focused on more urgent business, *The Enemy's House Divided* has been unknown in the English-speaking world, for all practical purposes, until the appearance of this translation. Lest the occasion be missed, I have supplied a longer-than-usual introduction, to help the reader get acquainted with the book, to give it a fighting chance to become well-known, and to establish its place more swiftly among the classics of our political and philosophic tradition.

The Enemy's House Divided seeks to identify the internecine causes of the collapse of the German war effort in 1918 and of the subsequent dissolution of the German Empire. The German people had shown astonishing energy and discipline on all fronts. Through four years of gruesome warfare and starvation, they held themselves together and responded with amazing vigor in every adversity. To all appearances, the Wilhelmine Empire was a prodigiously effective political entity, capable of concerted action on the grandest scale. Then, in 1918, after sustaining every previous strain, all the ligaments gave way. To explain this sudden collapse of morale and social discipline, de Gaulle concentrates upon the principal men in authority, whose duty it had been to honor and strengthen those ties. According to his account, they had not passively suffered these moral bonds to be destroyed. To the contrary, they had themselves—on and by their own initiatives—severed the crucial ligaments. They seemed to have taken this course with their eyes open. And because their attitude manifestly defied common sense, de Gaulle invites us to wonder why these redoubtable men undertook such dubious initiatives.

De Gaulle argues that their refusal of duty resulted from their convictions. Contingency, accident, and force play the dominant part in war, according to de Gaulle; but this particular fiasco was rather an outcome of reflection, character, and choice. He introduces us brusquely to the debate about responsibility that had galvanized "all thinking Germany" during the decades before the war. De Gaulle contends that the younger generation of German military officers had already taken sides in this great prewar *querelle de l'homme,* or argument over humanity.[1] Thus his work on the German debacle was not simply a professional historian's assessment of recent military events. *The Enemy's House Divided* dwells on the philosophical initiative that decisively influenced German military and political conduct. According to de Gaulle, the Great War—like some massive shift of the earth's tectonic plates—triggered the dynamite of Nietzsche's radical teaching. It magnified the impact of his powerfully persuasive writing and brought the moral consequences of his thought to light in the actions of the German officers. De Gaulle conceived his first book—and with it, introduced his statesmanship to the world—as a deliberate and studied response to Nietzsche's catastrophic philosophical initiative.

In due course we shall clarify these claims and make good on them. The part that de Gaulle's first book was intended to play in the quarrel will become evident as we review how it came to be written, beginning when the young Captain de Gaulle, seriously wounded and unconscious, was taken captive and transported to a hospital behind the German lines.

▬▬ Prisoner of War

The Enemy's House Divided was the harvest of de Gaulle's internment in Germany during the Great War. Captured in March 1916, he was a prisoner until his final escape in November 1918. Between escape attempts, he worked over German news reports, piecing together what was happening on the battlefields and studying the German political and military leaders. Only later—some six years after the war ended—did these efforts yield the book we have, de Gaulle's analysis of the capital errors that led the Germans to disaster. In the words of his biographer Jean Lacouture, "There in five chapters, was the slowly matured fruit of his thirty-two months of captivity. It was the whole secret mechanism of Germany, brusquely revealed."[2]

In prison, de Gaulle was preoccupied with problems of morale. He was himself endangered by the corrosive melancholy of his grand, stymied ambition. Unable to fight on the battlefield, he was thrown back upon the captive warrior's feud—with the mirror and his combative passions. He sought ways to prevent confinement and enforced inactivity from souring his ardor.[3] Drawing upon "the great library of his memory," he returned to the philosophical moralists he had read and sharpened his own moral insights by writing aperçus in the tradition of Pascal, La Rochefoucauld, Chamfort, Balzac, and Flaubert.[4] One year into his imprisonment he wrote his mother about the quotidian successes his comrades shared with him:

> The winter has definitely ended. Apart from frequent snow flurries, the temperature has become clement. You often ask if I go for walks. Indeed, for at least two hours a day inside the fort. What is most comforting in our situation is the excellent camaraderie that prevails among us, which prevents us from ever being alone in a moral sense.[5]

In prison, spirited men, desperate for action, left "alone in a moral sense," will turn almost inexorably against themselves. It is evident that de Gaulle's efforts to combat this tendency did not dispel his own melancholia. At best, they just kept it at bay. He admitted as much in writing to his mother: "Once again, do not concern yourself at all with my health, which is quite good. For the rest, my situation is of no interest, since I am good for nothing."[6] It was almost unbearable, when his country was fighting for its life, to be immobilized; and de Gaulle was twenty-seven, full of energy and courage. Even the exaltation of victory in 1918 was shadowed by his heartsickness, over an occasion that could not be retrieved:

> Without doubt today the crowning of so much effort is quite close. Once more, after a long road through the night, after a long series of blasted hopes, of numberless illusions shattered, of lethargies furiously conquered, success has smiled on the stronger will! In the immense joy I share with you over these events, it is true that for me there is mingled—more bitterly than ever—the indescribable regret of not having played a better part. It seems to me that this regret will never leave me for the rest of my life.[7]

Although chance had dealt him a paltry part in the French war effort, de Gaulle managed to dominate his regret throughout his imprisonment. He kept it from degrading his character. In the suffocating, constricted role that fell to him, he found duties of considerable scope. Indeed, as we shall see, the very meagerness of his part became a subject of inquiry; in it he discovered stores of strength and inspiration hitherto untapped.

De Gaulle's moral and intellectual strengths had already been recognized, most memorably in a now-famous epitaph. When it appeared that de Gaulle had been killed (rather than merely wounded) in the Battle of Verdun—at Douaumont—Colonel Philippe Pétain had been obliged, as his commanding officer, to submit an obituary report:

> Captain de Gaulle, commanding the company, reputed for his high intellectual and moral quality, while his battalion, undergoing a frightful bombardment, was decimated and while the enemies were pressing the company on all sides, led his men in a furious assault and fierce hand-to-hand fighting, the only solution he considered compatible with his sentiment of military honor. Fell in the fray. A peerless officer in all respects.[8]

Yet, disposed as he was to a certain moral seriousness, perhaps de Gaulle had not coordinated his faculties in quite this way before his capture. He took the restraints imposed by the prisoner-of-war camp as a goad to reflection and moral action. *The Enemy's House Divided* amply testifies to the fecundity of the peculiar moral experiences he went through in this desert. De Gaulle sought to locate the moral center of prison life and to work outward from it in defining his duties. As one traces the course of his reflections, from his prison notebooks to the book he finally wrote, one is struck by the gradual concentration of his thought on this problem: "What is most comforting in our situation is the excellent camaraderie that prevails among us, which prevents us from ever being alone in a moral sense." De Gaulle proved uncommonly intrepid in finding—along paths visible only to his pioneering faculties—ways to prevent his comrades from becoming morally isolated. Two modes of activity that had previously been fairly distinct—the intellectual and the moral—here became more tightly interwoven.

This convergence may become evident if we reflect on a vivid prison portrait that Jean Pouget has drawn, based upon interviews with de Gaulle's fellow prisoners. Let us dwell awhile on this portrait, as if we were standing before it in a museum; I shall point to other exhibits from time to time, to highlight what Pouget's word-painting reveals.

The Germans had sent Captain de Gaulle eastward from the first prison depot in Osnabrück. It appears that while en route, his guards caught him contriving an escape by boat on the Danube. For at the end of April 1916 he was in a remote camp "for retaliation," at Sczuczyn in Lithuania—an old wooden factory converted into a temporary prison.[9] There we take up Pouget's account:

Life at Sczuczyn flowed on like Time—useless, dreary, monotonous. To avoid wasting either, Charles de Gaulle tied himself to a kind of timetable and definite tasks. There were few things to do. Readings were scarce, beyond novels and books of leisure with stained pages, which were passed around from hand to hand. But outside the camp, in the world of free men, the war, on which the fate of the prisoners depended, continued.[10]

De Gaulle took it upon himself to reduce their sense of isolation by enabling the men in his camp to follow the course of the war. Opening a window to actual events in the world was a task of considerable difficulty. The Germans intended to keep the prison sealed off from the Allied armies. However, security proved to be lax:

Through some German soldiers of Alsatian origin, Roederer managed to obtain, from the guardrooms, some local newspapers and old publications that had been confiscated from the Russian dispositions. After the various physical occupations of rising, Captain de Gaulle gathered all the press documents and, installed on his bed, undertook to pluck them bare. The newspapers were not always the latest but each of them contained a scrap of news, or at least conveyed a confirmation, a subject for reflection. De Gaulle methodically analyzed the information, classified it, and worked out his syntheses.[11]

De Gaulle seems to have performed this office in all the camps to which the Germans transferred him. His companion Remy Roure has described him later at Ingolstadt:

. . . often alone, deep in the study of German dailies, noting down his impressions, searching relentlessly in the victory bulletins of the enemy for the barely discernible signs of a turn of the tide, studying the characters of the military and civilian leaders with minute care, looking for weaknesses in their armor.[12]

The disproportion between the poverty of de Gaulle's resources of information in prison and what he was able to do with them is quite striking. Because the Free French represented a great cause, after 18 June 1940, but had almost no resources, such poverty of means was to be a constant theme of his *War Memoirs*.[13] Throughout the Second World War, de Gaulle's capacity to identify the minimal, irreducible strengths on which he could build served him well. But in addition to making him more inventive with very limited means, the prison camp experience crystallized de Gaulle's thinking about the moral dimension of *renseignements,* or military intelligence. As de Gaulle began to understand, for men of action, knowledge is the nucleus of a moral relation, a bond of interdependence. Without means of communicating intelligence, there could be no responsibility or accountability for action. The violation by the German High Command of this essential condition of executive responsibility became a major theme in the first chapter of *The Enemy's House Divided.*[14]

When we left Pouget's account of the Sczuczyn camp, de Gaulle was methodically analyzing the news sources and working out his syntheses:

His solitary reading went on for an hour or two; everyone in the hayloft respected his meditation. Then, his work complete, he raised his head. That was the signal. All the officers in the barrack-room gathered around him to hear the news of the day. It was not a discussion—de Gaulle never took part in discussions—it was an exposition. From the communiqués of the German High Command, which were always much more accurate than the French communiqués, he deduced the intentions of the opposed leaders, toted up the results obtained, gave a measured critique of the doctrines of war. . . .[15]

Under the severe constraints imposed by prison camp, de Gaulle tested what he could accomplish, even with very limited information, through the adroit coordination of analysis and intuition, *esprit géométrique* (geometric spirit) and *esprit de finesse* (spirit of finesse). In Pouget's account of his effort to distinguish serious initiatives from mere feints—conjecturing, probing, comparing accounts—we see de Gaulle submitting to the necessities he later discussed in his essay on "the philosophy of action," *The Edge of the Sword*. These are the necessities imposed by an enemy's capacity for choice:

The action of war in essence assumes the character of contingency. The result that it pursues is relative to the enemy, who is preeminently variable. The enemy can present himself in an infinite number of ways; he disposes of means whose exact force one does not know; he can pursue his intentions along many different paths.[16]

Because of these contingent options, intelligence and analysis alone can seldom adequately anticipate the enemy. Hence, de Gaulle warned against the tendency, especially strong in French strategic thinking, "to abstract systematically from all the variable things, and above all, the enemy."[17] Restrained from such overreaching, reason can play a critical role:

> But if intelligence does not suffice for action, it goes without saying that it plays a part in it. Elaborating in advance the data for the assessment, intelligence clarifies them, makes them precise and reduces the scope for error. The enemy, to be sure, is contingent, variable. No study, no reasoning can disclose with certainty what he is, what he will be, what he is doing and what he is going to do. Nevertheless, intelligence, sensibly sought, ingeniously exploited, can limit the problem to which hypothesis opens pathways. Thus, judgment possesses, in some measure, the solid and defined material that it requires.[18]

For many readers, viewing *The Enemy's House Divided* in retrospect, what will seem most noteworthy is its initial precept: "that in war—save for some essential principles—there is no universal system, but only circumstances and personalities."[19] For this clearly points ahead to de Gaulle's teaching in *The Edge of the Sword*. And several entries in his prison notebooks, under the heading "Undertake the philosophy of action," prove that de Gaulle was at work on this treatise well before he wrote a line of *The Enemy's House Divided*.[20]

One can surely find a wealth of anticipations in this first book, since de Gaulle impressed his forceful character on all his actions and writings. However, much is to be gained from resisting this temptation. While de Gaulle began *The Edge of the Sword* in 1916, he chose to postpone its completion until 1932. He chose to crystallize *The Enemy's House Divided* beforehand. If we try to understand his first book first, we shall be in a better position to understand his subsequent actions and writings as de Gaulle himself conceived them.

I believe de Gaulle intended his account of the German debacle to be both initial and fundamental. *The Enemy's House Divided* was more than incidentally his debut as an author. It is the proper introduction to de

Gaulle's statesmanship; it forms the foundation of his political science and of his philosophy of action.

According to the precept we have just quoted from *The Edge of the Sword,* the primary contingency, the wellspring of contingency, is the enemy. In *The Enemy's House Divided,* the imperative to make the most of what one knows about an enemy is followed out to the limits of de Gaulle's ability. This is the most sustained of de Gaulle's studies of an enemy.

It is also the only work he devoted exclusively to France's traditional German enemy. *The Enemy's House Divided* thus has a certain priority for students of de Gaulle. It is the foundation for everything he wrote in the 1920s and 1930s, in the shadow of German resurgence, and for much of what he said and did after the Nazi victory in June of 1940.

Nor was this just a book about Germany. The Great War of 1914–1918 was the seminal catastrophe of the century, precipitating many subsequent calamities. It has long been a commonplace (endorsed by both Churchill and de Gaulle) that the Second World War was a continuation and consequence of the First. Moreover, as de Gaulle unfolds it, the German debacle of 1918 was the greatest moral disaster ever to befall a modern, civilized political community, before the fall of France in 1940. *The Enemy's House Divided* is a diagnosis of the profound crisis of civilization that unfolded in Germany during World War I. According to de Gaulle, the German military leaders brought that crisis to a head by embracing a radical critique of civilization, a critique of the science and morality by which civilized men had heretofore been guided. As we shall see, he argued that the essential causes of the German defeat were moral: the question the debacle raised was primarily a "moral question." This became a prominent theme of his subsequent thought and action. In 1940, De Gaulle understood the fall of France, above all, as a *moral* catastrophe for the French. The insights and precepts formulated in his later works thus lead us back to de Gaulle's first book, because they are deeply rooted in it.

De Gaulle's Practiced Reserve

To clarify the book's foundational character, let us return to Pouget's passing remark about de Gaulle's style in these prison camp discourses: "It was not a discussion—de Gaulle never took part in discussions—it was an exposition." No doubt this describes his customary distance from his fellow officers. The reader may be jarred by the harsh contrast between de Gaulle's appreciative remark about camaraderie, in his letter to his mother, and the impression of remoteness from his comrades conveyed by his manner. Some comrade! Does this reserve signal the pseudo-aristocratic disdain that Nietzsche encouraged in his readers?—the *hauteur* of Zarathustra's dictum, "Wherever the masses have gone to drink, the fountains are poisoned"?[21] Upon inspection, the evidence supports a subtle (but in practice decisive) moral distinction: de Gaulle's reserve is a sublimation, rather than a denial, of comradely fellow feeling.

An entry from his prison notebook may serve to elucidate this distinction:

> The best method of succeeding in action is to know how to dominate oneself perpetually; or better, this is an indispensable condition.
>
> But dominating oneself ought to have become a sort of habit, a moral reflex, acquired by a constant gymnastic of the will, notably in small things: dress, conversation, conduct of thought, studious and diligent method in all things, notably in work.
>
> One must speak little, one absolutely must. The advantage of being a brilliant talker is not worth a hundredth part that of being retired within oneself, even from the viewpoint of one's general influence. Reflection ought to be concentrated within the man of worth. He does not betray himself outwardly.
>
> And in action, one must say nothing. The chief is he who does not speak.[22]

This 1916 notebook entry leads, by one path, to de Gaulle's treatise on the philosophy of action. He elaborated upon these thoughts in the central chapter of *The Edge of the Sword,* "On Prestige." By a rather different path, it leads to the climactic final chapter of *The Enemy's House Divided.* By tracing both paths in turn, we may reach a clearer view of the nexus between de Gaulle's first book and his later writings and statesmanship.

Paradoxically, these notes on self-control should be understood as social psychology first and only then as ethics for the individual actor. De Gaulle's man of action, like Aristotle's, is preeminently a social or political animal.[23] Although the focus of the passage is the individual "man of character," who is primarily responsible for initiating action, clearly the action de Gaulle has in view is concerted effort requiring the collaboration of many actors. What he says about individual discipline has a social setting in view. It is apt advice for every member of a paramedic unit, an ambulance squad, or a hospital emergency-room team. The "gymnastic" he recommends is obviously deduced from the extraordinary strains that make cooperative work difficult in times of crisis. The moral reflexes to be developed prepare one to work with others under conditions of severe stress, emotional exhaustion, and excitability. Hence the need to discipline all those features of one's appearance that may communicate or suggest extreme emotional states. Because a media anchorman who breaks down on camera may encourage a panic or a stampede, we insist that he take pains to appear reassuringly well groomed, calm, moderate, understated, and unflappable. These practices must be secured so firmly in habit or moral reflex that the gravest news is unable to dislodge them.

While the purpose of de Gaulle's moral gymnastic is emphatically public and social, it is training in mastery over the motions of one's own body and soul. One must undergo an ascetic regimen to strengthen self-command. That regimen should fortify one's capacity to reflect and choose deliberately in emergencies when most will lose their heads, besieged by violent emotions and unfamiliar, seemingly irresistible impulses. Character, as de Gaulle understands it, is a kind of capital. It is a fund of poise and self-command laid up against misfortune. The "man of character" prepares himself to withstand impulse and excitability in the face of accident and force. Habituated to self-mastery, in emergencies he can bring his full faculties to bear and use his professional knowledge and experience effectively in concert with his collaborators.

The meticulous attention to small matters that de Gaulle advised would be ridiculous if it were mere façade:

The systematic reserve practiced by the chieftain makes an impression only if it is perceived as the shield of his decision and ardor. Everyone knows of impassive people who are thought to be sphinxes, for awhile, but soon prove to be imbeciles.[24]

How does one know that it is necessary to prepare in this fashion for the stress of military and political responsibility? In *The Edge of the Sword,* de Gaulle suggests the necessity by an example:

Hoche, who became general-in-chief at twenty-four in an age of rhetoric, quickly learned to be silent. "Matured before his time by habituation to command," a biographer says, "his impetuous fury gave way to a cold dignity and his brilliant words to a laconic language."[25]

This appeal to Hoche's example is suggestive, but also somewhat opaque. We infer that he swiftly learned the dire consequences of breaking his silence; but we need a more articulate accident report to conceive these hardships clearly ourselves, so that we can let such realities work upon us inwardly.[26]

The Enemy's House Divided supplies such a disaster report. In the crisis of military defeat in 1918, the German High Command, the Kaiser, the opinion leaders in the news media, and the political leaders in Parliament all lost their heads and failed to control their tongues, according to de Gaulle. They managed to turn a manageable reverse into a catastrophe that destroyed Germany's governing institutions. He cites the just reproach of a socialist editorial: "Each man should measure his words [before speaking], in high places as well as low, on the throne as well as in the workshop." This was meant for the Kaiser, but de Gaulle shows amply that it applied across the board.[27]

The distinction we have drawn between dutiful reserve and self-centered disdain is one that de Gaulle's comrades in prison, many senior to him and superior in rank, were quite capable of making. They surely understood his morning labors as a valuable contribution to their morale and as comradely service. They took his reserve in stride as the outward sign of studious concentration on their behalf and as the protective shield enveloping his decision and ardor. Hence they did not stint in their appreciation. As Pouget suggests, they thoroughly enjoyed giving him his due:

> Following one of these expositions, in which the young captain had demonstrated a brilliant talent for strategy, Tardiù decided to give him the rank and title of "Commandant." For some days he was called by that name, but (the same causes generating the same effects) almost every day he received an additional promotion. After "Marshal of France" they called him "Constable" and the title remained his, both for lack of a higher rank and because it fit the natural majesty of his bearing as well as his knowledge.[28]

In reflecting on de Gaulle's reserve, we may have seemed to digress, but our path now offers us a clear view of an essential feature of *The Enemy's House Divided*. For it is in one respect de Gaulle's most reserved writing. It is the only book in which his own prestige as the proponent of a controversial reform, or as the embodiment of a great cause, was not at stake. In its studied silence about de Gaulle, it bears a unique relation to his own "ardor and decision." Here, long before the creation of the historic figure "de Gaulle," he had made a most thoroughgoing effort to efface himself. The silence of the book envelops and safeguards the austere ardor of an author-spectator who bears witness to tragedy, to the ghastly national humiliation of an enemy.

A spectacle of self-inflicted moral degradation is disclosed by de Gaulle's history. The pathos of his own stymied ambition, his thwarted love of grandeur, has been consigned to the background, along with his joy in France's splendid victory. It is as though he had written to assuage Max Weber's suffering, by telling us what Weber found so hard to bear in the spectacle of his country's political collapse in 1918.[29] By clarifying this harrowing drama, de Gaulle has made it possible for us, merely by contemplating the German tragedy, to purge ourselves of petty emotions, and to revive our ardor for great things. Just as the effects of his own sound and fury worked on Hoche, to purge him of his youthful follies, such disasters work upon the public-spirited reader; they are an indispensable touchstone for de Gaulle's man of character. They may purify his will for its gymnastic disciplines. By bringing before him the moral disasters that are truly to be feared, such sights keep his eyes on the prize through the long repetitions required for thorough and conscientious preparation. Reinvigorating a noble pathos, they may save his daily regimen in small matters from becoming a heartless routine. Perhaps that is why Marshal Pétain recommended this book to all young French officers.[30] It brings home to us the greatest evils we can bring upon ourselves by our own actions. There is a place for tragedy in de Gaulle's precept, "To prepare for war is to prepare captains."[31]

Yet de Gaulle's most reserved writing is in another respect his most outspoken about the moral dimension of political action. Perhaps the spectator-historian could reflect on the moral dimension of political and military life with a directness denied the historic figure de Gaulle. *The Enemy's House Divided* initiates the reader—and perhaps especially the German reader—into the moral world of self-government and brings the moral principles of constitutional politics to center stage. In this tragedy, impersonal moral-constitutional principles become actors, like the Euminides in Aeschylus, avenging themselves when they are violated; these principles bring ruin upon the German people as punishment for the hubris of their chieftains. Perhaps no writing by de Gaulle so sharply awakens curiosity about the moral dimension of his thought. Certainly none is harder to square with the view that his political science was Machiavellian.[32]

In September 1916, the Germans dissolved the Sczuczyn camp. But de Gaulle repeated the pattern of morale-building reportage and strate-gic analysis at his next abode, in Fort IX at Ingolstadt in Bavaria. There, according to Lieutenant Borgnis Despordes,

> Captain de Gaulle occupied himself in organizing the camp; he gave a series of lectures on the war. The authority with which he spoke struck us. He also took charge of editing communiqués that were then posted on the cell doors, since the news most often came to us in truncated form.[33]

By the end of 1916, Lacouture reports,

> He judged that his documentation was sufficient to propound to his companions—many of whom, higher in rank than he was, could only be astounded by this audacity—a vast canvas of the course the war was taking. These expositions, spread over six months from Decem-ber 1916 to June 1917, have come down to us, perhaps reworked later, in the form of four chapters. Two are grouped under the global title, "On the war," the other two entitled "On the supreme direction of the war."[34]

Thus, for nearly three years in German war prisons, de Gaulle kept up a vigorous program of study and reflection directed consciously toward moral objectives. On the one hand, through these duties he made his dis-tinctive contribution to morale and camaraderie, keeping his fellow offi-cers abreast of the course of the war and continuing their mental prepa-ration for future action. On the other hand, this work was conceived by de Gaulle as a gymnastic of the will, strengthening his own domination over himself, developing moral reflexes that he would need to keep his poise in positions of responsibility. He seized upon imprisonment as an occasion for deepening his understanding of the prison unit as a moral community. He sought out duties that united science and morals, bring-ing his rare gifts of intellect to bear on moral questions and rescuing himself and his fellow prisoners from moral isolation.

As the culmination of his imprisonment, *The Enemy's House Divided* reflects his austere concentration upon problems of morale. Its stunning synthesis of scholarship and morals grew from the regimen he imposed on himself during these bitter months of enforced inaction. He emerged from prison confirmed in his determination to shore up these mutu-ally supporting pillars of French civilization—indeed of civilization *tout court*—and to unify them in his own person. We may therefore conclude our commentary on the Sczuczyn scene with a statement of his underlying principle. Although these are not de Gaulle's words, they do justice to his principle:

> By civilization, we understand the conscious culture of humanity, i.e. of that which makes a human being a human being, i.e. the conscious culture of reason. Human reason is active, above all, in two ways: as regulating human conduct, and as attempting to understand whatever can be understood by man; as practical reason, and as theoretical reason. The pillars of civilization are therefore morals and science, and both united. For science without morals degenerates into cynicism, and thus destroys the basis of the scientific effort itself; and morals without science degenerates into superstition, and thus is apt to become fanatic cruelty.[35]

In retrospect, one can see that *The Enemy's House Divided* grew naturally out of de Gaulle's prison lecturing, and so Pouget's vignette is a good portal through which to enter his war study. Throughout the writing of the book, the steady exercise of his faculties on German materials, which Pouget describes so vividly, unquestionably undergirded his efforts. Pouget also enables us to appreciate how de Gaulle's writing affected his fellow officers, winning their esteem and trust. The book continued to win men over to de Gaulle thereafter, one by one. Catroux, the first of the imperial proconsuls to join de Gaulle after June 1940, seems to have formed his estimate in this way.[36] And we have the eloquent testimony of Gaulmier, who discovered de Gaulle's writings in a garrison library in the French Levant:

> I shall never forget that light-hearted intoxication, that enchantment of discovering so many solid and convincing pages; no one at Aleppo had ever opened the pages or looked under the green and maroon covers of the sad Berger-Levrault editions. There, where I sought only an expert on modern war, I encountered a thinker, a vigorous writer, a philosopher. There, where I only looked for reasons to hope, I found the certainty that we would be victorious.[37]

De Gaulle's first book was thus firmly grounded in his wartime experience and reflection. Yet, it would be a mistake to place *The Enemy's House Divided* in "the collection of great books written in prison camps during the war," as Fritz Stern has done.[38] Nor is Lacouture's judgment wholly accurate: "There in five chapters, was the slowly matured fruit of his thirty-two months of captivity." In large measure, de Gaulle based his study upon information he garnered after 1918, from the memoirs of "the principal personalities" on the German side. We would do better to assume that the book we have was conceived and written later than his imprisonment.[39] It does reveal "the whole secret mechanism of Germany," as Lacouture has said. However, De Gaulle was able to piece that puzzle together only by analyzing what the main antagonists divulged in their memoirs. None of the German memoirs was published prior to 1919; most of de Gaulle's "documentation" was not available before 1920, and in some cases not until two or three years later.[40]

▬▬ The Authors of Catastrophe Write Their Memoirs

The most reliable report on the research and writing of the book is provided by de Gaulle's brother-in-law, Jacques Vendroux:

> Two months before his marriage, Captain de Gaulle was appointed as professor at St.-Cyr. . . . At the end of 1922, he was inducted at the École de Guerre. *The Enemy's House Divided* is in part the fruit of his course at St.-Cyr. Its composition was facilitated both by his extraordinary capacity for work and the possibilities for documentation which the library and archives of the institution offered him. He devoted the vacation in the summer of 1923 almost entirely to the preparation of this first work.[41]

Access to an abundance of up-to-date documents from the library at St.-Cyr opened new vistas to de Gaulle's pioneering intellect, and disclosed new dimensions of the war drama for his consideration. The intrepidity, intellectual stamina, and moral imagination he had deployed on tiny scraps of information, at Sczuczyn and the other prisoner of war camps, he now trained upon authoritative intelligence sources and massive amounts of primary material.

The Enemy's House Divided may be the most penetrating study ever written on the memoirs of the statesmen and generals who ruled Germany during World War I.[42] We should also underscore the special importance of these particular materials for comprehending de Gaulle's writings. Long before he set his pen to paper to write his own *Mémoires de guerre,* de Gaulle had published a book on how to read works of this genre.

And what a reader he had become! Let us imagine a scene as instructive as Pouget's, from St.-Cyr rather than Sczuczyn, describing a seminar given by de Gaulle on the political history of the Great War.[43] Suppose that the most promising scholars are enrolled among the French officers in this class. We may also assume that he had their full attention: the young officers at St.-Cyr called de Gaulle *"le double-maître,"* "twice the master-teacher." Each has been assigned to report on one of these German memoirs. For several nights before each class convenes, the same scene is repeated. Bent over his desk, in uniform, a young man looks up for a moment from a page of Ludendorff, Bauer, Erzberger, or Bethman-Hollweg. He knows that in writing his own book, de Gaulle had undertaken to pluck these documents bare. The student has been told, however, that this is not the moment to study de Gaulle's findings: "Try, instead, to imitate Descartes's qualities of judgment and suspicion."[44] So he must not trust his memoirist further than he can throw him. Returning to the text, he methodically analyzes the information, classifies it, works out his syntheses. Tiring, he stands, paces, gazes out the window. Perhaps he pictures de Gaulle alone at work on the documents, immersed in the German war memoirs: searching relentlessly in the recriminations for barely discernible signs of what must have occurred at a crucial turning point; weighing the characters of the military and civilian leaders with minute care; looking for weaknesses in their armor; deducing from their passionate self-justifications an action taken, a fact that must be suppressed, a responsibility that could not be borne. Refreshed by this image of mental vigor, the student returns to his desk, composes his report, gives his measured critique of the memoir for which he was responsible, and makes his own judgments plain.

Next day in class, following the report, de Gaulle is silent. He has warned them against reading *The Enemy's House Divided* as yet; his own findings must not abort the development of their judgment and intuition. The book was to be held in reserve. Each young officer must reflect first on all the reports; together they will present the massive puzzle almost in its entirety. Only later, after the seminar has concluded, do these initiates permit themselves to read *The Enemy's House Divided* from cover to cover, to discover what de Gaulle had seen in each document, and in them all together. Only then are they able to form an estimate of how those thirty-two months of captivity, when he was reduced to the barest resources, had honed and refined de Gaulle's extraordinary faculties; of what he had become capable of accomplishing when adequate documentation was available for his scrutiny.

But de Gaulle's reliance on these memoirs also reminds us that *The*

Enemy's House Divided was a response to the circumstances of the post-war period, and not confined to the war itself. Many of these publications were attempts to influence public opinion and political debate in the Germany of the nascent Weimar Republic. In retrospect, it seems clear that they succeeded. As Daniel Mahoney observes:

> By the middle of 1917 Germany had for all intents and purposes been transformed into a military dictatorship led by Ludendorff. This regime lacked the moral and political confidence that belongs to legitimate civilian authority. It precipitously collapsed in the fall of 1918 after a series of military reversals and the impact of American intervention in the war began making itself felt. Lacking the elementary self-knowledge and refusing to accept their political responsibility, Ludendorff and the other military subverters of the German order blamed anyone and anything but their own insubordination for the German tragedy: hence, the subsequent claims of the famous "stab in the back" by anti-German democrats.[45]

De Gaulle's inquiry was thus based on newly issued tracts that were shaping the postwar political debate in Germany over the defeat of 1918, the collapse of German institutions, and the terms of the Versailles Treaty. Although with few exceptions each memoirist merely blamed someone else who held authority, the effect of this storm of recriminations was to teach the public that they all eschewed responsibility. This was not quite the principle of the *Dolchstoss* or "stab in the back" propaganda. Blaming each other, none of the memoirists argued that someone who held no position of authority and command was responsible for the defeat. But they thoroughly plowed the ground to receive this principle.

That de Gaulle originally conceived Chapter 5 as a contribution to this debate is clear from the earliest extant version of the chapter.[46] According to his Polish translator, Capt. Medvecki, de Gaulle lectured on the topic "Defeat, a moral question" on at least two occasions during his postwar tour of duty in Poland:

> At Rembertov, fifty kilometers from Warsaw, the French officers had the benefit of a vast camp. . . . From time to time, Commandant de Gaulle set aside the themes of combat properly so-called and gave a conference on more general subjects. The finest of these, entitled "Defeat, a moral question," was truly a great class. It had to be mimeographed because all the student officers wanted a copy of it. Better

yet, it reverberated all the way to Warsaw, and we were obliged to go there together, to present it again before an audience of generals and colonels, French as well as Polish. . . .[47]

I do not know whether mimeograph copies of this 1919 lecture remain. However, de Gaulle's papers included an article by this title that he had never published; it was made public in 1973, after his death. The French editors deem it to have been written in 1927 or 1928, but internal evidence places it in 1919 or 1920, when de Gaulle was in Poland. Its first sentence reads, "It is a commonplace to say that the war just ended [*aujourd'hui terminée*] — or that appears to have ended — was a war between peoples, and not merely a war between armies" (93). This locates us shortly after the war. Its peroration forcefully addresses the "stab in the back," the nascent *Dolchstoss* theme, in reply to very recent statements reported in German newspapers:

> When an army turns tail, or when it capitulates, it ill becomes it to boast of its troop strength, its artillery, the means of war that remain to it and which it delivers up to the enemy. It would be quite astonishing to behold it counting the advantages of the position which it has abandoned; it would be odious to hear it say with pride, "We are capitulating with our forces intact." And yet Germany is not afraid to adopt such terms. We have heard her glorying in having accepted the supreme humiliation, since her military resources were still very powerful. Yes, it is true! Germany had under arms, on the day of the armistice, 4 million men! Yes, her losses, proportionally to her population, were inferior to ours! Yes, her cannons still numbered in the thousands, and her machine-guns were beyond number. Yes, her troops were in enemy territory. Yes, her factories remained intact and her fields fertile. However, she surrendered. She preferred to throw down her weapons, give away her provisions, and submit to the hard law of the conqueror. She refused to make further sacrifices, hoping to end her suffering. That is and has always been the very essence of defeat. All the armaments [*moyens*] that remained at the disposition of Hindenburg on the day of the rout of the German people are nothing more than our trophies today. And in the future [they will be] the very symbol of our enemy's disaster.[48]

"Defeat, A Moral Question," was the basis for Chapter 5 as it appeared in the book. The body of this 1920 lecture contains the entire chapter almost verbatim. The transposed passages appear in the book version with only minor stylistic improvements, editing, and footnotes. Neither the opening, nor the peroration just cited, appears in Chapter 5.

I suspect de Gaulle withheld the lecture "Defeat, A Moral Question" from publication because it was inadequate to its task. In the book, de Gaulle took as his starting point what he had earlier advanced as the conclusion of the lecture: the Germans' inability or unwillingness to comprehend their defeat as a moral question. Assuming this same recalcitrance or political immaturity in his German readers, de Gaulle framed his study as a primer in moral responsibility. He simultaneously widened the scope of his inquiry. Losing the war did not make the 1918 Revolution inevitable, according to de Gaulle. Defeat and revolution were separable "questions." *The Enemy's House Divided* attempts to demonstrate that both are "moral questions," but distinct and substantially different moral questions. To understand how they became confounded, (and how that confusion could have been prevented), we must study how the German authorities discharged their military and political duties, during the war and its political aftermath. In the book, de Gaulle reframed his 1920 lecture as "The Debacle of the German People," making it the denouement of a long tragedy with four previous "acts." Here he no longer exclaims or protests. Instead, his exposition compels us to study the German defeat and the revolutionary sequel as distinct questions, and to do so in methodical detail. Each of the four preceding chapters of *The Enemy's House Divided* deals with a major turning point in the war; each shows the violation of a moral constitutional principle to be a cause of both the defeat and the final debacle. His statesmanlike understanding of political history exhibits the denouement as the result of moral causes and hence of remediable mistakes. In addition, by supplying an adequate education in constitutional principles, it leaves no reader the excuse of ignorance or dogma: there was nothing necessary or inevitable about the 1918 Revolution.

De Gaulle understood the culminating chapter of *The Enemy's House Divided* as a contribution to the postwar debate. Because the debate was wide-ranging and his contribution multifaceted, we confine ourselves to only one aspect here. De Gaulle attempted to make clear to French, English, and American readers the precariously lopsided character of that debate: in Germany great attention was centered on the end of the war, whereas the victors were exclusively preoccupied with its beginning. This disproportion reflected the Allies' failure to consider (much less to engage) the moral question of utmost urgency on the German side, on which de Gaulle concentrated. That question concerned responsibility—to the German nation—for the defeat of the Central Powers and for the destruction of the Wilhelmine Empire, along with the dismemberment of its ally the Austro-Hungarian Empire.[49] Later, this public abdication on the part of the victors bore strange fruit, insofar as it left the field free for Ludendorff and Adolf Hitler to monopolize "defeat as a moral question" in Germany. Just as *The Enemy's House Divided* appeared in the bookshops, in 1924, these two were exploiting the issue in a Bavarian courtroom, following the failure of their Beer Hall Putsch.[50]

Perhaps the first reason for the neglect of de Gaulle's history by historians lies in his implied repudiation of the premise of almost all historical writing on the Allied side in the two decades after the war. Not only does he resist the impulse to deploy his scholarship to allocate blame for the outbreak of the war; he does not even acknowledge the raging historiographic controversy on this topic. Perhaps de Gaulle (like Max Weber) thought it was an exercise in futility.[51] De Gaulle contributed to the postwar political debate (once again, like Weber) by focusing exclusively upon what the Germans themselves had done to Germany, above all upon those who held offices of trust and authority in the Imperial government and the military. In reading the highly charged memoir literature, he was fully cognizant that these authors wrote to shape the present and future. By promoting the *Dolchstoss* legend, which helped to bring down the Weimar regime and aided Hitler in his rise to power, some of these memoirs helped to perpetuate the original catastrophe of the war, bringing Germany to a new height of fury and depth of national degradation.

Decades later, when he came to write his own memoirs, de Gaulle had long understood that writing could be consequential political action. His memoirs were guided negatively by the loathsome qualities and deadly consequences of the worst of these postwar German memoirs and positively by his resolve to shape the present and future through a more responsible politics of memory.[52] Similarly, his actions after June 1940 reflect his resolve that France should be rescued from the moral degradation of the Vichy debacle. In this they were shaped and informed by his understanding of the 1918 German debacle. In both respects, the experience of writing *The Enemy's House Divided* had been formative and foundational.

His prison notebooks suggest that by 1916 de Gaulle was a keen reader of military and political memoirs, indeed a discerning aficionado of this genre.[53] In the postwar German memoirs he found the ordinary vices that one expects from honor-lovers desperate to justify their actions: all the petty injustices of wounded egotism, spiritedness, vanity, and pride. However, in *The Enemy's House Divided,* he argued that something far more original and ominous was at work, both in the actions and in the retrospective self-justifications of these authors.

▄▄▄▄ A Postwar Postmortem on the Philosophy of the Future

The Enemy's House Divided is a sustained critique of the principled irresponsibility that de Gaulle found in the actions of the German generals and politicians, and later in their public recollections. According to de Gaulle, the disintegration of Germany during the war reflected an ongoing philosophical argument about responsibility. The war memoirs continued to prosecute that quarrel; he found them consistent with the philosophy that the leading figures had embraced before the war began, and which guided their actions at its essential turning points. Through de Gaulle's account, the German military and political leaders come to light as perhaps the first governors of a modern civilized nation to repudiate their moral and constitutional responsibility on principle. In doing so, they destroyed their own regime and Germany's governing institutions.

In this respect, the book does not fit on the continuum we have traced from his prison studies. It develops a philosophical and moral theme that we could not have anticipated from his wartime notebooks and lectures. Moreover, by obtruding it upon our attention in his Foreword, de Gaulle fairly compelled his readers to judge the book by this point of departure. He deliberately gave his study the form of a reflection on the influence of Nietzsche's philosophy.[54] Rey-Herme puts this point most forcefully:

> Even if these studies are technical on their face, they are all curiously surrounded by a properly political perspective since they evoke the relations between the allies, the relations between military and civil power, including parliamentary intrigues and backstairs maneuvering. This captain intends to study a military situation with all the intellectual and human faces that it presents. Moreover, the conclusion that he draws in his Foreword is pregnant with significance. If the military leaders, despite their eminent qualities and their remark-

able efforts, led the German people to disaster, "It is perhaps due to the influence of Nietzsche's theories of the elite and the superman."

Thus from the first pages Charles de Gaulle wrote, it is the philosophical aspect of the conduct of beings that represents the final explanation. He inaugurates his work by asserting that behind the failures of Ludendorff and Hindenburg stand Nietzsche and Zarathustra. This theme is repeated like a leitmotif throughout the development [of the work].[55]

In many quarters, de Gaulle has been interpreted as a Nietzschean of some sort. Because that claim has wide influence, Rey-Herme's claims to the contrary deserve close scrutiny. Rey-Herme contends that *The Enemy's House Divided* is a philosophically fundamental book for understanding de Gaulle. It reveals the extent to which de Gaulle's statesmanship was a deliberate and carefully premeditated response to Nietzsche's influence over men of action and over educated opinion. The foundation of de Gaulle's understanding of military and political action was his sustained reflection on the significance of Nietzsche's philosophic influence for political life, for serious citizenship and statesmanship. His first book indicates that from the outset, de Gaulle joined *la querelle de l'homme* (the argument or strife over humanity) as an agon with Nietzsche and the Nietzscheans.[56] Insofar as Nietzsche's philosophy of action is the great alternative to which de Gaulle opposed his own thought, it is the touchstone of de Gaulle's thought. Nietzsche had observed that one must be judicious in choosing one's enemies; Stendhal that one should enter society with a duel. In that spirit, de Gaulle singled out Nietzsche from the outset. *The Enemy's House Divided* was de Gaulle's duel with Nietzsche.[57]

Or perhaps one should say that it was only the beginning. For this duel was to go on; it was mirrored in de Gaulle's other works. The stylistic qualities of his later writings may be the result of de Gaulle's quest for an art of rhetoric equal to the challenge posed by Nietzsche's powerfully persuasive, formative writings. In this respect, *The Enemy's House Divided* might provide the fundamental political analysis on which all the writings of de Gaulle's maturity draw. Coming before his more rhetorical speeches and writings, this first book may be better suited to teach us about the presuppositions of the art of rhetoric that guided them. It may reveal more clearly the moral and philosophical foundation on which de

Gaulle based not only his statesmanship, but also the epic accounts of his statesmanship that he left for posterity.

According to Rey-Herme, in *The Enemy's House Divided* de Gaulle undertook to show that Nietzsche's thinking divided and brought down the Wilhelmine regime from within.[58] By embracing the suggestions of a philosophic assassin, the German rulers committed political and military suicide. This previously unthinkable Nietzschean *Dolchstoss* was self-inflicted. In this respect, de Gaulle's first book was his most "philosophical." It was more explicitly and directly engaged with the influence of a philosopher on the life "of a great and valiant people" than any of his later writings. It displays a philosophic doctrine as the cause of military defeat, the destruction of a regime, and the moral disintegration of a nation.

Let us survey the book in the light of Rey-Herme's thesis.

In his Foreword, de Gaulle says that he will investigate five essential turning points in the German conduct of the war that he believes were crucial to Germany's defeat. Each illustrates a lack of self-restraint, indeed a defiance of the limits laid down by experience, common sense, and law. De Gaulle tentatively attributes this defiance to the influence of Nietzsche's philosophy (presumably in the 1890s, in the years when the 1914 generation of German leaders was coming to maturity and forming its outlook):

> The German military leaders, whose task it was to guide and co-ordinate such immense efforts, gave proof of an audacity, of a spirit of enterprise, of a will to succeed, of a vigor in handling resources, whose reverberations have not been stilled by their ultimate defeat. Perhaps this study—or, more precisely, the disclosure of the events that are its object—may make evident the defects common to these eminent men: the characteristic taste for immoderate undertakings; the passion to expand their personal power at any cost; the contempt for the limits marked out by human experience, common sense, and the law.
>
> Perhaps reading this will cause the reader to reflect that the German leaders, far from combatting these excesses in themselves, or at least concealing them as defects, considered them instead as forces, and erected them into a system; and that this error bore down with a crushing weight at the decisive moments of the war. One may per-

haps find in their conduct the imprint of Nietzsche's theories of the elite and the Overman, adopted by the military generation that was to conduct the recent hostilities and which had come to maturity and definitively fixed its philosophy around the turn of the century.

The Overman—with his exceptional character, his will to power, his taste for risk, his contempt for others who want to see him as Zarathustra—appeared to these impassioned men of ambition as the ideal that they should attain. They voluntarily resolved to be part of that formidable Nietzschean elite who are convinced that, in pursuing their own glory, they are serving the general interest; who exercise compulsion on "the mass of slaves," holding them in contempt; and who do not hesitate in the face of human suffering, except to hail it as necessary and desirable.[59]

If Nietzsche's doctrine was at work, it was not so much as a theoretical tenet, therefore, but rather as what de Gaulle called a philosophy of action. Put somewhat differently, Nietzsche's thought does not always act on men as an intellectual doctrine that informs their reasoning; often its influence is more intimate and insinuating, forming their characters or personalities "from within." It would make itself evident in "how one becomes what one is," in one's willing and one's way of fighting.[60] De Gaulle obviously saw Nietzsche's influence as an alternative "gymnastic of the will," rather than as a cosmology or philosophy of history. It is a teaching that became embodied, through an obscure but nonetheless intelligible process of incorporation, in the habits of will of the German leaders, and hence in their actions. Its product is not a system or method but a self, a type of warrior.[61] Nietzsche's thought would therefore have to be discerned in the development of each man's morality, or (as Nietzsche put it) in the genealogy of the relations of rule between his drives.[62]

So the tentative, suggestive phrasing of the Foreword we have just quoted is apt. De Gaulle is directing the reader's attention toward events in the soul that must be very difficult to corroborate. In making his subject Nietzsche's influence, as the fountainhead of German morale, he asks us to consider the German commanders as they understood themselves. *The Enemy's House Divided* inducts us into the German Army as its officers saw it, from within, illuminated by the sources of morale or strength of character they had adopted, from Nietzsche, as their own. Somehow, these secret mechanisms or dynamics in the soul are to be exhibited in de Gaulle's history.[63]

One may well wonder whether a sober and matter-of-fact history can bear this weight. Such a history might be hard pressed to demonstrate de Gaulle's leading argument, that Nietzsche's thought, and the style of action he inspired, was what divided the German enemy's house and brought it down in World War I. However that may be, de Gaulle not only claimed to have understood how Nietzsche's thought shaped the course of the war at its decisive turning points; in the Foreword he somewhat tentatively promises that these five episodes will justify this conclusion, enabling us to corroborate it.

This inducement is powerfully reinforced, when de Gaulle takes up Nietzsche's influence again in Chapter 1; and the hesitancy of his Foreword seems to be replaced by categorical certainty in that chapter. It focuses on General von Kluck's refusal to obey orders from the Supreme Command in August–September 1914, a decision that led swiftly to the German defeat at the Marne. De Gaulle claims that Kluck was following a pattern established under Moltke the elder in the campaigns of 1866 and 1870. As Supreme Commander, Moltke was meticulous at the stage of preparation but extraordinarily self-effacing when it came to execution. At that stage, he issued a few broad directives but left subordinates largely unsupervised, neglecting to secure the communication links that a closer supervision and a more comprehensive responsibility for execution would have required. De Gaulle argues that Moltke's system afforded very great opportunities for self-assertion. Under the impact of Nietzsche's influence, the next generation of German commanders took these opportunities to an extreme. De Gaulle exhibits the faults of this system in 1866 and 1870, arguing that the German military historians, instead of subjecting the flaws to thorough criticism, allowed the pattern to be admired and emulated. The French under Joffre at the Marne exploited precisely these flaws.[64]

The fundamental "division" examined in this opening chapter bears crucially on the political debate over the responsibility for Germany's fate during the war. For de Gaulle demonstrates that from the outset the German command structure was a house divided against itself. Indeed, it had been divided, since before the founding of the Wilhelmine Empire, by the founder of the modern Prussian military system, the elder Moltke, whose victories in 1866 and 1870 made possible Bismarck's unification of Germany. Contrary to Allied war propaganda, the Wilhelmine Empire was not a coherent aristocratic regime, nor was its predominantly Prussian military system a cohesive moral-political formation united by a common military culture and authoritatively governed by its High Command. Already in 1866 and 1870, in the very battles that created the Wilhelmine Empire, it was evident that Moltke's great victories owed far too much to the incompetence and lethargy of the enemy. The duty of German military historians was to warn that the system would produce catastrophe as soon as it was tested against a resourceful opponent. Rather than prepare through a comprehensive critique of their system's weaknesses, the men responsible for training German commanders joined unthinkingly in the celebratory mood and institutionalized its imbecilities for six decades (1866–1914).

In the meantime, the impact of Nietzsche's thought completely transformed the moral and intellectual milieu. The essential division laid open to our view in this first chapter is between the two essentially antithetical regimes or military cultures that shaped the minds and souls of German officers after 1870. The Junker ethos of the old Prussian officer class, which Hindenburg exemplifies for de Gaulle, increasingly became an empty shell or facade, while the younger generation adopted a Nietzschean morality or "gymnastic of the will." De Gaulle draws this distinction explicitly:

> Marshal Hindenburg did not belong to the unbridled generation, that victorious Prussia molded on the morrow of 1870, and of which Ludendorff is the prototype. The marshal had received his intellectual formation, consolidated his philosophy, and completed his military apprenticeship, before 1866. A more fervent cult of duty, a greater moderation of judgment, a moral sense better developed, an almost religious taste for "service," also distinguished Hindenburg, in our opinion, from the younger, more supercilious, more subjective Prussians who surrounded him in the General Headquarters, and who were also more abreast of the times.[65]

Thus, what other historians have characterized as "the problem of German militarism" was not a single problem at all, according to de Gaulle.[66] By 1914, German militarism was an unstable compound of two antithetical moralities of self-discipline and self-assertion, as well as of collective discipline and corporate assertion in war. There was no agreement or unity of principle in the Prussian-German officer class. France's salvation at the first Battle of the Marne in 1914 revealed this essential incoherence, in the form of Kluck's insubordination.

Moltke's system thus predated the influence of Nietzsche's thought within Wilhelmine military circles, but its structure permitted Nietzscheans to thrive and develop throughout the army and to rise to the highest levels of command. To uninformed outsiders, the military system might appear to be an impressively organized regime. De Gaulle portrays it to the contrary, as a house deeply divided against itself, in which a traditional ethos of duty to fatherland, empire, throne and pulpit was at war with a revolutionary Nietzschean moral doctrine of liberated will:

> It was from Nietzsche that the leaders, like all thinking Germany, had drawn their philosophy. Enthusiastically adopting the cult of the Overman, each was thus naturally disposed to consider himself the center of the world. Each inclined, on the one hand, to develop his character to an extreme and put it to the test with a constancy and audacity that have not been sufficiently noted. But on the other hand, each leaned toward exaggerated independence and was determined to act on his own in all situations.
>
> Militarily, their leaders had been formed by studying Moltke's campaigns, and it is understood that they treated them as models. The "manner" of the old marshal appeared to them as the ideal, not only in consideration of his success, but precisely because it encouraged such distorted initiative in subordinates and because it consecrated unlimited independence.
>
> The commanders of the army of 1914 dreamed of following the example of Frederick-Karl before Königgrätz or on the eve of Gravelotte. They were all disposed and resolved in advance to form their own personal conception of the situation and to act accordingly, regardless of what the higher command might prescribe.[67]

Following the manner or fashion that Moltke crystallized, and giving that manner the added intensity and revolutionary scope of Nietzsche's radical teaching, the German officers squandered their own prodigious accomplishments. According to de Gaulle, they did so not by inadvertence but, as it were, on principle, following the Nietzschean doctrine of the self they aspired to embody.[68]

By the middle of the first chapter, therefore, it has become evident that de Gaulle is not at all in doubt that Nietzsche exercised the decisive formative influence on the German commanders. The several *"peut-être"* of the Foreword have been replaced by unqualified conclusions. Thus far, the reader has every reason to assume that de Gaulle will develop the

Nietzschean theme methodically, as Rey-Herme has suggested, throughout the remainder of the book.

What then do we find if we examine precisely how the themes of the foreword are developed in the later chapters?

Chapter 2 follows Admiral von Tirpitz's struggle against Chancellor Bethmann-Hollweg from before the war through the fateful decision for unlimited submarine warfare, which brought the United States into the war. This is the first chapter on the insubordination of the German military to civilian authority. It sets the stage for the later, far graver conspiracy that finally brought down the chancellor, and transformed the empire into a de facto military dictatorship (the subject of de Gaulle's Chapter 4). This chapter is a subtle account of Tirpitz's brutally single-minded effort to compel Bethmann's resignation, a campaign the chancellor was able to repulse so long as Wilhelm II retained his authority. Without removing Bethmann, Tirpitz did manage to circumvent his authority, to exploit the weakness of his character, and to paralyze him for future action. Faced with a fait accompli on the unlimited submarine war, Bethmann acceded, against his better judgment, and then found his position increasingly compromised and untenable. De Gaulle does not speak of Nietzsche in this chapter. He describes Tirpitz as a man of wide culture, differing in this respect from most of the "old Prussians."[69] He does not tell us whether that culture included Nietzsche or to what extent Nietzsche's influence shaped Tirpitz's thinking and character. His only allusion to the Nietzschean theme of the Foreword is relegated to a footnote.[70]

Chapter 3 is a study of the relations between the Austro-Hungarian and German empires and the causes of the German failure to establish a unified military command. Here again, as in Chapter 1, de Gaulle shows that Allied assumptions about German thoroughness and system were unfounded. Instead of taking the direct route (which was to court the Habsburg emperor Franz Joseph and assure his goodwill), the German rulers threw away their early opportunities.[71] Falkenhayn similarly discarded every chance for a good working relationship with the Austrian commander in chief, General Conrad von Hötzendorf, largely because Falkenhayn staked his future on victory on the stalemated Western front, while Conrad wanted action in the East.[72] The Germans evidently did not appreciate the necessity for command unity, and this crippling disagreement was not set aside until Hindenburg took Falkenhayn's place as head of the General Staff, in late 1916. Chapter 1 exhibits individualistic Nietzschean commanders, at loggerheads with their military superiors and impatient of the discipline imposed by the high command. In contrast, Chapter 3 displays German overbearing conduct toward an ally who had to be treated as equal and independent. In Chapter 2, De Gaulle had underscored the difference between Hindenburg and Ludendorff, between the old Prussian ethos of service and duty and the regime of unbridled self-assertion. One might see that contrast faintly in Chapter 3, in the difference between Emperor Franz Joseph and Wilhelm II, between the Habsburg ethos of duty and the rule of subjective will to power.[73] But this is a subdued echo, rather than a trumpeted development, of the Foreword's philosophic theme. Again there is no discussion of Nietzsche in the chapter, nor of his influence upon its protagonists.

Chapter 4 describes the overthrow of Chancellor Bethmann-Hollweg in midsummer 1917 by the German high command in collusion with some parliamentary politicians—chiefly the Catholic Centrist deputy Matthias Erzberger. Both Erzberger and Ludendorff felt capable of assuming responsibility for the entire empire and its institutions. Erzberger saw himself as Bethmann's replacement and so failed to consider the real danger of a military regime ruling through a puppet chancellor. De Gaulle's account in this chapter of how Ludendorff outmaneuvered and then discarded Erzberger sets the stage for the next. The military dictatorship of Ludendorff and Hindenburg could rule only on condition that the dictators won an overwhelming military victory. They therefore discarded a promising opportunity for a negotiated peace on very good terms for Germany.[74]

In Chapter 5, de Gaulle applies a pattern familiar to military historians: the phases through which a military unit passes as its morale breaks down in the stress of battle. But he applies this commonly observed sequence in an uncommon—indeed, shockingly unconventional—fashion, to explain the moral collapse of the entire German nation in the late summer of 1918. In an age of total mobilization for war it is possible for an entire civilized nation to experience the panic disintegration of a fighting team. De Gaulle is not uncritical of the part played by parliamentary party politicians and German journalists in this debacle. However, he follows the hierarchy of official responsibility, laying primary responsibility on the highest political and military authorities, beginning at the top with the Kaiser and the Supreme Command. By subverting the constitutional authority of their own government (through the kinds of actions described in Chapters 2 and 4), Germany's leaders crippled her for action. They insured that in the nation's hour of greatest need, the German people would be without the capacity to act as an organized political community.

Ludendorff is the protagonist in de Gaulle's fourth and fifth chapters. Although he does not comment directly on Ludendorff's writings on the total mobilization of the nation for war, de Gaulle subjects Ludendorff's thinking to a devastating trial by fire in Chapter 5. He develops the analogy just described, which begins from the most elementary moral knowledge a commander must have. According to de Gaulle, Ludendorff apparently never learned what common sense and experience have taught about the stages through which a battalion or division passes as its morale weakens and finally dissolves. We may infer that Ludendorff did not understand the moral implications of his own theory of total mobilization and, indeed, could not do so because he was not morally competent in what every battlefield commander has to know.

Surveying the book with an eye to Rey-Herme's thesis, how does his thesis stand up? We see that de Gaulle's claim about Nietzsche's influence, first advanced in the Foreword in a rather tentative or conditional formulation, was strengthened, for a brief moment in Chapter 1, into an unqualified assertion. Yet when we subject later chapters to scrutiny, seeking further elaboration of Rey-Herme's challenging assertion, they prove strangely disappointing. The theme suddenly vanishes after Chapter 1, and for the duration. Nietzsche's name drops from the narrative; there is no further allusion to his thought.

This is a perplexing and wholly unheralded reversal. De Gaulle does not obtrude it; indeed, his misdirection disguises it. Yet once noticed, it cries out for explanation. Can it be that de Gaulle has (already!) abandoned the argument he so confidently put forward as the great philosophical theme of his book?

Before we pursue these questions, let us consider how the argument of *The Enemy's House Divided* conceals them from view. Rey-Herme has overstated his thesis, but he is following an impression conveyed by de Gaulle's book. To put the point sharply: de Gaulle creates the illusion that his critique of Nietzsche (and his claim regarding Nietzsche's prodigious influence) is further developed in Chapters 2–5. To see how, let us return to his Foreword.

De Gaulle's assertion about Nietzsche's influence is part of a larger argument. He seeks to enable the reader to judge the defects of "the philosophy of war" (or more comprehensively, the philosophy of action) that guided the German commanders and statesmen. These defects are shown in two ways. First, by their fruits: German errors led to defeat. But in practice it is never clear that a doctrine led to defeat, unless one has a standard—an alternative doctrine—by which to identify and judge mistakes. So the second way puts the burden of these consequences squarely on the German leaders and their philosophy of war. It requires that de Gaulle clarify the true principles, or adumbrate the superior philosophy of action, by which one should be guided. He does so in this passage:

> Perhaps, finally, in meditating upon these events, one may wish to measure with what dignity we should clothe that superior philosophy of war which animated these leaders and which could at one time render futile the harshest efforts of a great people and at another constitute the most universal and surest guarantee of the destinies of the fatherland.[75]

That is, a nation must not take its bearings by a philosophy of war that once provided the most universal and surest guarantee of the destinies of the fatherland, if the next time round it can render futile the harshest sacrifices of its people. De Gaulle's irony reminds us that we require principles to be immutable. The immutable principles, according to de Gaulle, correspond in some fashion to "the classical rules of order":

> This study will have attained its object if it helps in its modest way to induce our military leaders of tomorrow, following the example of their victorious models in the recent war, to shape their minds and mold their characters according to the rules of classical order. It is from those rules that they may draw that sense of balance, of what is possible, of measure, which alone renders the works of energy durable and fecund.[76]

The principles of greatest concern to de Gaulle are few and immutable. Yet they are not simply self-evident or accessible to everyone. One must train one's mind and character by "the classical rules of order," if one is to draw from them the sense of proportion that makes action productive in particular circumstances. Those who adopt Nietzsche's gymnastic of the will, by contrast, train themselves to ignore or override these classical rules of order. De Gaulle uses the debacles of the German war effort from 1914 through 1918 to dramatize the consequence of Nietzsche's teaching, pointing out how it overpowered "that sense of balance, of what is possible, of measure, which alone renders the works of energy durable and fecund." The German commanders and soldiers exerted themselves with extraordinary energy and industry, but their works were sterile and short-lived.

De Gaulle's formulation is quite precise; his argument turns on an acquired virtue. The quality of mind that alone renders the works of energy lasting and fertile is a "sense of balance, of what is possible, of measure." Because Nietzsche's doctrine is hostile to the classical rules of order, his influence might lead a man—who would otherwise be capable of moderation and practical wisdom—to scorn these virtues. Still, Nietzsche's influence is by no means a necessary condition or cause. It will be quite enough that you are by nature a bully, a berserker, or an imbecile; you have all that it takes, without Nietzsche, to make a mess of things. Nor will the classical rules of order make you adroit and prudent.

As de Gaulle's political history unfolds, therefore, we should not be surprised that he becomes less concerned about the source of unmeasured and imbalanced choices. It suffices to show that Admiral Tirpitz, General Ludendorff, and Reichstag Deputy Erzberger lacked a "sense of balance, of what is possible, of measure"; that their actions violated immutable principles; and that, as a consequence, their works were transient and futile.

The rules of classical order shape the mind and form character toward self-mastery and devotion to the duties of a defined office. Hence the melancholy aspect of every social order governed by such rules:

> In the classical French garden, no tree seeks to stifle the others by overshadowing them; the plants accommodate themselves to being geometrically arranged; the pond does not aspire to be a waterfall; the statues do not vie to obtrude themselves upon the admiring spectator. A noble melancholy comes over us, from time to time. Perhaps it comes from our feeling that each element, in isolation, might have been more radiantly brilliant. But that would be to the detriment of the whole; and the observer takes delight in the rule that impresses on the garden its magnificent harmony.[77]

De Gaulle said consistently that the moral and philosophical perspective he spoke for, and from which his books are written, was "classical" in character. Here he makes an analogy to "the classical French garden," and some observers have assumed that by classical he meant French. But to understand de Gaulle's classicism as exclusively French is to contract his horizon. It is also to forget what the classics of antiquity taught the

French before their revolution. To be sure, for de Gaulle, France under the old regime was a great and memorable example of "the rules of classical order" in action:

> The policy of seventeenth-century France was formed by circumstances. It fought shy of abstractions, preferring facts to fancies, usefulness to sublimity, and opportunity to glory. For each particular problem it sought the practical rather than the ideal solution. Though unscrupulous as to the means employed, it showed its greatness by keeping a nice proportion between the end in view and the resources of the state. What was true of policy was true of its instrument, the army. Its recruitment and its organization were based not on law but on experiment. Its discipline and its code of honour were based on fact rather than theory. Strategy and tactics took as their guide common sense, experience, and a wise opportunism, unhampered by formulae.[78]

De Gaulle was justly proud of Louvois. However, he regarded the policy of the ancien régime as a rediscovery of the *phronesis* of Odysseus and of Aristotle's serious citizen, the *spoudaios politikos*.[79] The classical measure appears in de Gaulle as the standard for man as man, and France in the ancien régime has the glory of measuring up by that standard. To convey his classicism, de Gaulle refers, in one passage of *The Edge of the Sword*, to "the highest philosophical and religious ideals" for clarification.[80] In another, the term is illustrated by a page from Homer.[81] And in the most famous passage of his *War Memoirs*, he brings us into this perspective by sharing with us "a certain idea of France" that has been before his eyes throughout his life.[82] In every case the classical perspective is what Aristotle spoke of, in his *Politics*, as a political-moral opinion, meaning that it concerned the whole and put the citizen in an emotional and intellectual rapport with the whole. De Gaulle invokes a "classical" perspective in order to conjure up *l'ensemble*, or the whole, in its proper *rapport* with the citizen as a constituent part of the whole.[83]

De Gaulle has several ways of acknowledging the inherently problematic, challengeable status of this classical perspective. In the beginning of *The Enemy's House Divided*, he broaches the most comprehensive challenge to "the classical," Nietzsche's philosophical challenge. But one might say that every one of the leading German "personalities" poses his own peculiar challenge to "the classical." By repudiating the constraints of *l'ensemble*, by asserting himself in his own cause, each of the partisans whom de Gaulle notices in this first book defies the classical standard in his own, uniquely perverse way.

As a practical matter, that challenge must be met by authoritative action. In addition to shaping the individual's ethos from within, the rule must impress its magnificent harmony on the garden by imposing a discipline from without. Men of war are not statues; they vie to obtrude themselves and must be restrained. In politics, the "plants" do not accommodate themselves to being geometrically arranged; every puddle wants to be a waterfall. So the appropriate principles must be upheld by vigorous action. Their authority must be asserted by men like de Gaulle, whose character has been formed by the rules of classical order.

It fell to Bethmann-Hollweg to assert the appropriate principles, to sustain their authority and his own authority as chancellor of the German Empire, at the climactic turning point in July 1917. In the passage of *The Enemy's House Divided* that I believe he always remembered best, de Gaulle explained why the chancellor was unequal to the challenge:

> Perhaps, had he suddenly exploited this political turmoil for his own benefit, Bethmann-Hollweg could have succeeded in retaining power, by placing himself resolutely on the ground of peace without conquests and of the democratic transformation of the empire; dismissing from the government the likes of Helfferich, Stein, and Capelle; grouping behind him the majority of the Left and Center in the Reichstag; and appealing to public opinion against the pan-Germanists. But for that he would have had to talk frankly and firmly to the Kaiser, break Ludendorff, silence Tirpitz and Reventlow, form a parliamentary ministry, order the submarines to return to their ports, proclaim before the world that he was ready, without conditions, to evacuate Belgium and Northern France. From the bottom of his soul, the chancellor wished to see Germany follow this path; but he lacked the energy to open it for her. Not with impunity had he bowed his convictions and his conscience, on terrible occasions, before the will of the warriors, accepting the invasion of Belgium, tolerating "unrestricted warfare," and allowing the drowning of civilian passengers. A character abased, a heart made vile, refused to serve with courage a mind that remained lucid.[84]

In this portrait, we may discern de Gaulle's best answer to critics who notice the contradiction between his claims about Nietzsche's influence in the Foreword and Chapter 1, and his deliberate neglect of those claims in the last four chapters. The statesman's lucidity of mind can be sustained in action only if he can summon a heart that has not been made vile and a character that has not bowed and abased itself. These are the indispensable moral elements of civil courage in action; for in these deciding moments, prudence must command more than cunning and violence.

As we have seen, theoretical consistency and professional probity would require that de Gaulle provide a more sustained account of Nietzsche's influence. The terms of his duel, however, demand that the essential defect of Nietzsche's thought not only be disclosed but also be redressed. In the Foreword and Chapter 1, de Gaulle has sufficiently revealed Nietzsche's devaluation of the classical concern for measure in the character and self-restraint in the heart of the statesman. According to de Gaulle, Nietzsche teaches us to despise these concerns as merely moral and "human, all too human." Justly, and by example, de Gaulle goes forward in Chapters 2–5 to teach serious citizens—and the political historian—to forgo that Nietzschean imperative in favor of classical prudence.

▰▰▰ Coda

I have encouraged the reader to look forward to de Gaulle's book through the eyes of his fellow prisoners of war and to view his later career from the perspective of this first writing. For too long, *The Enemy's House Divided* has been eclipsed by the brilliance of de Gaulle's great public actions and his later reflections upon them. The reversal proposed is more than chronological, however. Looking backward, we are tempted to view de Gaulle's career as an ascent from obscurity to a lofty public prominence. Yet he may have seen that motion in some measure as a descent. For although de Gaulle had grand practical goals, he differed from many captains and statesmen in his ultimate measure, assigning a relatively low rank to the man of action:

> To one of his ministers of the Fifth Republic, who asked him to rank the categories of men—and women—in the order of his admiration, he could reply: "First, great writers; next, great thinkers; third, great statesmen; and fourth, great generals." The minister, it need hardly be said, was astonished, but also deeply impressed.[85]

Here is the standard of an intrepid thinker and imaginative writer who knew that his highest faculties could not be fulfilled in action but whose duty required that he devote his life almost exclusively to action. It reminds us that the closing remarks of his Foreword may apply even (or perhaps most stringently) to de Gaulle the thinker and writer.[86] If the classical French garden imposes its magnificent harmony upon the general, the statesman, the thinker, and the writer by ranking them as de Gaulle's standard ranks them, why would the author of this remarkable book submit to labor so long and so arduously in the two lower ranks? Understanding human excellence in these terms, why did de Gaulle choose so single-mindedly to protect the French political community and its moral life, as a statesman? However one answers these questions, de Gaulle's choice challenges the thinker and writer to become truly comprehensive—by doing justice to what is humanly great and memorable in the life of action.

According to de Gaulle, nations do not die. Yet without perishing, they may so demoralize and dishonor themselves as to become incapable of repenting their downward course. The Germans were soon to travel about as far down this path, from dishonor to unrepentant self-assertion, as it is possible to go. This is a moral suicide from which timely national action (and only such deliberately shared action) can save a people; or so de Gaulle sought to prove by his later actions. Here he prepared himself and the reader for such actions by thinking and writing on a nation's mortification. *The Enemy's House Divided* is an inquest. I can think of no better way to sum it up than to borrow the words of another tragedian, which, though applied in another context entirely, are no less true here:

> This is the story of the Wilhelmine Empire's suicide, of the events that led up to it and followed it and of the place in which it happened. There are the action, the people, and the place; all of which are interrelated but in their totality incommunicable in isolation from the moral continuum of human affairs. . . . There was no inquest, no trial in the judicial sense. Since then people have said there was a trial of sorts going on.[87]

The Enemy's House Divided

The Enemy's House Divided
Foreword to the First Edition (1924)

The German defeat cannot deter French opinion from rendering our enemies the homage they earned, by the energy of their leaders and the efforts of those who carried out their orders. But the exceptional extent of the warlike qualities they demonstrated, from one end of the drama to the other, better enables us to measure the errors that they committed.

We can do so all the more easily because almost all the German personages who played a role of the first rank in the conduct of the struggle have now published their memoirs. And, while it would not be fitting to make use of these writings without very seriously weighing the spirit of self-justification in which they were written, it is possible—by comparing them one with another, by counterpoising the theses they maintain, and by grouping their affirmations and negations—to discern more or less the principal reversals,[1] and to form a judgment about the action of these personalities.

Among the multiple acts of this drama, the present study is concerned with the episodes that appear to be most freighted with consequences for the course and outcome of the war. Moreover, these seem to be most characteristic of the spirit and conduct of the personalities who were involved in them. It also happens—as is easily explained—that the memoirs of the actors are particularly expansive and impassioned in regard to these events.

The five chapters to follow thus have for their subjects, respectively,

- The indiscipline of von Kluck, who from the 2nd to the 5th of September 1914, created the conditions favorable to our offensive at the Marne and called forth our victory;
- The unremitting struggle waged by Grand Admiral Tirpitz against Chancellor Bethmann-Hollweg from 1914 to 1919, to compel him to declare unlimited submarine warfare, which he by no means wished to do, and which induced the Americans to take up arms;

- The inability of Germany to establish a unified command in the coalition of central states, even though all the circumstances combined to offer it to them;
- The governmental crisis, thenceforth incurable, provoked at Berlin in 1917 by the intrigue of Ludendorff, who was resolved to seize de facto dictatorial power and did not hesitate, in order to achieve this, to overthrow Chancellor Bethmann, compelling the Kaiser's will, rousing up political parties, and creating a fatal agitation in public opinion;
- Finally, beginning on July 18, 1918, the abrupt and complete moral collapse of a valiant people, a degradation all the more grandiose because this people had, until then, been able to muster a collective will to conquer, an obstinacy in staying the course, a capacity for suffering that deserved the admiration and astonishment of its enemies from the first day of the war, and will assuredly secure the homage of history.

The German military leaders, whose task it was to guide and coordinate such immense efforts, gave proof of an audacity, of a spirit of enterprise, of a will to succeed, of a vigor in handling resources, whose reverberations have not been stilled by their ultimate defeat. Perhaps this study—or, more precisely, the disclosure of the events that are its object—may make evident the defects common to these eminent men: the characteristic taste for immoderate undertakings; the passion to expand their personal power at any cost; the contempt for the limits marked out by human experience, common sense, and the law.

Perhaps reading this will cause the reader to reflect that the German leaders, far from combatting these excesses in themselves, or at least concealing them as defects, considered them instead as forces, and erected them into a system; and that this error bore down with a crushing weight at the decisive moments of the war. One may perhaps find in their conduct the imprint of Nietzsche's theories of the elite and the Overman, adopted by the military generation that was to conduct the recent hostilities and which had come to maturity and definitively fixed its philosophy around the turn of the century.

The Overman—with his exceptional character, his will to power, his taste for risk, his contempt for others who want to see him as Zarathustra—appeared to these impassioned men of ambition as the ideal that they should attain. They voluntarily resolved to be part of that formidable Nietzschean elite who are convinced that, in pursuing their own glory, they are serving the general interest; who exercise compulsion on "the mass of slaves," holding them in contempt; and who do not hesitate in the face of human suffering, except to hail it as necessary and desirable.

Perhaps, finally, in meditating upon these events, one may wish to measure with what dignity we should clothe that superior philosophy of war which animated these leaders and which could at one time render futile the harshest efforts of a great people and at another constitute the most universal and surest guarantee of the destinies of the fatherland.

This study will have attained its object if it helps in a modest way to induce our military leaders of tomorrow, following the example of their victorious models in the recent war, to shape their minds and mold their characters according to the rules of classical order. It is from those rules that they may draw that sense of balance, of what is possible, of measure, which alone renders the works of energy durable and fecund.

In the classical French garden, no tree seeks to stifle the others by overshadowing them; the plants accommodate themselves to being geometrically arranged; the pond does not aspire to be a waterfall; the statues do not vie to obtrude themselves upon the admiring spectator. A noble melancholy comes over us, from time to time. Perhaps it comes from our feeling that each element, in isolation, might have been more radiantly brilliant. But that would be to the detriment of the whole; and the observer takes delight in the rule that impresses on the garden its magnificent harmony.

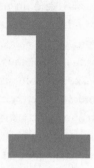

The Disobedience of General von Kluck

Returning to Berlin an emperor[1] and victorious,[2] and receiving in the name of Germany his subjects' congratulations, Wilhelm I declared publicly, "You, Moltke—thanks to your labor in time of peace, and your methods in time of war—have conducted our armies to victory."[3]

Military Germany thenceforth consecrated an unreserved admiration to [Marshal] Moltke and his system of command. All the German commanders trained themselves by studying the "manner" of the marshal and his glorious subordinates.[4] In 1914, they went off to battle animated by the will to imitate their great predecessors, not only in their success but also in their procedures.

That obsession, that superstition about the past, was recognized by Kaiser Wilhelm II and was encouraged.[5] All his proclamations at the outbreak of the war called it to mind. And for such sentimental reasons, he was determined that he too should have a Moltke as chief of staff.[6]

On the two days during which Prussia's fortune was determined, the 1st of July 1866 and the 15th of August 1870, the application of Moltke's system had, at the decisive times and places, brought success.[7]

On the days that determined the result of the Great War, the 4th and 5th of September 1914, General von Kluck was charged with the principal mission.[8] This commander, who was justly and universally respected, imitated in a striking fashion the conduct of the great victors of Königgrätz and Metz [see Figure 1].[9] That was the origin of the disaster. . . . There is a clear analogy between the doctrine and procedure of the Prussian commanders in the earlier victories and those of the German generals in the defeat. This manifest analogy serves to prove that in war—save for some few essential principles—there is no universal system, but only circumstances and personalities.

I

The personality of Field Marshal von Moltke was perfectly suited to preparation but was systematically self-effacing when it came to execution. It was the marshal who had chosen and molded the entire General Staff. It was he who assigned the officers to each post in it, according to their talents and the confidence he placed in them. Owing to him, the whole Prussian army embodied a unity of doctrine that has rightly evoked such astonishment and admiration. He prescribed the thorough study of enemy arms carried out by the General Staff. It was he who drew from that study the famous hypotheses, concerning enemy calculations, which he made the basis of his initial strategic conceptions. It was under his immediate, attentive, scrupulously careful direction that the plans for mobilization, concentration, and transport were studied, settled, and drafted.[10]

But once the campaign began, Moltke refused on principle to determine anything beyond extremely general intentions, expressed in a few very broad directives. It was to subordinates that he confided the execution in its entirety, admitting a priori that they would be better and more quickly informed than he would of changes in the situation. And he left them, most often, to coordinate their efforts themselves, in the light of his unified doctrine.

A crown prince,[11] a Frederick-Karl,[12] a Steinmetz,[13] superb leaders, seeking responsibilities, could thus give free rein to their initiative. They never lacked it. Moreover, they became accustomed to act exclusively by their own conceptions and to consider those of the chief of the General Staff, literally, as secondary. Besides, Moltke, consistent with himself, did not fail to approve them after the fact, disdaining all authorial vanity and concerning himself only with results.

This manner [of doing things] had two consequences that, in their turn, became causes.

Moltke did not maintain independent means of keeping himself informed: all the cavalry went to the commanders, none to the generalissimo. Consequently, the field commanders were better informed than the supreme commander most of the time, and believed themselves to be so in all cases. Even more reason for them to judge their own conceptions better justified than judgments from higher echelons.

FIGURE 1.
The Disobedience of von Kluck, First Battle of the Marne, September 1914

Disobeying orders from Moltke, Kluck marches south, exposing his right flank, and the entire German line of battle, to envelopment by Maunoury's newly formed Sixth French Army.

Sources: *For this figure and Figures 4a–e, I have drawn information from the maps in Bülow, Hausen, Kluck, Kuhl, Moltke, and Tappen, all cited in the Appendix. Since even the maps in these memoirs are apologetic and tendentious, I have also drawn from plates in sources that de Gaulle does not cite:* Wilhelm Muller-Loebnitz, Der Wendepunkt des Weltkrieges: Beitrage zur Marne-Schlacht am 5. bis 9. September 1914. Kritische Beitrage zur Geschichte des Weltkrieges *(Berlin: E. S. Mittler & Sohn, 1921);* George Herbert Perris, The Battle of the Marne *(London: Methuen, 1920); and* Frederick Ernest Whitton, The Marne Campaign *(London: Constable and Co., 1917).*

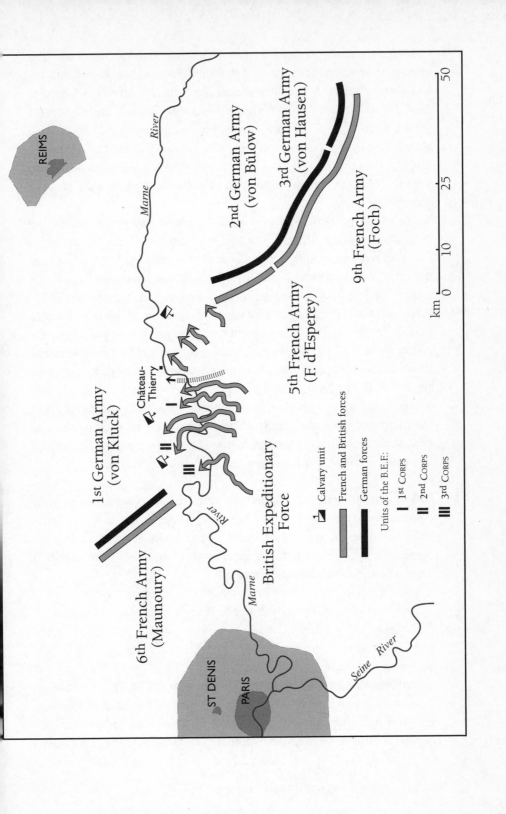

Moreover, transmissions between General Headquarters and the armies were entirely neglected. On 1 July 1866, Moltke gave his directive for the decisive battle against Benedek.[14] He himself was at Gitschin; Frederick-Karl was at Horitz, twelve kilometers distant, and the crown prince was at Königinhof, a distance of forty kilometers [see Figure 2a]. No one had thought to connect these three command posts by telegraph. They had not even set up a chain of cavalry riders. It fell to colonels from General Headquarters, who galloped all night through the rain, to carry the orders. . . .

On 18 August 1870, Moltke passed the whole day at the side of the king, near "La Point du Jour" behind his right flank.[15] He saw his right flank beaten and almost put to flight. It was with his left that he had mounted his operation. It was from his left that he anxiously awaited news. That left flank, under the crown prince of Saxony, attacked Saint-Privat at 6:00 P.M., eight kilometers away from Moltke's command post. A simple relay of riders would have brought blow-by-blow intelligence, barely an hour old, to the commander in chief. Instead, he would know nothing. No one even thought to keep him up to date. Not until 11:00 P.M. did he learn what had happened.

Due to this system and its consequences for means of information and communication, Moltke's army commanders acted by themselves, and against the intentions expressed by the High Command, at the decisive moments in their victorious campaigns.

■■■■ On July 1, 1866, Benedek was occupied in concentrating his army corps between the Elbe River to the south of Josephstadt and the Bistritz River facing to the west and the north. The Prussian Army of the Elbe (commanded by Herwarth von Bittenfeld), placed under the orders of Frederick-Karl, was toward Chlumetz.

The First Army (Frederick-Karl) was to the south of Horitz.

The Second Army (Crown Prince of Prussia) was toward Königinhof. [See Figure 2a.]

Moltke had been at Gitschin only a dozen hours. The evening before, he was still at Berlin with the King.

Furthermore, he had no cavalry at his disposal. In fact, the armies momentarily lost contact with the enemy. Behold the chief of the General Staff without military intelligence! He was going to base his conception for the battle upon an hypothesis, and that hypothesis was false.

FIGURES 2A–C.
The Battle of Königgrätz/Sadowa, 3–5 July 1866

By placing his headquarters (⊠) at Gitschin and neglecting communications with his commanders, Moltke encouraged them in "an exaggerated independence." His false hypothesis is shown in Figure 2a. Moltke believed the Austrian forces were east of the Elbe River, between Josephstadt and Königgrätz; they were actually ten kilometers west. Moltke's conception for the battle is shown in Figure 2b: the First Army and the Elbe Army were to circle to the south of Benedek and attack him from the south and southeast. But had Frederick-Karl obeyed Moltke's orders to March south along the Bistritz River, his army would have been exposed to a mortal threat from Benedek's entire army, as shown in Figure 2b. Had the Austrian commander seized the opportunity exhibited in the figure, he could have destroyed the Prussian First Army. Alerted to Benedek's actual position, Frederick-Karl ignored Moltke's command, and marched straight toward Benedek, asking the Crown Prince of Prussia to attack from the north. As shown in Figure 2c, the Prussian armies converged on the Austrian position from three sides, winning a victory that gave Prussia immense prestige and hegemony among the German states.

In 1866, the result of following orders would thus have been disastrous. Yet the cause could have been removed. Had headquarters been moved and communications to the supreme command secured, Moltke's information could have been as reliable as that of his commanders; or Frederick-Karl could have apprised Moltke quickly of the Austrian location.

Sources: *Figures 2a–c are based on Henri Bonnal,* Sadowa; étude de stratégie et de tactique générale. L'esprit de la guerre moderne. *(Paris: R. Chapelot, 1901); the label of 2a is taken from one of Bonnal's maps.*

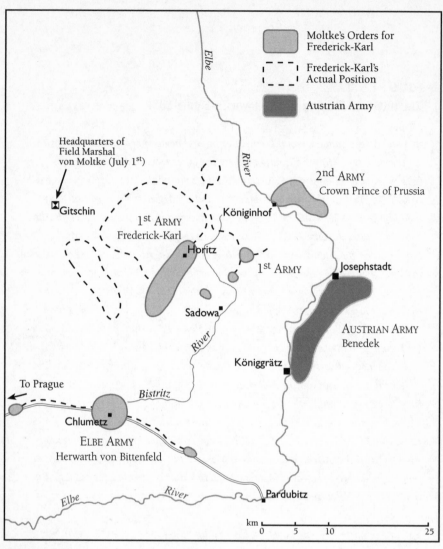

FIGURE 2A.
Dispositions ordered by von Moltke for 3 July

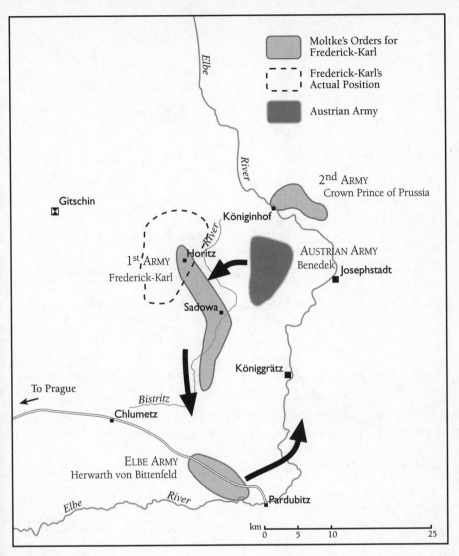

FIGURE 2B.
Outcome had Frederick-Karl obeyed von Moltke's orders

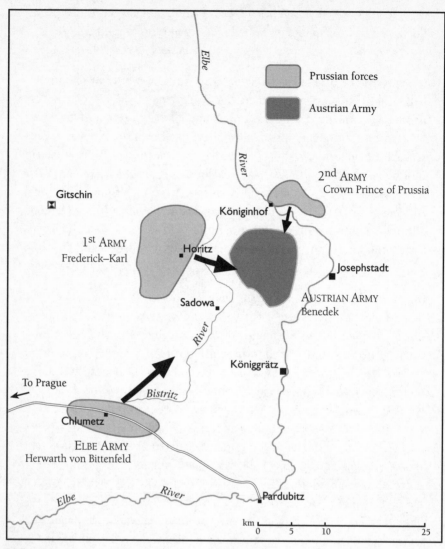

FIGURE 2C.
Actual result of Frederick-Karl's disobedience

He supposed that the enemy was to the east of the Elbe River, between Königgrätz and Josephstadt, and his orders for 2 July stipulated that

- the Army of the Elbe was to cross the Elbe at Pardubitz to turn Benedek's left.
- the First Army was to follow the movement of the Army of the Elbe, and to detach a flank-guard between the Bistritz and the Elbe. If that flank-guard encountered few significant Austrian forces east of the Elbe, it was to attack them.
- the Second Army was to remain in place. [See Figure 2a.]

However, on the morning of July 2nd, the cavalry of Frederick-Karl spotted very considerable masses of Austrian forces (at least four army corps), on the east bank of the Bistritz. The commander of the First Army immediately took it upon himself

1. not to execute the movement ordered by Moltke, which would result in making the Army of the Elbe and the First Army march in file, exposing its flank to the concentrated Austrian forces [see Figure 2b];
2. to bring himself with all his forces against the enemy masses east of the Bistritz River, and to engage them there in battle;
3. to call directly for the assistance of the Crown Prince of Prussia [see Figure 2c].

Frederick-Karl made his decision, dictated his orders, and had them largely put into execution even before advising General Headquarters, which was twelve kilometers away. Moltke would approve completely. The commander of the First Army had intelligence not possessed by the commander in chief; it was only right that he should do things his own way. Moreover, his decision conformed to the unity of doctrine: march straight to the known enemy. The marshal was fully satisfied.

A lieutenant colonel from General Headquarters mounted his horse on the night of 2–3 July and went alone under the beating rain to Königinhof (forty kilometers), to bring the order to support Frederick-Karl. And if that colonel had fallen into some ditch en route, nothing would have changed. For the crown prince, who had been ordered to remain in place, had already, on the evening of 2 July, ordered his army to march toward the enemy. The First Army and the Second Army had launched the operation, each independently and on its own, without taking account of intentions or orders from above. The result was Königgrätz. The entire German military, considering the victory, would have nothing but praise for the system.

■■■■■ On 15 August 1870, the French Army of Metz had been retreating toward Verdun since early evening.[16] The indecision of its leader, the wretched marching conditions, and the confused fighting at Borny on the 14th had delayed it in the extreme.[17] The Army used the day's march to concentrate itself on the left bank of the Moselle, to the north and northeast of Gravelotte [see Figure 3a].

The First German Army (Steinmetz) had been engaged at Borny. On the evening of the 15th, it was concentrated to the southeast of Metz, in the angle formed by the Seille and the Metz-Saint-Avold Road, facing to the northwest. The Second Army (Frederick-Karl), extremely dispersed, was on horseback on the Moselle from Novéant to Marbache, oriented to the west along a forty-kilometer front, forty kilometers deep.

Moltke was at Herny. He had received intelligence reports about the progress of the engagement at Borny only quite belatedly and slowly. Furthermore, he had no cavalry. Indeed, it would take more than six hours for him to communicate with Pont-à-Mousson, the headquarters of Frederick-Karl.

Toward the middle of the day, however, the chief of the General Staff had been able to form a correct idea of the situation thanks to a personal reconnaissance that he had conducted, led by his chief quartermaster General von Podbielski. From the heights of Flanville, he could see that the French army had evacuated the right bank of the Moselle, proof that it was beating its retreat, but that it had gained only very little ground toward the west. He therefore made his decision for the 16th and expressed it to Frederick-Karl by an order dispatched at 6:00 P.M., which arrived at Pont-à-Mousson at 11:00 P.M.:

> The advantage gained yesterday at Borny by the First Army cannot be directly pursued by it. It is solely by a victorious offensive of the Second Army against the roads from Metz to Verdun by Fresnes and by Étain that we can harvest the fruits of victory [see Figure 3a].
>
> The commander in chief of the Second Army is ordered to conduct that operation according to his own inspiration and with all the means at his disposal.

Moltke thus wanted, for the 16th, to cut off Bazaine's retreat to Verdun by interposing the entire Second Army.

However, as on 1 July 1866, Frederick-Karl formed a wholly personal conception of the situation. This time, again, his conception in no way agreed with that of General Headquarters. This time, again, he was going to act according to his own view and to consider received orders as peripheral.

Frederick-Karl had believed since the 12th of August that the French were retreating from the Moselle to the Meuse. Alerted to the Battle of Borny, he was inclined to see it only as a rear-guard engagement of the enemy. The evening of the 15th, he was convinced that Bazaine had gained considerable ground toward the west and that there was no hope of overtaking him before the Meuse. The prince judged that the task for his army was to reach the Meuse south of Verdun as quickly as possible, and only then would he be able to head north without encountering merely empty terrain [see Figure 3b].[18]

At 7:00 P.M., he gave his orders to the Second Army for the 16th: "The enemy is in retreat toward the Meuse. Consequently, the Second Army will follow the adversary without stopping, in the direction of that river."

The bulk of the army was oriented squarely toward the west. Only two corps of the right flank, the Third and the Tenth Corps, were pushed toward the northwest up to the road from Mars-la-tour to Verdun [see Figures 3b, 3c].[19]

At 11:00 P.M., Moltke's order came to Frederick-Karl, directing him to "mount a vigorous offensive against the roads from Metz to Verdun by Fresnes and Étain with all means at your disposal."[20]

The commander of the Second Army had more than enough time to modify his previous order and to orient his army toward the north and northwest.[21] He did nothing about it. Not a word that he had written beforehand was changed.

The next day, near Gravelotte, the Third and Tenth Corps were about to throw themselves alone against the entire French army, intact and reassembled. It would require the systematic inertia of Marshal Bazaine to save them from a complete disaster [Figure 3d].[22] However, military history has been unwilling to recognize the mortal peril risked on the decisive day. The result having been attained on 18 August, everything that had preceded and led to it was proclaimed glorious and reasonable. The unlimited independence of Frederick-Karl was, as after Sadowa, universally cited as exemplary.[23] The system of Moltke found itself definitively consecrated in it. On this occasion, however, the application of the system, and of the independence which was its fruit, had come within a hair's breadth of ruining Prussia's fortune. . . .

■ II

The Imperial Army of 1914 claimed it would assure the definitive triumph of that fortune.

It was from Nietzsche that the leaders, like all thinking Germany, had drawn their philosophy. Enthusiastically adopting the cult of the Overman, each was thus naturally disposed to consider himself the center of the world. Each inclined, on the one hand, to develop his character to an extreme and put it to the test with a constancy and audacity that have not been sufficiently noted. But on the other hand, each leaned toward exaggerated independence and was determined to act on his own in all situations.

Militarily, their leaders had been formed by studying Moltke's campaigns, and it is understood that they treated them as models. The "manner" of the old marshal appeared to them as the ideal, not only in consideration of his success, but precisely because it encouraged such distorted initiative in subordinates and because it consecrated unlimited independence.

The commanders of the army of 1914 dreamed of following the example of Frederick-Karl before Königgrätz or on the eve of Gravelotte. They were all disposed and resolved in advance to form their own personal conception of the situation and to act accordingly, regardless of what the higher command might prescribe.

That command, furthermore, was steeped in the same principles. Following the example of the great marshal, the command had minutely regulated the preparation, the plans, and the initial missions. But it had decided a priori to give to subordinates only extremely general and infrequent directives in execution and to sanction all their initiatives on principle. Perhaps an authoritarian personality of the stature of a von Schlieffen, only recently chief of the General Staff, whose superiority was acknowledged by the whole army, would have acted differently.[24] But in 1914, the chief of the General Staff was Colonel-General von Moltke, a hard-working and well-prepared man, but with only half his energy and, moreover, ill. Rightly or wrongly, his ambitious and troublesome lieutenants considered him to be a man of the second rank. For

FIGURES 3A–D.
The Battle of Gravelotte, Franco-Prussian War, 15 August 1870

Figure 3a shows that had Moltke's orders been followed, Frederick-Karl's Second Army would have been well-concentrated and strongly positioned, cutting off the lines of Bazaine's retreat from Metz. Figure 3b displays Frederick-Karl's contrary conception, illustrating his false hypothesis that Bazaine was retreating rapidly toward Verdun. Following this hunch, he tried to outrun the French by racing up the Meuse Valley. The result is shown in Figure 3c: part of the Second Army is out of the picture, on the Meuse; another part is strung out along the road to Fresnes; and only the small Tenth and Third Corps are near the French positions. The real vulnerability of these numerically small units is shown graphically in Figure 3d.

In 1870, at Gravelotte, disaster could well have resulted — not from obedience to Moltke, as in 1866, but from Frederick-Karl's disobedience, which exposed these units of Alvensleben and Voigts-Rhetz to vastly superior French forces. Moreover, in 1866, he had solid evidence that at least four corps of the Austrian army were close. In disobeying Moltke's order he was conforming to the "unity of doctrine," marching straight toward the known enemy. In 1870, however, his intelligence was not superior to Moltke's; he was guessing as to Bazaine's whereabouts. In fact, he was marching away from the enemy and removing his forces from the battle.

Sources: *Figures 3a–d are based on Henri Bonnal,* La manoeuvre de Saint-Privat, 18 juillet — 18 août 1870. Étude de critique stratégique et tactique, *3 vols. (Paris: R. Chapelot, 1904–12); the detailed troop dispositions in 3c and 3d are based on one of Bonnal's maps.*

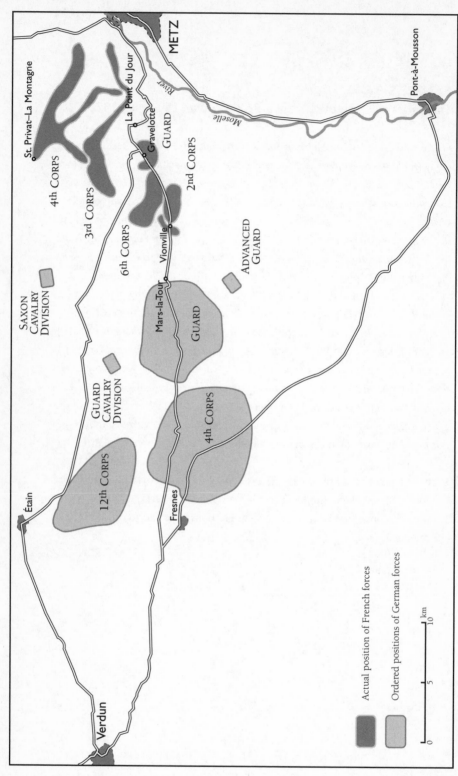

FIGURE 3A.

Actual position of French forces

Ordered positions of German forces

0   5   10 km

METZ

Pont-à-Mousson

St. Privat–La Montagne

La Point du Jour

Gravelotte

GUARD

2nd CORPS

4th CORPS

3rd CORPS

6th CORPS

Vionville

Moselle River

ADVANCED GUARD

Saxon Cavalry Division

Mars-la-Tour

GUARD

Guard Cavalry Division

4th CORPS

12th CORPS

Étain

Fresnes

Verdun

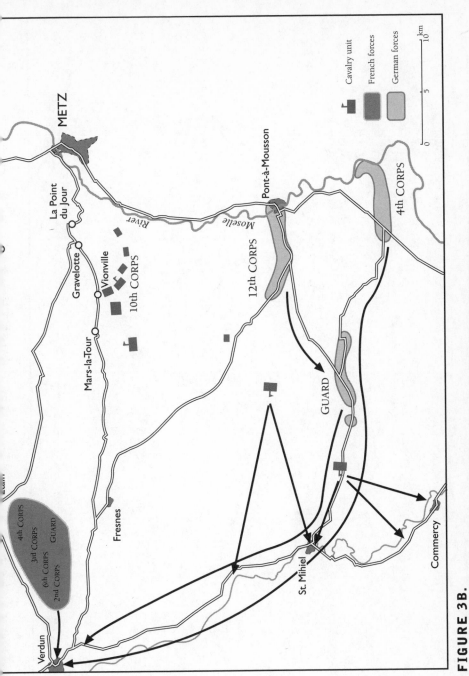

FIGURE 3B.
Frederick-Karl's guess and his emplacement of the German Second Army

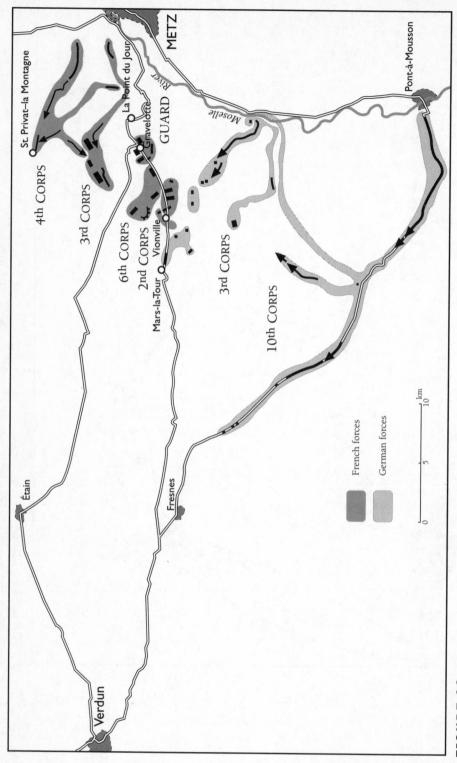

FIGURE 3C.

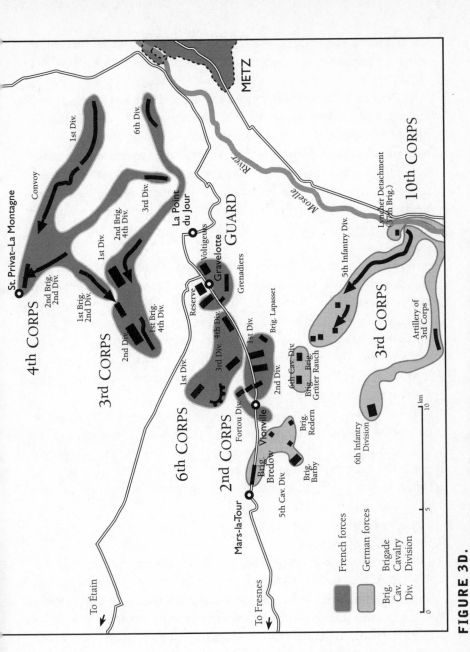

FIGURE 3D.
Third and Tenth German Corps prepared to face the entire French army

Kluck, Bülow, Hausen, and the like, Moltke really owed his position to being the nephew and namesake of "that gentleman who had so much talent."

On September 2, 1914, the Imperial General Headquarters was at Luxemburg.[25] [See Figure 4a.] Much has been said about the disadvantages of that emplacement. It was much too far removed from the line of battle, especially from the right where the main maneuver was executed. Its communications were highly precarious, since it took at least fifteen hours to drive (given the conditions of the roads and bridges) from Moltke to Kluck. Nor could telephone lines be run, or a telegraph set up, quickly enough. In fact, communications were reduced to the radio transmitter.

In the thick of the Battle of the Marne, Lieutenant Colonel von Hentsch of General Headquarters was to be charged on two occasions with a mission to von Kluck (First Army) and von Bülow (Second Army). Because of the distance involved and the precarious communications, this unfortunate officer was unable to keep himself up to date on a general situation that was rapidly changing. He would issue inopportune instructions, on behalf of the High Command, which would precipitate the defeat, and aggravate it.[a]

But the choice of a headquarters so far removed—that kind of negligence on the part of a chief of the General Staff with respect to the means of information and communications at his disposal—was precisely the "manner" of the great Moltke. The nephew, like the uncle, would be able to judge the situation only very late and through the eyes of his lieutenants. In addition, up to the 2nd of September, his conception regarding the maneuver of his right (First and Second Armies) was identical to that of Kluck.

We know that the commander of the First Army continued to believe, after [the Battle of] Guise, that the British army as a whole was at the extreme left of Joffre's forces and that everything swirling around farther to the west could be deliberately ignored [Figure 4b].[26] As his overall mission and intention consisted in enveloping the Allies' left, Kluck judged he should devote all his efforts to the pursuit of [the English commander Sir John] French.

Also, from the 31st of August, in agreement with Moltke, he had begun

[a] Colonel von Hentsch was killed on the Romanian front in 1916.

to bend toward the southeast and crossed the Oise River between Compiègne and Noyon.

However, beginning on 2 September, the Imperial General Headquarters began to modify its way of seeing things. By aerial reconnaissance of all the armies and by certain other means of information, they got the feeling that the French were massing and reinforcing important units in the immediate vicinity of Paris. Hence the radio message of that day: "The intention of the supreme command is to repulse the French to the southeast of Paris. The First Army will follow the Second in echelon. It is charged, in addition, with covering the flank of the armies." Moltke wanted to have his right in echelon formation toward the rear in order to be able to cope with every contingency.

Yes . . . But that was not the conception of von Kluck, who denied there was any serious peril from Paris. The commander of the First Army therefore would not obey. Like his illustrious predecessors of 1866 and 1870, he would ignore the directive of his superior. Like them, moreover, he sincerely believed that he was judging the situation better than one could from General Headquarters and that he was duty-bound to act according to his own inspiration.

That is what he did. He was ordered to hold himself behind the Second Army; he continued to march ahead. He was counted upon to cover the flank of the entire German disposition; he did not cover it.

On 3 September, he crossed the Marne, as quickly as he could, between La Ferté-sous-Jouarre and Château-Thierry. Clinging to his conception, he did not even advance toward his right the cavalry corps (von der Marwitz) under his command, nor did he orient it toward Provins. And he experienced no embarrassment whatsoever in informing Moltke in what manner he was interpreting his mission. His radio message of the 3rd says tersely: "The French are executing a change of front around their right wing. The English are to the north of Coulommiers. The First Army crosses the Marne today. Tomorrow it will continue its movement beyond the Marne, through Rebais and Montmirail."

And Moltke did not react at all. Such is the weight of the past.

However, on 4 September, he received (from Armies other than the First, notably from the Second Army) aerial reconnaissance reports on the movements of French trains from east to west, such that he could no longer doubt that a grave danger was becoming evident on his right. At 7:00 P.M., he gave the order by radio: "The First and Second Armies must operate in concert against the front east of Paris. The First Army between Oise and Marne."

At that moment, von Kluck had barely crossed beyond the Petit Morin. Had he obeyed on the 5th, he would have been able to bring the bulk of his army back into the region of Lizy-Betz. Then, on the 6th, during the Maunoury offensive, the French Sixth Army would have marched headlong into his five army corps and his whole cavalry corps.

But Kluck had not modified his personal conception of the situation; he therefore would not change his orders. On the 5th, he continued his march toward the southeast and reached the Grand Morin. A solitary corps (the Fourth Reserve) and one lone division of cavalry (the Fourth) were left as a flanking guard on the north of the Marne [Figures 4c, 4d1].

And only late in the morning on the 5th, when his troops had completed the better part of the day's march, did he give General Headquarters an account of his manner of seeing things and of the dispositions he had taken: "I consider it disruptive to move the First and Second Armies. I propose to pursue the enemy as far as the Seine and only afterwards to besiege Paris. If we were to carry out that siege as you ordered it, the enemy would be free in his movements."

Then, while his radio message was being deciphered at Luxemburg, the commander of the First Army finally received from Moltke a written order and intelligence bulletins that made clear to him the extent of his error:

> The enemy has reached the outskirts of Paris with some component units. He is proceeding to reorganize his forces and to marshal large numbers in the vicinity of Paris.
>
> Consequently, the First and Second Armies must continue to press on the Paris front. Their mission consists in countering the enemy initiatives coming from Paris.
>
> The First Army is to remain between Oise and Marne!

But it was too late; the French offensive had begun.

■ On the 2nd of July 1866, Prince Frederick-Karl had received the order to encircle the Austrians from the south. Instead, he marched directly upon them toward the east, and determined the outcome of the battle and the victory at Königgrätz.

On the 15th and 16th of August 1870, Prince Frederick-Karl, despite the orders he had received, had pursued the enemy toward the Meuse, where the enemy was not to be found. He had strung out his dispersed army within range of massed French troops, assembled unbeknownst to him on his right flank, and had risked what might have been a decisive disaster.

On the 5th of September 1914, General von Kluck, despite the repeated orders of Moltke the nephew, had rushed toward the Seine. Believing he was holding the enemy's left, he extended his troops in file beside the Sixth French Army, which was concentrated on his right flank. Maunoury stood forth before him.[27] The strategic surprise of Kluck was complete. The entire German strategic position was to pay the price, with an irremediable defeat.

As we have seen, the chief of the German General Staff of 1914 had conformed very closely to the manner of his illustrious predecessor of 1866–70. The commander of the First Army had acted no differently from his glorious counterparts in that happy epoch. Moltke's system, as regards execution, was rigorously applied by the German command in the course of those immortal days of September 1914. That system had formerly produced Sadowa and Saint-Privat. It was now the cause of the Marne.

In studying victories, German military history deferred to national pride and constrained itself not to discern the faults committed; it refused to heed the warnings. What had succeeded against a Benedek, or a Bazaine, was rendered disastrous by a Joffre.

FIGURES 4A–E.
The First Battle of the Marne, 6–9 September 1914

Figures 4a–e exhibit Kluck's vital mission and his failure to carry it out. Figure 4a shows how rapidly the German armies pushed the French and British into positions from which they could not protect Paris—or so it appeared. The strategic conception is on a much grander geographic scale than the 1866 and 1870 operations; the reader will see that the German line of battle extended from the German border near Strasbourg to above Verdun, and then from Verdun to Paris. The idea was to swing the whole front around the hinge at Verdun and thereby drive the Allied armies south and east of Paris. But to keep the French armies moving, the entire German line had to face them to the south and maintain a continuous fighting line. They were especially vulnerable, therefore, on Moltke's far right. If the right flank of the line were turned, a complete revolution in German strategy would follow. (The reader may recall Figure 1, on the effect of Kluck's disobedience.) The taking of Paris, and the hope of a quick victory in the West, had to be abandoned. The only option was to extend the line from Verdun to the coast; both sides then began their "race to the sea."

Kluck's hunch was originally well founded; the British Expeditionary Force (BEF) under Sir John French was to the left of the French Fifth Army under Franchet d'Esperey. Unbeknownst to Kluck, however, Joffre began to form a new army under Maunoury, to the north and east of Paris, while the BEF was executing the turn-about shown in Figure 4b.

Figures 4c and 4d show how poorly prepared Kluck was for Joffre's counterstroke. Figure 4c shows Kluck's guess and his emplacement of the German First Army. Kluck's hunches were just as wrong as Frederick-Karl's had been in 1870. In 1914, as in 1870, the German chief of staff had more accurate intelligence of the enemy's movements. Kluck was commanded to keep his units in echelon formation against the danger of a French attack from the west. Then he was ordered to march straight to the known enemy, outside Paris. Instead, he left minimal units to guard his right and plunged south, achieving the positions shown in 4c. Figure 4d shows him withdrawing in response to Maunoury's army, which was enveloping him from his right.

Figure 4e indicates the consequences of Kluck's error. His Fourth Corps, which the reader will see well east of Coulommiers in Figure 4c, had crossed the Grand Morin River. Kluck was forced to withdraw it back to the Ourcq River (Figure 4d), and finally to put it on his extreme right, to prevent Maunoury from turning his flank (Figure 4e). His Second Cavalry Division had also been below Coulommiers (Figure 4c); he had to withdraw it north near Château-Thierry. His Third Corps had been below the Grand Morin south and slightly west of Montmirail; he had to withdraw it northwest of Château-Thierry, a retreat of more than twenty kilometers (Figure 4e).

Sources: *See Figure 1.*

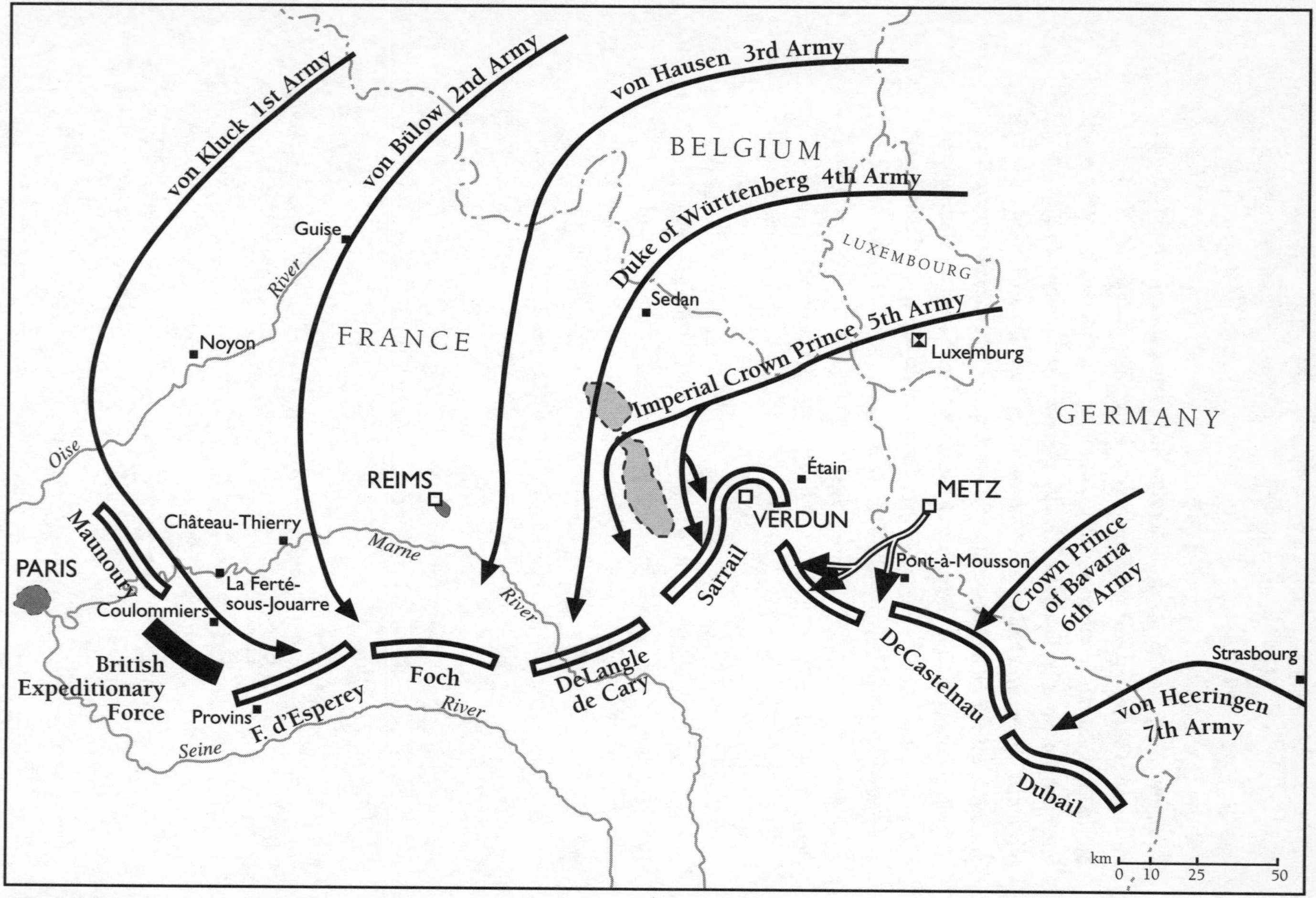

GERMANY

BELGIUM

LUXEMBOURG

FRANCE

Strasbourg

von Heeringen 7th Army

Crown Prince of Bavaria 6th Army

Dubail

DeCastelnau

Pont-à-Mousson

METZ

Luxemburg

5th Army

Imperial Crown Prince

Étain

VERDUN

Sarrail

Sedan

Duke of Württemberg 4th Army

DeLangle de Cary

von Hausen 3rd Army

River

Foch

River

Marne

REIMS

von Bülow 2nd Army

River

Guise

River

Noyon

Château-Thierry

La Ferté-sous-Jouarre

Provins

F. d'Esperey

Seine

von Kluck 1st Army

Oise

Maunoury

Coulommiers

British Expeditionary Force

PARIS

km

0   10   25   50

FIGURE 4.4

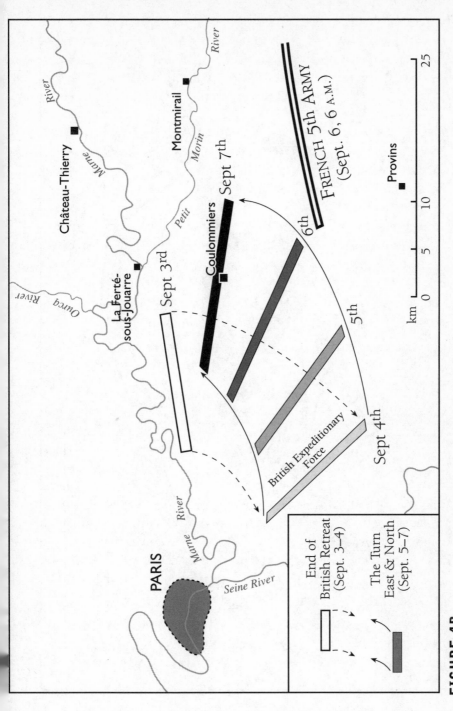

FIGURE 4B.
The British turn-about

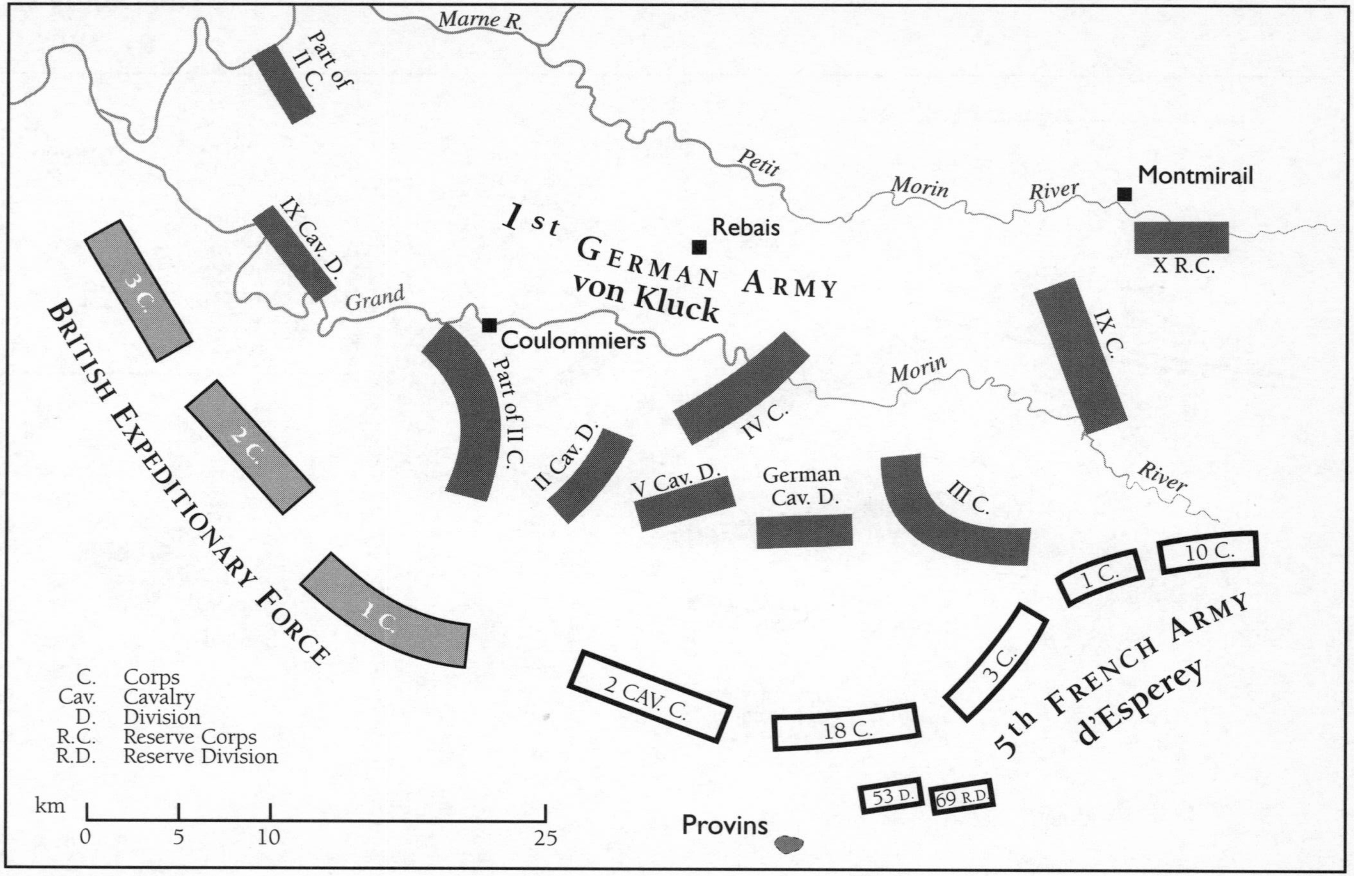

FIGURE 4C.
Kluck's moves and his positioning of his forces

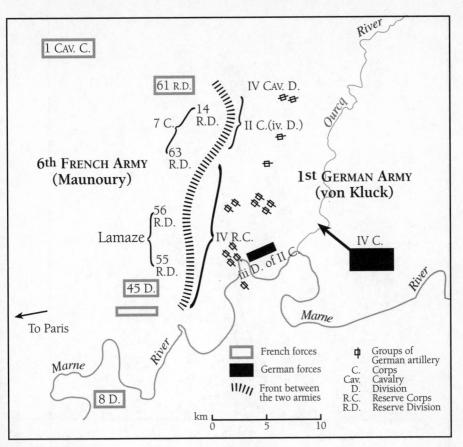

FIGURE 4D.
The Ourcq Front, afternoon of 6 September

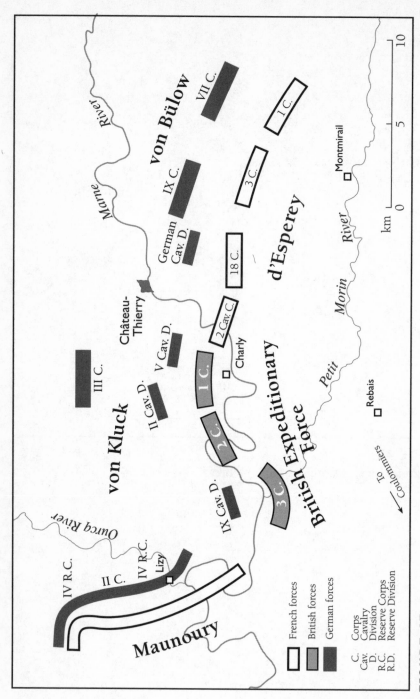

FIGURE 4E.
The Marne recrossed, morning of 9 September

2

The Declaration of Unlimited Submarine Warfare

The proclamation of an unlimited submarine blockade was bound to entail the gravest foreign policy consequences. There is no doubt that in this matter it was the chancellor of the Empire, the head of government exercising political direction of the war, who logically should have had final disposition over the decision. As we shall see, his authority was disputed furiously and at length, then torn away from him in the final reckoning.

A relentless battle between the government and the navy was allowed to go on around the weak mind of Wilhelm II over the course of two years. That struggle took every form: political controversy, sly intrigue, violent outbursts. In each of the two camps, the impossible was accomplished to assure the support of public opinion and of men of influence. What ought to have remained a question of utility and opportunity, at all costs, became a great affair of political parties and the standard by which personalities were to be judged. The conflict was finally resolved in the worst way and at the worst moment. This injected into German public opinion the gravest acrimony and divisiveness, from which it never recovered. And this resolution, decided contrary to the only man who ought to have been acquainted with it—against the head of the government, against the chancellor—was the direct cause of the German defeat.

If the logic of principles had been respected—if the government of the Empire had been allowed to conduct the war as it wished, if it had abstained from launching intensified submarine warfare in February 1917 —then Germany would have pulled it off. Without American intervention and the hope that the Entente drew from it, the events of this period —the Russian Revolution and the peace with Russia some months later, the failure of the French spring offensive combined with the moral crisis which was its consequence, and the efforts of Lansdowne and Ramsay MacDonald in London—would have placed the Empire in highly favorable circumstances to negotiate peace with the aid of the mediation that President Wilson had just offered.

I

Until the spring of 1916, Grand Admiral von Tirpitz was secretary of the Navy. Already well before the war, Chancellor Bethmann-Hollweg and Tirpitz were locked in a continuous, if veiled, struggle.

Bethmann, who was a jurist and a democrat, and Tirpitz, a quintessential Junker and an "old Prussian" despite his breadth of mind and culture, could not easily understand each other.[1] The grand admiral had properly been the father of the German fleet; and he was the soul of the naval challenge to England. The chancellor, however, desiring to achieve a rapprochement with England, had favored the visit of Lord Haldane to Berlin and accepted the principle of a limitation on naval construction. It was Tirpitz who prevented any agreement. Bethmann and Tirpitz never forgave each other for their respective parts in the episode.[2]

From the first day of hostilities [in 1914], the grand admiral's opposition to the war policy of the chancellor was entirely unconcealed. Bethmann never gave up hope of one day reconciling Germany and England; he intended to make Russia bear the costs of the conflict. Tirpitz, like many of the Old Prussians, dreamed of an alliance with the Tsar and of crushing the democracies of the West. Furthermore, his entire life had been devoted to preparing for war against Great Britain. He wanted to see the naval enemy smitten.

By 2 August 1914, the opposition between the admiral and the chancellor appeared plainly. That day a conference was held before the Kaiser, between Bethmann, the Minister of Foreign Affairs Jagow, Chief of the General Staff von Moltke, the Minister of War Falkenhayn, and Tirpitz. It was a question of reaching agreement on the dates for sending the different declarations of war. A violent altercation took place between the admiral, supported by Moltke, and the chancellor. The latter, very much annoyed, left the meeting. When he was gone, Tirpitz said to the sovereign, "For several years now our Foreign Ministry has not functioned. It is not my role to give you advice in this matter, but the gravity of the hour constrains me" — (already!) — "to overstep the limits of my function. As the Chancellor is my superior, I do not wish to judge him. But as for Jagow, he must be replaced by Hintze, whom you will recall from Mexico."[3]

Recalled or not, Admiral von Hintze, minister to Mexico, in fact returned from there immediately. He found the means to open a route for himself all the way into the headquarters of the Kaiser. But from there, Bethmann, who had retaken the advantage, succeeded in sending him to Peking.[4]

Tirpitz, whose normal place was in Berlin, wished to follow the Headquarters of the General Staff, hoping to be able to exercise his influence on it. There [in Charleville]he chafed at the reins. He was held in distrust by the Kaiser's cabinet, was viewed in a rather bad light by the General Staff of the Army (which, under the orders of the moderate Falkenhayn,[a] judged him "tiresome and unrestrained"), and he was in open conflict with the chancellor's people and with Jagow's.[b] He avenged himself for this coldness by making pessimistic and sarcastic remarks about the military.[c] He had flatly proposed that the fleet should sail out at the first favorable occasion and seek battle. But this project enthused neither the Kaiser, nor the sailors themselves, nor Falkenhayn. Heartbroken, the grand admiral thus saw his life's work rendered vain. In an excess of bitterness, he naturally blamed his old adversary and threw himself into a shrill and dogged campaign of insinuation against the chancellor, claiming that "he was afraid to excite England" and that he was the cause of the inaction of the fleet.

[a] Recall that Falkenhayn had replaced Moltke, disgraced after his defeat at the Marne.

[b] At Charleville, Tirpitz had been lodged at the Place Carnot (the Maison of Madame G. Gailly), as far as possible from the Kaiser, who lived close to the station (Maison of M. Corneau). "Very few people come to see me," he wrote, "and only at night, hugging the wall in order not to compromise themselves." (*Wartime Letters of Tirpitz*).

[c] At the "Hotel du Lion d'Argent" at Charleville, the officers of the departments of the General Staff had their "casino." There, toward the end of 1914, it was said, "There is only one man at Charleville who does not wish to believe that the war will be over by 1 April 1915; that man is Grand-Admiral von Tirpitz." (*Wartime Letters of Tirpitz*). [See Tirpitz, *Memoirs*, 2:229.]

On 4 September 1914, through his friends in the Reichstag, Tirpitz was able to mount a demonstration in his favor. A motion was made, inviting the government to quickly present new legislation for naval construction. And Count von Reventlow, a personal friend of the grand admiral, opened a campaign along the same lines in a series of vigorous articles in the *German Daily News*.[5] On 4 September 1914, before the Marne, the entire world believed that the war would be quickly terminated. In any case, who believed that it would last more than three years? Now, three years would be required to construct new battleships. To put such a project into execution would be to proclaim that a war without quarter would be waged on England. The chancellor had the motion buried. His resentment against the admiral increased; and in return, the admiral fully reciprocated.

Tirpitz saw that he could not vanquish the opposition of the Kaiser and of many naval officers (notably von Pohl, the chief of the naval general staff, and von Müller, the chief of the Kaiser's naval cabinet) to his plans for a great naval battle. So he resolved, although without any enthusiasm, to devote his efforts to submarine warfare. An exclusive partisan of great combat ships, in peacetime he had systematically scorned the grandiose projects for mass producing submarines, projects that pitted against his own plans a certain number of officers and engineers, some theoreticians and publicists, and (in the Reichstag committees) politicians preoccupied with economizing.[6]

Once he had resolved on submarine warfare, however, Tirpitz wanted to see it begun only when the means existed to conduct it on a very grand scale. With good reason he judged that the moral and material results would be infinitely better if the maximum impact were obtained at a single blow. This would leave no time for the Entente to find a means of defense, or for neutrals—America in particular—to crystallize their attitude and perhaps to prepare their intervention.

According to him, it was expedient, therefore, prior to taking any action, to construct a considerable number of submarines, to arrange ports, to make sure that repairs would be possible, and to prepare for the action at sea.

But this was not the opinion of the chief of the Naval General Staff, von Pohl. This man of narrow, ambitious, and vain intellect was above all jealous of Tirpitz. He was inclined to propose (as if on principle) the contrary of whatever the grand admiral recommended. Moreover, it seemed clear that Pohl owed his position to this notorious hostility and to the hope entertained by the chancellor and by the Kaiser's cabinet that they might use him to neutralize Tirpitz and be left in peace to some extent.

Von Pohl was determined to put the submarine war into effect immediately. He felt haste was all the more necessary because he was preparing to take command of the fleet and did not wish to leave the General Staff before he had put his name on the orders launching this new form of naval warfare for the first time in history.

Chancellor Bethmann had no technical understanding whatever of naval questions. But he understood that submarine warfare waged on commercial ships would be the start of a series of possibly very grave difficulties. His common sense, the reports of German ambassadors, in particular those sent by Count Bernstorff from Washington, and the declarations of U.S. Ambassador Gerard, all left him in no doubt whatever. He was sure that the destruction of neutral vessels and of English and French ocean liners (on which many Americans voyaged) would lead to acute complications with the United States and perhaps with other neutral powers. And in regard to the "unrestricted submarine warfare"[d] that was contemplated by the chief of staff of the Navy, the chancellor was rightly convinced that it would lead to a conflict over principles with Wilson and to war with America. Bethmann was resolved to do everything to insure that this new enemy did not join the Entente. Beyond the moral and material reinforcement that it would give to the adversaries of the Central Powers, he foresaw the dashing of his hopes for American mediation at the favorable moment.

From the moment Tirpitz became aware of the chancellor's opposition to submarine warfare, his resolve to impose it was immediate and implacable. The same passion, tenacity, and energy that he had previously brought to condemning it, he now put into recommending it, praising it, demanding it. To force it upon the government, which did not want it at all, he deployed every means and used every channel.

He threw the question into the political arena. He made it into a struggle over personalities, putting himself up against the chancellor before the public, thereby imparting to this controversy a fierce and furious character that we can hardly imagine today.

[d]Unrestricted submarine warfare consisted in sinking encountered vessels without giving warning or even surfacing, thus depriving passengers and crew of all possibility of saving themselves.

At the end of December 1914, Admiral von Pohl proposed to the Kaiser to declare the submarine blockade of the coasts of Great Britain and Ireland and to set the launching of operations for the end of January. Tirpitz made plain his disapproval of the date, finding it premature, but openly gave his assent to the principle. As the chancellor saw, the Kaiser and the High Command were dejected by recent setbacks on the Yser, and by the prospect of a whole winter of stalemate.[7] They were thus disposed to lend an ear to the hotheads in the navy, who claimed shrilly that with submarine warfare they had the means "to bring England to its knees in six weeks." To gain time, he tried to reconcile himself with Tirpitz; he knew Tirpitz was disposed to defer the proclamation of the submarine blockade for lack of resources. He had several conversations with the grand admiral on this subject. During the last, on 27 January [1915], he received assurances from Tirpitz that he would oppose von Pohl's hastiness. Reassured, Bethmann consented to have jurists and the staffs of the Ministry of Foreign Affairs go to work on the text of a declaration of blockade. This would gain several months. In the spring, great military events would surely develop, and the Kaiser would be thinking about something else.

What game did the grand admiral play during the few days that followed? The details are not known. However, enough is known to confirm that he was neither loyal nor above-board. On 4 February, von Pohl took advantage when the Kaiser was visiting the port of Wilhelmshafen by ship, far from the chancellor and Jagow. Taking this as a sign that slumbering naval ambitions were reawakening in the Kaiser, von Pohl had him approve the text of a declaration of blockade that had been drafted in his headquarters. He swore to Wilhelm II that he had obtained the approval of the chancellor in advance; and he had this text published immediately. Tirpitz was present but in no way opposed it. He limited himself to having a few details modified.[8] What is one to think of this change of face? Until we are more fully informed, are we not justified in concluding that the grand admiral's hatred of Bethmann, his desire to inflict a defeat on him, and no doubt also his hope that Bethmann might submit his resignation, prevailed in Tirpitz's mind and conscience, over his convictions and his word?

Bethmann could do no more than record the fait accompli. He discerned the series of new perils to which it exposed Germany. But since his character was too mediocre to oppose the thing squarely, he hoped the future would offer him the occasion to unravel this web, whose weaving he had not been able to prevent.

II

On 12 February [1915], an American note was received in Berlin protesting the declaration of blockade and warning Germany that she would be responsible for all damages caused by submarines to the life and property of U.S. citizens. That threat had been easy to foresee; Ambassador Gerard in Berlin and Count Bernstorff in Washington had warned of it clearly.

The U.S. note restored the chancellor's energy. On 15 February he obtained from the Kaiser the decision to wait until further notice to start the operation. But distrusting the independent spirit of Tirpitz and of the new chief of the Naval General Staff, Bachmann,[e] he took the additional precaution of having it stipulated directly and specifically to all the submarine commanders that they were to spare all neutral vessels within the blockade zone. Finally, determined to cut off at their source the incredible rumors about the possibilities of submarine warfare that were streaming into the political world, the press, the salons, and the streets, he persuaded the Kaiser's cabinet to send Tirpitz the following telegram: "The Kaiser wishes that you may make known to him, without reticence, whether and in what measure you can guarantee that within six weeks the new commercial war will constrain England to capitulate. Respond by telegram."[9]

Twenty days previously, Tirpitz had declared to Bethmann, and had even written to the Kaiser, that in his opinion they ought to defer the beginning of the submarine war, because sufficient means to conduct it were lacking. Carried away this time by the passion of the personal fight into which he had thrown himself, seeing only the combat with his adversary Bethmann, who must be defeated, he had the audacity to respond, "The Secretary of State, Tirpitz, and the Chief of the General Staff of the Navy, Bachmann, are persuaded that England will be brought to capitulate six weeks after the commencement of the new submarine war, provided that, from the outset, all the available means are energetically engaged."[10]

[e] Admiral Bachmann had replaced von Pohl, named commander of the High Sea Fleet.

That promise removed the hesitations of the Kaiser's cabinet, and on the 20th of February 1915, the order to execute the policy was launched.

Of course, once the submarine blockade was announced, Tirpitz and Bachmann never ceased to intensify it, despite the entreaties of the Wilhelmstrasse. They began by excusing the submarine commanders from sparing neutral ships encountered in the blockade zone, under the pretext that all Allied commercial vessels sailed under a neutral flag. At first free passage was reserved for Swedish and Norwegian boats; later that privilege was denied them. Finally, alleging that the security of German crews outweighed all other considerations, the submarines were authorized to sink enemy ships without surfacing, which amounted to suppressing all prior warning.

Despite all the prayers and recommendations the chancellor sent to the navy, no account was taken of any of them. The foreign situation, however, should have inclined Germany toward moderation. Italy was reorienting itself toward the war. Bulgaria was beginning to propose its cooperation. To calm the one and draw the other along, it was absolutely necessary that the policy of the Central Powers not be condemned by neutral powers pushed to the limit; above all it was absolutely necessary that the ties between Berlin and Washington not be severed. Bethmann understood that quite well. But while he was responsible for the whole, he had neither the power to command this nor the character to insist on it.

On 7 May, the *Lusitania,* an English liner filled with American passengers, was sunk. As is well known, the incident triggered a truly national outburst of anger in the United States. Wilson immediately protested violently and demanded indemnities. The chancellor believed the moment had come to retake the offensive against the naval command.

General Headquarters, greatly preoccupied with the French attacks at Artois and with the advance march of Mackensen, after Gorlice, and now altogether skeptical about the results that would be "obtained against England in six weeks," no longer took any interest in submarines.[11]

Moreover Falkenhayn, overwhelmed by Austrian lamentations since Italy's entry into the war, absolutely insisted that Bulgaria be persuaded to fight and that the neutrals be kept neutral. At last the Kaiser and political opinion were, for the moment, favorable to the chancellor. His projects, of making a peace without annexations in the West and gaining much more advantage in the East, seemed to many to be good sense itself, since Mackensen had pierced the Russian front and the French had leapt with one bound as far as Vimy.[12]

Thus on 31 May, at the council of war held at Pless,[f] when Tirpitz and Bachmann found themselves alone in proposing to continue submarine warfare as it had been conducted, Bethmann declared that "he wanted no responsibility for this." Falkenhayn approved that, as did also those from the Kaiser's cabinet; Wilhelm II therefore signed the order to spare all neutral vessels and, some days later, the order not to sink passenger liners, even those of enemy powers.

In order to apply balm to the wounds thus inflicted on the grand admiral, the Kaiser bestowed on him "the Order of Merit." On receiving it some weeks later, Tirpitz said, "I am greatly moved by this privilege, but not happy. Given the manner in which the war on the seas is being conducted, there is no more joy for me."

He was not, moreover, of a character to accept defeat in exchange for a ribbon. Seeing that he was persona ingrata to the Kaiser and the Supreme Command, he resorted to his political friends. In the corridors of the Reichstag, the battle against the chancellor became more and more ardent. There one saw the cold face of Count Westorp, the leader of the Conservatives, "take on an expression of contempt" when Bethmann's name was mentioned. One saw Bassermann, the leader of the National Liberals, incite the deputies, declaring to them that the resignation of the grand admiral was imminent. He read them a letter from von Pohl, commander of the fleet, addressed to the Kaiser, demanding to be relieved of his post "in view of the conditions imposed by the chancellor on the naval war." There one even saw Dr. Kämpf, the venerable leader of the Center and president of the Reichstag, shaking his prophet's beard and invoking the shade of Bismarck. It was hard going for the defenders of Bethmann. Among them were Jagow, stiff and phlegmatic, but a conscientious minister and loyal to his chancellor; Payer, skeptical and eloquent, disdainful of the military men and instinctively opposed to their conceptions; and above all, Erzberger: agitated, insinuating, his gaze lowered, gliding over the carpets, "his shoulders bent as if ever afraid of a blow from a baton," but devoured by ill-concealed ambition, detesting the political right, who paid him back amply in kind and

[f]In the spring of 1915 the headquarters of the Imperial General Staff was moved from Charleville to Pless, for the offensive against the Russians.

treated him as "a dangerous Jew." All these men, moreover, had neither the inclination to make a decision in this matter, nor the power to do so, but were all the more irritated and uncertain. Their agitation was not hidden from the public. In order to have some peace, the chancellor adjourned the Reichstag. At the last session of the "Principal Committee"[8] on August 15th, the right sharply pressured Jagow, who was representing the government: "You are afraid of America!" Jagow was obliged to promise, not without irony, that "The American attitude will in no way influence us regarding submarine warfare."

Some days later, the *Arabic* was sunk by the naval officers, without warning and in formal violation of the orders they had received from the Kaiser not to sink passenger steamers. This time Bethmann acted with vigor. In Washington, Count Bernstorff ran to Wilson to declare that the misfortune was solely due to the error of a submarine commander, that the officer had been punished and that Germany was ready to indemnify the victims. Tirpitz and Bachmann were called urgently to Pless. When they arrived on the morning of 26 August, they first met the chancellor, who immediately challenged them:

> Ambassador Gerard tells me that the situation is grave with regard to our relations with America. That is also the opinion of our naval attaché, in Washington . . . I have had enough of walking upon volcanoes! . . . I want to be able to telegraph, without lying to Washington, that we will no longer torpedo any passenger steamer without warning, and without the passengers and crew being put in a position to save themselves.[13]

Then he bitterly revisited the *Lusitania* affair, in which the naval officers refused to recognize their errors: "I will accept the judgment of a tribunal of arbitration. It will fix the indemnities that we shall pay."[14]

Thereupon they were received at the Kaiser's. Here Tirpitz did not show his usual arrogance. He even proposed to withdraw all the submarines from British waters and to dispatch them to the Mediterranean.

---

[8] The Reichstag had elected from its bosom a committee, called the "Principal" or Main Committee. The leaders of all the parties were members; it was charged "to keep itself current on all questions concerning the foreign and domestic conduct of the war, and to manifest at their discretion the sentiment and intentions of the representatives of the German people." The committee did not hold public meetings, and its discussions have not been published.

He agreed that a conciliatory note would be sent to America and insisted only that it should not sacrifice the principle of submarine warfare. Bachmann showed less pliancy, saying that this was no time to send Washington "a declaration of weakness."[15] If one was absolutely determined to appear conciliatory, he argued, one should restrict oneself to "an invitation, made by the chancellor to the Navy, to have measures taken for saving the passengers of torpedoed liners," an invitation that would be published in the newspapers. And Tirpitz and Bachmann discussed the content and form of what the chancellor was to write; no one saw fit to invite them to mind their own business.[16]

Lunch was announced and the Kaiser cut off the conference to dine.

The next day, von Treutler, Bethmann's confidant and his representative at General Headquarters, came to Tirpitz's quarters and announced to him that Wilhelm II, acting upon the advice of the chancellor, had ordered the Foreign Office to send Washington the note Bethmann wanted. And when the admiral exclaimed that one ought at least to have taken his advice on the wording, Treutler replied, "The note has already gone off."[17]

During the day, Tirpitz and Bachmann were sent the Kaiser's order not to send any new submarines into the commercial war "until the situation has been clarified."

That same evening, Tirpitz, the Secretary of State for the Navy, Bachmann, the head of the Naval General Staff, and von Pohl, the Commander of the Fleet, demanded to be relieved of their functions.

To von Pohl, a mediocrity, the reply was limited to saying "that he had no right to protest his Majesty's orders." Bachmann, an excellent soldier without political experience or any taste to meddle in politics, was dismissed. But they were afraid of Tirpitz, knowing that he was a man who could cause great trouble out of office. His resignation was therefore refused, while he was reprimanded severely by the Kaiser: "Much previous experience has convinced me that all collaboration between yourself and the chancellor is impossible in all naval questions which touch upon politics, that is to say, almost all those concerning the conduct of the war at sea. I shall therefore forgo consulting with you regularly in regard to these questions. . . ."[18]

Despite the authoritarian brusqueness of the imperial letter, Tirpitz surely sensed that he was feared. If he was unaware of it, moreover, he would have learned of it quickly enough, upon seeing the crowd of personalities that paraded to visit him in Berlin during these days of crisis, to assure him loudly of their devotion. Half the Reichstag came to see and acclaim him. So did the boards of the six great German economic associations, "The Union of Farmers," "The German Association of the Peasantry," "The Group of Christian Peasants," "The Central Union of German Industrialists," "The Union of the Middle Classes of the Empire," and crowds of functionaries, businessmen, publicists.

Thus shored up, the grand admiral reiterated his resignation, declaring "that he could not remain at his post if he were not consulted in those questions which were the reason for the existence of his charge." The sovereign gave in and sent him this imperial promise: "It is entirely in accord with my intentions to request your advice in regard to all important naval questions."[19]

An extraordinary retreat of the supreme power, and unchallengeable proof of the crisis of authority, which (despite certain appearances) was the true moral cause of the defeat of the Empire!

III

The relations between the chancellor and the secretary of state of the Navy at this time had the character of open and public hostility. When, contrary to Tirpitz's advice, Admiral von Holtzendorf was named to replace Bachmann as head of the Naval General Staff, Tirpitz noisily refused to receive him. Everywhere it was said that Bethmann would be forced to depart and that Tirpitz would take his place. The grand admiral made every effort to bring people of weight around to his point of view: military men, politicians, businessmen. The empress, the crown princess, and Prince Henry of Prussia escaped him no better than Ballin, Cuno, or Stinnes. Hindenburg, already renowned, whom a large body of public opinion wanted to see made generalissimo, and moreover embittered because the Kaiser and Falkenhayn had rejected his strategic projects,[h] received the admiral's visit at his headquarters in Lötzen. What did Tirpitz propose to him? The Marshal has remained quite discreet on this point, but there are reasons to believe that the admiral offered him an alliance. "If I become chancellor, you will be generalissimo!" The

[h] At the beginning of 1915, Hindenburg had proposed that the Western front be substantially reduced, at the risk of losing some ground there, and that an offensive of very great scope be mounted against the Russians, to completely destroy their army. Falkenhayn preferred an effort conducted with limited means.

victor of Tannenberg detested politics and intrigue. But his chief of staff, Ludendorff, disdained neither.

Falkenhayn and the General Headquarters saw the second winter of the war arriving, and were obliged to halt the march on Russia; they began again to think favorably of the submarine weapon. In addition, Bulgaria had now intervened. Moreover, the offensive against Verdun, which it was hoped would be decisive, was being prepared, and it was considered imperative to disrupt English maritime traffic to the maximum, before and during the effort. Tirpitz could momentarily count on the cooperation of the Army Command.

The Reichstag, having returned from adjournment, began again to work itself up. The position of the chancellor there was difficult now because the right could not forgive his "softness," while the left found him insufficiently democratic and wanted to make him propose universal suffrage for Prussia, which would immediately have embroiled him with the Kaiser.

The grand admiral opened his door to all the politicians and held the most frank discussions with them. Remarkably, he declared to Erzberger, "It is my unshakable conviction that our navy is in a position, thanks to unrestricted submarine warfare, to bring England to its knees in six weeks, and to make it capitulate unconditionally."[20]

During the winter of 1915–16, such remarks, repeated on all sides, had become virtually the refrain of conversation for all Germans. The great economic associations named above offered a petition to the chancellor covered with signatures, protesting to him "that Germany's consideration for American interests ought not to go so far as to throw down the most redoubtable weapon she has at her disposal for conducting economic war against England."[21]

The right-wing press—above all the *Deutsche Tageszeitung,* followed by the *Gazette de la Croix,* the *Lokal Anzeiger,* and the *Gazette de Cologne* —treated America and Wilson like declared enemies and called with great clamor for a Bismarck to direct the policy of the Empire. Erzberger recounts:

At the beginning of February, there was seen developing in the public, at whom fantastic statistics were being thrown, a movement of opinion in favor of unrestricted submarine warfare, comparable only to the movement in Rome in May 1915 which by pressure from the streets compelled the Italian government to go to war. To my knowledge it was the first time in Germany that the people in the streets had taken part in politics. When I returned from the Orient, a veritable frenzy reigned in Berlin. Any man who was not a partisan of unrestricted submarine warfare found himself treated as an enemy of the nation, as an anti-patriot, a defeatist, etc. When it was squarely put to all these heroic armchair sailors what would become of Germany if America declared war on her, they fell silent or replied, "We shall see later," or "The submarines would act so swiftly that the Americans would not have time to enter the war."[22]

Tirpitz judged that the moment had come for him to move to the decisive attack. Reconciled for the moment with Admiral von Holtzendorf, chief of the Naval General Staff, he assembled at the home of the minister of war, Wild von Hohenborn, a council of conspirators, who met on 30 October 1915 and 5 January 1916. There Grand Admiral Holtzendorf and Wild von Hohenborn preached to Falkenhayn, whose support was indispensable. Falkenhayn declared himself decided, saying that if he had heretofore shown himself hostile to submarine warfare, it was in order to be assured of Bulgarian intervention. That intervention having taken place, there was no further obstacle, provided that the Navy promised to succeed. Tirpitz and Holtzendorf accepted this obligation with a light heart, and the agreement was made.[23]

On 7 January, Holtzendorf sent a categorical report to the Kaiser: "If we remove the trammels imposed on submarine warfare, we can affirm as certain, taking as a basis experiments already made, that the resistance of England will be broken in at most a half-year."[24]

At the same time, and with the same ink, Tirpitz wrote to the chancellor.

Once again in doubt about the undulating mind of Falkenhayn, the grand admiral sent to him at General Headquarters on 11 February a trusted aide, Ship's Captain Widenmann. This sailor, charged with creating a broil between the chief of the General Staff of the Army and the chancellor, touched Falkenhayn on a sensitive point. He insisted on the fact that Bethmann's peace projects were most unfortunate, for he meant not to keep any conquest in the West and to abandon Belgium, on the pretext that it would never be possible to crush the French and the British. Falkenhayn, who was completing preparations for the offensive against Verdun, was greatly moved by the argument. Indeed, he counted on reaping a decisive victory in the next few days. But he knew that his project for an attack against the French had been strongly criticized by Bethmann's entourage, who agreed in this matter with his fortunate and menacing rival, Hindenburg. Thus cleverly outmaneuvered, Falkenhayn took his supreme decisions and replied to Tirpitz's messenger, "We are all in accord in thinking that England will fight until the decision. The decision is the possession of Belgium. If we let go of Belgium, we are lost!" And then, "I have decided in favor of submarine warfare, and I firmly count on its implementation. In order to insure that, I will fully commit myself to it, and I will obtain it. . . ."[25]

Finally, on 23 February, profiting from the arrival of the Kaiser at Wilhelmshafen and from the exaltation produced in his spirit by the first news of the assaults on Verdun, Tirpitz brusquely took it up: "It is with a profound joy that I learned of your Majesty's intention to conduct a serious struggle against English tonnage. The question of tonnage is the decisive question of the whole war. It is no longer possible to postpone it, for it is a question for Germany of its very existence. . . . It is necessary that you come to a decision. . . ."[26]

Bethmann saw the storm approach, and understood that it was high time to subjugate Tirpitz or resign his post. He maneuvered, notably, toward the side of the accessible Falkenhayn. On 6 March, the Kaiser's cabinet was called together to study the question of submarine warfare: Bethmann, Falkenhayn, and Holtzendorf.

Tirpitz, apprised, urgently demanded of von Müller, the chief of the naval cabinet, if the Kaiser had called him as well. "No," replied Muller. "His Majesty has not ordered that the Secretary of State for the Navy be present."[27]

What occurred during the course of that conference?

On 6 March, precisely, Falkenhayn found himself newly inclined toward moderation, because General Pétain had just restored the critical situation of the French at Verdun. . . .

In brief, the council decided, at the instance of the chancellor, to postpone submarine warfare until an indeterminate date.

The next day, Grand Admiral Tirpitz, secretary of state for the Navy and creator of the German fleet, reported sick. A telegram from the Kaiser invited him immediately to request a leave of absence, which he received on 17 March.[28]

If the chancellor had waited such a long time to make his implacable adversary leave the government, it was because he foresaw that an independent Tirpitz would cause him more trouble than a Tirpitz with official duties.

The grand admiral left the Naval Ministry amidst intense popular and political emotion. The entire press on the right, and even the *Germania* from the center, outdid each other in celebrating him. In the Reichstag, Mr. Basserman, leader of the National Liberals, had his group pass a dithyrambic order of the day. In a brochure composed by him and distributed throughout the country, he wrote, "The faithful pilot has just left the ship." He extolled "the great statesman Tirpitz" and declared "that they would invade his retirement to beg him to enlighten the country with his counsels."[29]

The Conservatives demanded that a public session should be held on the incident, in which they intended to overwhelm the chancellor. He succeeded in avoiding this drama, but had to submit to very severe challenges in the "Principal Committee."

Popular demonstrations, the first since the mobilization and the last before the Revolution, were organized in favor of Tirpitz in Berlin and had to be prohibited by the military authorities and disbanded by force.

Tirpitz doubtless did not need these displays to convince him to pursue the battle against his enemy [Bethmann]. His conviction, his character, and his resentment were entirely sufficient for that. But he found in the public, and notably in the elite, all the desired elements for assembling a party. And this great military leader did not wait two weeks to create that party, "of the fatherland." He did not hesitate to traverse Germany, presiding in uniform over impassioned and tumultuous gatherings. Taking the floor to speak, he used all his powers to overstimulate the three sentiments that were agitating Germany: anxiety over the outcome of the war; greed for the benefits that would crown so many exertions; and finally, hatred of the enemy. And he threw out to the masses a tripartite demand for action: the resignation of the chancellor, the annexation of Belgium, and merciless submarine warfare.

Prince von Salm, president of the Naval League, accompanied Tirpitz everywhere, sending to the Kaiser's cabinet letters of this kind: "Nothing could make us happier than American intervention. At least we would thus recover the freedom of action that we have, alas, lost. . . . Unrestricted submarine warfare would be welcomed by the people with a cry of joy."[30]

Moreover, the resignation of the grand admiral had not increased the authority of the government over the Navy. On 24 March 1916, the French ocean liner *Sussex* was sunk, without warning, with several American passengers on board. To the indignant protestations of Wilson, the chancellor at first replied that the submarines surely had nothing to do with it, given the orders that they had received. Then, when it was proven that despite these orders, a submarine had torpedoed the *Sussex*, he had to make profuse excuses and promise reparations.[31] Tirpitz, in the name of the "Party of the Fatherland," sent the Kaiser a dispatch entreating him not to give way to Wilson's threats. And from everywhere in Germany, committees of the party showered on the General Headquarters and the Chancery what was henceforth called a "heavy bombardment of telegrams," all conceived with the same message and signed by recognized and weighty names. The Kaiser, nevertheless, declared that Bethmann was right and ordered that the commander of the submarine be punished. But the secretary of state, von Capelle, would not agree to pronounce the punishment. Nor would the chief of the Naval General Staff, the commander of the fleet, or the Flanders commander of the naval corps. The Kaiser had to do it himself.

The redoubled blows with which the enemy struck Germany during the summer of 1916 restrained for some months the propaganda of the Party of the Fatherland and the political agitation directed against Bethmann-Hollweg. The offensive on the Somme, the victories of Brusilov, the taking of Monastir by the French and the Serbs, the intervention of Romania, made the pan-Germanists fall silent and gave courage to the moderates.[32] The press no longer spoke of annexations, nor of the crushing of the Anglo-Saxons. What the public read now was no longer the frenzy of Reventlow in the *Deutsche Tageszeitung,* nor the fiery articles of the *Cologne Gazette,* nor the reports of Karl Endres in the *Lokal Anzeiger.* They hardly had a taste for anything except the pessimistic irony of Theodor Wolf in the *Berliner Tageblatt;* the acidic and bitter insinuations of the *Frankfurt Gazette,* and Georg Bernhard's theories in the *Voss Gazette* on reconciliation with the French.

The committees and corridors of the Reichstag were now anxiously quiet. Bethmann and Jagow no longer heard themselves criticized there. And the chancellor found no opposition when he shouted, raising his fists toward heaven, "If we conducted unrestricted submarine warfare, as Tirpitz advocates, the entire world would rise up to destroy Germany as if she were a rabid dog."[33]

But on August 29, the Kaiser, crushed with anxiety, decided to relieve Falkenhayn, and to make Hindenburg Chief of the General Staff.

Nothing can convey an idea of the enthusiasm which seized the whole of Germany when it heard the news. The popularity of Marshal Hindenburg, the confidence that he inspired, the affection shown for him by the troops and the populace were literally indescribable. The victor of Tannenberg, of the Masurian Lakes, and of Niemen owed his extraordinary prestige to these successes, without a doubt. Also to the defeats that others had suffered and to the fact that he had advised against Verdun. But it was due still more to the disinterestedness of his character, to his profound calm, and to that obscure awareness of the downtrodden masses that he was a sympathetic and compassionate man as well as a resolute leader.[i]

People are often surprised by the rapidity and seeming ease with which tottering Germany righted herself at the end of 1916, and restored her imperiled situation. The prestige of Hindenburg suffices to explain them.

Bethmann-Hollweg understood, from the moment the nomination of the field marshal and his imperious adjutant Ludendorff was in question, that these military men would exercise a moral dictatorship, against which all the rights of the civilian power would have no weight. But he had to choose between their supremacy and the defeat of the Empire. The chancellor made the most of their good fortune.

He welcomed them all the more, furthermore, because he believed he was in accord with them on the way the war should be conducted. Hindenburg and Ludendorff were the men of the Eastern Front. They had often declared that peace ought to be made at the expense of the

---

[i] Marshal Hindenburg did not belong to the unbridled generation, that victorious Prussia molded on the morrow of 1870, and of which Ludendorff is the prototype. The marshal had received his intellectual formation, consolidated his philosophy, and completed his military apprenticeship, before 1866. A more fervent cult of duty, a greater moderation of judgment, a moral sense better developed, an almost religious taste for "service," also distinguished Hindenburg, in our opinion, from the younger, more supercilious, more subjective Prussians who surrounded him in the General Headquarters, and who were also more abreast of the times.

Russians. Above all, the very day after their installation at General Headquarters, discussing with Bethmann the question of unrestricted submarine warfare, they characterized it as "folly," protesting that "they had quite enough enemies to fight without adding America, Holland, and Denmark."

The unfortunate Bethmann believed he would henceforth be able to interpose the glorious person of the new leader between himself and his opponents from the "Party of the Fatherland." He modestly declared to Hindenburg that "since he did not want the submarine war, it would not be declared, and that in this matter he would act as the General Headquarters desired him to do." Thus he signed in advance the capitulation of the civil power to military authority, which was now without a counterweight.

In October, Germany had regained confidence. The offensive on the Somme reached its limit. Brusilov no longer advanced; the Romanians had been crushed. This was the moment for Tirpitz and his partisans to retake the advantage. The grand admiral was all the more moved to hatred because his pet ideas regarding a separate peace with Russia now appeared to be realizable. In Petersburg, Sturmer and his party clearly displayed their intention of entering into negotiations with Berlin. If the occasion were seized and moderation were shown toward the Russians, an armistice in the East was possible. And then one could turn all one's efforts to the West, annex Belgium, and perhaps even more. But to succeed, Bethmann had to cede his place, and the Party of the Fatherland had to redouble its attacks upon the chancellor without scruple.

Bethmann now no longer had any hope of preventing the entry of new enemies against the Empire and catastrophe, except by American mediation; so he actively prepared for it, Wilson having made it known in October that he would voluntarily accept the role of arbitrator. . . . Some weeks later, moreover, Wilson published the famous December Note, in which he declared "that in this war there should be neither victor nor vanquished," and in which he invited the belligerents to make known their respective conditions. But if American action were to produce these results, it would be necessary at all costs to gain a few months and to prevent unrestricted submarine warfare during this time. Tirpitz and his people would do everything to snatch these few months from the chancellor.

At the end of October, they once again chose as the arena for their attack the "Principal Committee" of the Reichstag. The Conservatives, the

National Liberals and the majority of deputies of the Center carried out a furious assault against Bethmann over the submarine war. Jagow brutally declared to them that if they prevailed, it meant war with America. Using statistics, the vice chancellor and economist Helfferich proved to the deputies that the submarine blockade would end in a fiasco, and that England could not be starved.ʲ But the opponents [of the chancellor] found a vigorous collaborator in the person of the secretary of state for the Navy, von Capelle, once the adjutant, now the successor, but always the friend of Tirpitz. This minister declared that unrestricted submarine warfare must commence immediately, that in six months at the most England would be at bay, that a child could calculate the tonnage.

"All right! Let us suppose that England may be overcome," Erzberger said. "But how will America be overcome? Do you see any means of doing so?"

"There is no means for doing so," cut in Jagow, "and that is why there must be no submarine warfare."

"There must be!" cried Capelle. "The entry of America means zero!" And as that extraordinary affirmation raised murmurs, the admiral reiterated, "It is zero! It is zero!"[34]

The Conservatives and the National Liberals left the meeting proclaiming that "Nevertheless, the question of submarine warfare is not within the jurisdiction of the chancellor, but of Hindenburg." The Center voted a pharisaical order of the day:

> The Chancellor alone is responsible for the political conduct of the war. But his decision ought to be essentially supported by that of the military High Command. If their decision is to conduct unlimited submarine warfare, the Chancellor can be certain of the Reichstag's approbation.[35]

Only the Progressives took the part of Bethmann, declaring that "in these very grave circumstances, it was vital to avoid all unqualified pressure, from whatever direction it may come." The Socialists themselves did not have the courage to condemn submarine warfare forthrightly. They declared evasively, "That their way of seeing this matter did not depend

---

ʲ Helfferich, moreover, soon passed to the side of the partisans of submarine warfare. "Some weeks later," Erzberger recounts, "he demonstrated its necessity, with the help of the same statistics that he had used to combat it." [Erzberger, *Erlebnisse im Weltkrieg*, 221.]

on that of the military command, and that they rejected the submarine weapon, if one were obliged to employ it without taking account of the interests of neutrals, provided that these interests were justified."[36]

A few days after this frenetic session, Jagow resigned.

Thus the desperate propaganda conducted in public by Grand Admiral Tirpitz had succeeded everywhere.

Furthermore Hindenburg, more and more discontented with Bethmann's policy, became more and more unpleasant toward him. The proclamation of Polish independence in November brought to a head the irritation of the marshal, who was systematically opposed to the resurrection of Poland.

Besides, having restored the military situation, Hindenburg and Ludendorff lent a willing ear to the assurances of the Naval General Staff. Beginning in November they declared to the chancellor "that they judged the time had come to re-impose the blockade on England." Bethmann succeeded in obtaining a respite by announcing his upcoming proposal for a general peace. But as soon as the negative response of the Entente became known, Hindenburg formally posed the question. And in response to a small hint of independence from Bethmann, he replied overbearingly, "With all my strength, and in full awareness of my responsibility for the victorious outcome of the war, I will make sure that what appears good to me from a military point of view will be done."

On 9 January 1917, the Marshal convened a decisive council of war at his headquarters at Pless. There the chancellor once again sketched out what consequences the submarine war would have for Germany. Not only would Wilson's mediation become impossible, but it was certain that they would soon see the United States join the battle. The chief of the Naval General Staff, Holtzendorf, reiterated the familiar assurances that with English tonnage so reduced within six months, London would have to beg for mercy. Hindenburg, finally, declared that he was going to call for unrestricted submarine warfare and that he would propose it to the Kaiser. Wilhelm II had only to nod for it to be done. He did so. The commencement of the blockade was fixed for the 1st of February.

Some days later, Bethmann made a new effort to obtain at least a delay from Hindenburg. On the 17th, he had received from Bernstorff a telegram that he then transmitted to General Headquarters: "The postponement of submarine warfare is highly desirable. Wilson believes he can obtain a peace on the basis of the equality of all nations."

But Hindenburg and Ludendorff wanted nothing of such a peace, and their power was such that no one could dream of fixing the conditions of an eventual treaty without their approval. Bernstorff's appeal could not change their decision.

On the 29th of January, Bethmann arrived in Pless to make a final attempt. He brought a new telegram from Bernstorff: "Wilson," the ambassador says, "wants a peace to be made on the basis of the status quo ante bellum."

The military men protested loudly, and Ludendorff, seated at the corner of a table, set to dictating the minimal conditions demanded by the military command. This final discussion lasted hardly more than a few minutes. It unfolded amidst a general irritation increased by certain inconvenient material details. The Kaiser had received everyone in a room encumbered by presents that he had just been given on the occasion of his birthday. People disappeared among the parcels. It was difficult to find a seat.

Two days later, Germany notified Washington of the commencement of a merciless blockade. The die had been cast. An exasperated America went into the war, bringing to the Entente an endlessly expanding military assistance and, above all, a decisive moral reinforcement.

Some weeks after the proclamation of the blockade came the Russian Revolution, then the defeat of the French offensive. Some months later the peace of Brest-Litovsk and the peace of Bucharest were signed. But the hope of American relief restored courage in Paris and London. Having taken Tirpitz's advice, Germany no longer found President Wilson an accommodating mediator but instead a determined enemy. It was at the precise moment when the German Empire was unquestionably in a position to seize an advantageous peace that it condemned itself to destruction.

History, when it is provided later with documents and testimony that we lack today, will be in a better position than this summary study to measure the faults of the men who unleashed unrestricted submarine warfare. However, without waiting for her to render her sovereign judgment, we know enough of the matter to be astonished at the fact that neither Grand Admiral Tirpitz nor General Ludendorff have acknowledged their responsibility in it. The former protests that submarine warfare would have been decisive had it been initiated a year earlier, but that all the misfortunes that it called down on Germany, are due to Chancellor Bethmann-Hollweg, who set it in motion in 1917! The latter disloyally insinuates that the chancellor agreed to do it, that he was the head of the government, and that he ought to answer for the consequences.

In this gloomy and pitiful subject, History will recognize greatness only in this conclusion of Field Marshal von Hindenburg. After announcing that the decision was taken by him because he judged it to be good, he wrote:

> When a leader on the field of battle throws his last reserves into combat, he does what the country rightly expects of him, and nothing else. He accepts the total responsibility and gives proof of the courage which consists in taking the supreme decision, without which there would be no victory. . . . If he fails, then he will see himself inundated by the outrage and fury of the weak and cowardly. . . . But that is the destiny of the soldier. . . .[37]

Giving all due homage to the moral courage of the field marshal, however, History will doubtless blame him for having employed his incomparable authority to violate a great principle.[38] It will not forgive Grand Admiral Tirpitz and the naval officers whom he inspired for having sought by every means to force the hand of the chancellor of the Empire in a political question of the first order and for unleashing in the nation a furious and fatal tempest.

3

The Relations with the Allies

It has long been thought that in the course of the recent war Germany was swiftly able to coordinate the efforts of the Central Powers, by imposing on her allies the authority of her own military leaders. Today we know that nothing of the sort was done. Hardly had the logical organization begun to function when it was reduced to nothing by the young emperor of failing Austria, who inaugurated a policy and a strategy of renouncing victory.

Two years had passed, during which the Central Powers could have better exploited the superiority of their resources, on condition that they be managed by a single chief. But their efforts remained at odds. From 1915 onward, Grand Admiral Tirpitz could with justice write, "For us, this is the war of missed opportunities. . . ."[1]

I

Germany and Austria-Hungary were constitutionally organized in such a way that they could easily have resolved the problem of unitary command. In each of the two empires, the sovereign personally commanded the army. Consequently, a personal agreement between Franz Joseph and Wilhelm II would have sufficed to regulate the collaboration of their military forces.

Obviously, everything should have induced the Central Powers to choose a German general as military head of the coalition. But to accomplish such unity, the Emperor Franz Joseph would have had to be favorably inclined toward his ally and hold him in enough esteem to make this concession to him. It would also have been necessary that he should care to exercise sufficient personal direction over his army to make it accept foreign tutelage. None of these conditions was realized.

Politically and militarily, Franz Joseph maintained a majestic and, as it were, systematic reserve from the day of the declaration of war until his death.

The Austro-Hungarian peoples, who observed this reserve, tried at the time to explain it in a thousand different ways. "The Emperor," it was said everywhere, "is nothing but a shadow. His intelligence and his will, already very weakened by age, have finally been overwhelmed by the weight of events." And the Viennese banterers passed around silly jokes on the subject. "The Emperor confuses the present war with those he saw in the days of yore." Receiving Potiorek after the defeat of Chabatz in Serbia, they had him say, "Stand fast, Monsieur le Maître de camp, these Magyars are going to be beaten, I am sending you my loyal Croats."[a]

To Conrad, who spoke to him in praise of a Saxon corps engaged in the Carpathians, they had him say, "Brave men, these Saxons! We must protect them: I don't want the Prussians to take a single boot from them."[b]

Others claimed that the illustrious old man, preyed upon by an incurable neurasthenia, driven beyond his limit by the assassination of the Archduke Francis Ferdinand, wished to think only about the afterlife and refused to take an interest in [public] business.

Some insiders were certain that the ministers of Vienna and Budapest had agreed with Wilhelm II that a vacuum would have to be created around Franz Joseph under the pretext that Berlin feared malicious initiatives and belated disavowals coming from him.

In reality, the emperor remained completely lucid until his last day, despite his great age, and never ceased to keep himself perfectly up to date on all political and military events, judging them with a sagacity and sangfroid for which he was ceaselessly admired by all who came near him. Moreover, the manifold and tragic misfortunes of his family did not affect him beyond measure. He steadily met them with a sort

[a] At the time of the Hungarian revolution of 1848, the Croats and their leader Jellachich had relieved Vienna and crushed the insurgents on behalf of Franz Joseph.

[b] In 1866, the Saxon army, driven back in Bohemia by the Prussians, had been shielded by Benedek, who was moved to advance solely by the personal intervention of the emperor.

of haughty fatalism that some of his intimates characterized simply as coldness of heart.[2]

And if Franz Joseph was the one man in Austria most compelled by personal motives to find the Prussian alliance unpleasant, he was also the one whose fidelity to the engagements he undertook could be trusted to remain most complete, come what may.

Above all, Franz Joseph was a gentleman. He would endure the worst rather than renege on his word. Despite the mortal perils into which his empire was brought by standing with Germany in the war, despite the blunders of the Berlin people, he would never allow the idea of a separate peace even to be mentioned in his presence. The impulses to bring that about were born in Vienna on the day of Franz Joseph's death.

The reserve in which the emperor of Austria encased himself cannot be explained by a weakening of mind, nor by an excess of personal misfortune, nor by the precautions of an entourage devoted to Berlin. Its principal cause was the sovereign's lack of confidence in the outcome of the war. His profound experience and his natural pessimism left him with hardly any hope. He judged accurately the grave internal weaknesses of the monarchy. As to the army, he was concerned with it, knowing its leaders personally, ignoring nothing about its organization and materiel, following its operations in detail. But the enthusiasm was not there, and Franz Joseph let that become visible. At Solferino, as a confident young sovereign, he had personally witnessed the defeat of his loyal troops in 1859. And the complete, brutal disaster of 1866 had stripped him of his last illusions. In 1909, he said bluntly to Conrad, who was discussing future operations with him, "Are you sure of your troops?"[3]

Franz Joseph did not love the Prussians and had a very limited opinion of their sovereign. Sadowa was not only a matter of patriotic regret for him. In the depths of his soul he had never ceased to consider the disaster as a personal injury; and time had scarcely diminished its bitterness.[4]

The humiliated Emperor of 1866 beheld Prussian Germany much as the lord of a crumbling chateau might have looked upon the new palace of his own steward, who had dishonestly enriched himself. In addition, the very person of Wilhelm II was profoundly antipathetic to him. The majestic Habsburg was distant, very sparing in public gestures, and highly sober in his speech; he despised from his depths the Hohenzollern's agitation, his familiarity, his taste for being seen. "The German Kaiser keeps such poor company," Franz Joseph often said. No doubt the alliance with Berlin was personally painful to him, and he had always kept to a bare minimum the occasions when it compelled him to meet with the Prussians. Even the war did not cause him to alter this rule of conduct. The two sovereigns, whose capitals were separated by a night's railway travel, saw each other only once between the declaration of war and the death of the old emperor. As to their acting in concert, sharing their views, and coordinating their efforts, there was never any question.

However, in the first weeks of the war, Franz Joseph suspended his skepticism, and although it deeply wounded his Habsburg pride, already vanquished in Serbia and Galicia, he took it upon himself to congratulate the victorious Hohenzollern in public and without reservation. In September, he had the Great Cross of the Order of Maria Theresa dispatched to Wilhelm II in Luxembourg, and sent Moltke the same honor with a signed letter of praise. His messengers arrived at the German headquarters convinced (as all Austria was convinced, taking on faith the official dispatches) that the armies of Wilhelm II were making a short halt before Paris and were going at any moment to deliver a deathblow to the French army. However, despite the efforts of every department of the General Staff to conceal at all costs the reverses suffered at the Marne, at Luxembourg the Austrians observed the icy wind of defeat passing over these angry and anxious faces. The delegation nevertheless delivered the insignia of victory to the disconsolate Kaiser and the disgraced Moltke; they were received a bit like a bad joke.[5]

Franz Joseph did not forgive Wilhelm II and the Prussian general staff for thus deceiving him. The Battle of the Marne, and the fact that the reverses and the outcome had been hidden from him, deprived him of the better part of his confidence and his esteem in regard to his allies. Henceforth, it was not to be expected that he would spontaneously agree to have his troops under the direction of the German command.

II

At least, the complete latitude that he continued to give to Marshal Conrad von Hötzendorf, the chief of the Austro-Hungarian General Staff,[c] would still have made it possible to achieve the commonsense

---

[c] In truth, Archduke Frederic, the cousin of Franz Joseph, was the Emperor's representative to the armies and theoretical commander in chief. But in fact, he exercised no authority, and his quite self-effacing personality found this perfectly acceptable.

solution without the emperor's intervention. To have their direction recognized, the Germans could not have dreamed up a more accommodating personality to head the Austro-Hungarian army than Conrad's. He was a soldier loyal and disinterested in the extreme, profoundly conscious of his worth and with a very exact sense of his authority. But he loathed all personal notoriety and was indifferent to fame. Moreover, he was much too intent on victory, his character was far too just, and his learning far too comprehensive, not to recognize the immense advantages that Austria and Germany would gain from a complete coordination of their efforts by the choice of a common commander. But once again, it would have required that Conrad and the Austrian army be spared the wounding, disdainful, and unreasonable methods that were employed by the German commanders. It would also have required that the German army itself be commanded by a leader of sufficiently elevated character and demonstrated abilities, to whom Conrad could give his complete respect. There was nothing of the sort for more than two years. Then it was too late; Austria's wounds were beyond healing and her will to fight was destroyed.

However surprising it may seem, the German and Austrian general staffs never undertook a single project together prior to the crisis of July 1914. Moreover, they had not even communicated to each other their respective plans of concentration and operations. It was known in Vienna that in the event of a war on two fronts, the General Staff in Berlin intended first to mount the principal effort in the West; but the form and the scope of that effort were not known. And the Germans never let the Austrians know what forces they assigned to the Russian front.

Vienna had repaid the secrecy of her allies with secrets of her own. The disdain of one, the jealousy of the other, their reciprocal lack of confidence, had accomplished this result: that two empires, formed by their politics and geography into a bloc, who never questioned that they would have to conduct the war side by side along a common front—and what a front!—had never coordinated their action before the decisive events, events that they had foreseen, if not provoked.

In July 1914, it was no longer doubtful that the war with Serbia was going to unleash a Russian mobilization, and that this would drag Germany and France into the conflict. The chief of the Austro-Hungarian General Staff wanted to reach agreement with Moltke as to what would be done in the first weeks on the Eastern Front. Moltke thought only of the grandiose maneuver mounted in the West and refused to believe there could be a serious Russian threat before six weeks of hostilities had passed. Conrad was much less reassured. He pressed Moltke to tell him at what time he could count upon the intervention of substantial German forces in the East. "Toward the 39th or 40th day of the mobilization," was the response.

Nevertheless, it was understood that each would assure the defense of its territory; they would exploit the lead they thought they would have over the Russian mobilization, in order to reduce the salient formed by Poland between Eastern Prussia and Galicia, and to extend the front on the Vistula toward Warsaw and Ivangorod. They agreed upon a concentric offensive of the German army of East Prussia (General Prittwitz und Gaffron) and, from the left, of the Austro-Hungarians (the armies of von Dankl and Auffenberg). However, the question of the date was not broached; and as to the question of the unitary command which would be needed to conduct these coordinated operations, it was not even touched.

It was under these conditions that hostilities were opened along the immense common front. As is well known, the anticipated offensive in Poland changed quickly. The invasion of East Prussia by the armies of Rennenkampf and Samsonov and the defeat of General Prittwitz und Gaffron, thrown back upon Königsberg, prevented the Germans from taking part there. As to the Austrians, after they had pushed their left as far as Lublin, they watched as their army of Eastern Galicia, under the command of Brudermann, was penetrated by the Russians at the end of August. After trying in vain to reestablish themselves below Lemberg, they had to withdraw in all haste, quit Poland, evacuate Galicia, and reconstitute their armies on the Dunajec and the Carpathians, severely strained both materially and morally.

The defeat of the Austrians was greeted by the German High Command with paroxysms of anger, all the greater because it coincided with the crisis of the Marne. "The Austrians have broken down abominably," wrote Tirpitz from Luxembourg. "Now it is necessary for us to take the whole affair in hand."

It was in fact necessary, and the circumstances were favorable.

The Austro-Hungarian High Command, after the disasters of Serbia and Galicia, was inclined toward anxious moderation. On the other hand, the prestige of a great German military name began to fill every mind. Hindenburg had just rescued Eastern Prussia in a few days, destroying the invading Russian armies (at Tannenberg and the Masurian

Lakes); and his victories appeared all the more brilliant because the news of them arrived at the same time as the defeats in France, Serbia, and Galicia. Perhaps Conrad would have accepted directives for an operation executed in common, had they come from a Hindenburg, a plain soldier, personally disdainful of publicity, and visibly older than himself. But for this it was necessary that the German High Command should choose to send substantial reinforcements to the East; and that its new chief should know how to silence an odious jealousy in his heart and to make the most, in the general interest, of the fame of a comrade. These two conditions were not fulfilled.

███ III

Falkenhayn had replaced Moltke after September 14th. Having achieved the supreme command, he immediately became highly controversial. General Headquarters, full of men loyal to Moltke, made its displeasure obvious, all the more so, as Moltke was still there.[d] Falkenhayn was accused of being above all a politician, a protégé of Bethmann and Valentini, owing his appointment solely to the favor of the Kaiser.

Falkenhayn registered this opposition with all the sensitivity of a considerable natural vanity that was intensified by the ups and downs of a career filled with sudden favors and excessive disgraces. He was all the more inclined not to let any glory overshadow his own.

Moreover, the new chief of the General Staff was determined to play again the decisive role on the Western Front that had been compromised by his predecessor. He intended to succeed where Moltke had failed. The Russians would be taken up afterward. Telegrams from Conrad insisted that German reinforcements be sent to Silesia and reminded him of the promise made by Moltke to transport considerable forces to the East "toward the 39th or 40th day of the mobilization." Despite these, Falkenhayn held firm to his own conception of keeping in France all he found there and of expediting all available reinforcements to it.

He could not dream, however, of leaving the Austrians on their own, because a new withdrawal on their part would mean an invasion of Upper Silesia, infinitely more threatening than the invasion of East Prussia.

[d] He dragged himself there, sick and discouraged, and was maintained at General Headquarters by the Kaiser, who feared that the news of his disgrace would broadcast the defeat at the Marne to the fatherland and the Allies.

His first act of command was therefore to order, on the 14th of September, the creation of an Army for Silesia, which would be formed near Breslau, under the orders of General von Schubert, by means of two army corps detached from Hindenburg. The latter was no longer to do more than remain waiting on guard in East Prussia with the vestiges of his Eighth Army.

This designation of von Schubert to command the army of operations, by which the victor of Tannenberg saw himself reduced to the condition of leading a border-guard, is difficult to explain, other than by motives of personal rivalry. But what cannot conceivably be defended from any standpoint was the wish to deny Hindenburg his chief of staff, Ludendorff. That officer received the order to go to Breslau to put himself at the disposal of von Schubert. And the whole world already knew that the brilliant maneuvers against the Russians had been conceived and realized less by a man than by a trio. "Hoffmann has imagination,"[e] it was said, "Ludendorff gets things done, Hindenburg accepts the risks and shoulders the responsibility."

The general interest required that these men, who complemented each other so well, be left to work together. Falkenhayn appeared not to understand this and made several attempts to separate them.

But the trio did not intend to let that be done. It was to Moltke that they turned. Moltke, again present at General Headquarters, took the matter in hand and succeeded in imposing his will for one last time. It was arranged that the Army of Silesia be entrusted to Hindenburg and formed of all his available forces. He was to establish contact with Conrad to draw up an agreed-upon plan of operations.

In an interview that Ludendorff held with Conrad at the Austrian General Headquarters in Neu-Sandec, they seemed to be in agreement on the main lines of a coordinated offensive. The Austro-Hungarians in Galicia would advance toward the San, raise the blockade around Przemysl and then push on beyond the San, toward Chelm. The Germans declared their intention to march rapidly upon the Vistula, toward Ivangorod and Warsaw. Conrad proposed, with his habitual reserve, to conduct the whole of these operations. It was in fact logical, given the proportion of forces each would have engaged in it. Ludendorff categorically refused, and the Germans and Austrians immediately set their

[e] Colonel [Max] Hoffmann, chief of the Operations Section of the Eighth Army (Hindenburg) [and author of *The War of Lost Opportunities*].

preparations in motion without further concerning themselves with each other.

On September 28th, Conrad was not a little surprised to be informed, by a simple telegram from Hindenburg, that the Ninth German Army had commenced its march. On 4 October, he in turn took the offensive.[6]

The Austro-German counteroffensive in Poland, launched without a unitary leadership, without an agreed-upon plan, and without common reserves, ran a strong risk of turning into a grave defeat at the first unfortunate incident.

Toward the 20th of October, on the San, the Austrians fought arduously without succeeding in forcing a breakthrough. The Ninth German Army had reached the Vistula between Ivangorod and Warsaw, but these two places were still held by the Russians. The Grand Duke Nicholas was preparing to make use of the Warsaw bridgehead to put important forces across to the left bank of the river and outflank the very exposed northern wing of the Germans.

Hindenburg—warned of the enemy's intentions, as usual, by captured radio transmissions whose code he had broken—demanded reinforcements from Conrad to support Mackensen[f] in front of Warsaw. But Conrad was greatly offended by the conduct of his ally, who after refusing him direction of the effort, had begun the offensive without warning him in advance and had managed it in a manner of which he did not approve. Moreover, Conrad was himself in a bad enough situation on the San. So he refused to give Hindenburg Austrian troops. He proposed to him, however, to relieve the whole German right between Ivangorod and Novo-Alexandria, with his army corps, which would release assets for Hindenburg. The Germans' anger, the telegrams from Hindenburg to Falkenhayn and from Kaiser Wilhelm to Franz Joseph, those from Franz Joseph to Conrad, in no way altered the decision of the chief of the Austro-Hungarian General Staff. He therefore relieved the two corps on the German right.

These quarrels had consumed time. Hindenburg, sharply pressed on his north wing, was constrained to withdraw. He informed Conrad by a radio message sent when the movement of the retreat was already fully under way. The procedure succeeded in irritating the Austrian Supreme Command.

A few days later, however, an occasion arose to repay the Germans in

[f] Commanding Hindenburg's north wing.

their own coin. Hindenburg had hoped to be able to reestablish himself to the east of Tomashov. With his front reconstituted and his units restored to order, he was already prepared to repulse the Russian assaults when a telegram arrived to inform him that the Austrians were in retreat on the Radom. They had not been able to prevent the Russians from crossing the Vistula. Hindenburg, his right unprotected, could not maintain his position. The Germans and Austrians therefore withdrew to their lines of mid-September, mutually accusing each other of incompetence and bad intentions.

Was the fear of a common disaster going to lend some force to the voice of wisdom?—The Russians regained the offensive along the whole front. East Prussia found itself invaded once again; Posnia, Silesia, and Hungary were at great risk of being invaded in short order. But Falkenhayn was bent on seizing an improbable decision around Ypres and then on the Yser; he refused to listen to the appeals from "the men of the Eastern Front." At the end of October, he summoned Ludendorff to Berlin to announce to him that he did not intend to give him, any more than the Austrians, any appreciable reinforcement. When he was asked, at the very least, to unify the command of German forces in the East, he at first refused to do so, loathing to give new powers to Hindenburg, whose personality he found unaccommodating and whose glory annoyed him.[g] Furthermore, he did not like Ludendorff, whom he judged to be dictatorial and brutal, and with whom he had earlier had a bitter personal conflict.[h]

However, Conrad and Hindenburg had been able to measure what their recent disagreement had cost them. They both had the character to recognize their errors. In agreement they established the plan for a new common offensive, and they mutually consented to collaborate without

[g] Hindenburg was named commander in chief of the Eastern German front on November 2nd.

[h] In 1913, at the time when the famous law on the effective strength and organization of the army was under discussion, Ludendorff had demanded, as head of the Operations Section of the General Staff, and with the support of Moltke, the immediate creation of three new army corps. Falkenhayn, as minister of war, fearing a socialist uproar, had rejected the proposal. This led to an exchange of insulting remarks between General Headquarters and the minister, which was brought to an end by the transfer of Ludendorff, who was sent to Dusseldorf to command the Thirty-first Infantry Regiment there.

reservations in its management. It was decided that Hindenburg would concentrate all his combat-capable forces near Thorn and advance in the direction of Lodz, inside the Russian flank, which had crossed the Vistula. Conrad for his part undertook the direct defense of German Silesia and brought there the whole army of Boehm-Ermolli, withdrawn from the Carpathians. Finally, despite the very mediocre material and moral condition of his troops, the chief of the Austrian General Staff promised to attack on the Dunajec. Hindenburg did not hesitate to place under Conrad the German elements left in Silesia under the command of von Woyrsch. A little later, he placed a division at the disposition of the Austrians, to the south of Cracow.

Success crowned these well-coordinated arrangements. After a long and hard series of struggles, conducted all along the Eastern Front, the Russian effort there was wholly smashed. Except in East Prussia, they were unable to gain ground.

Conrad and Hindenburg, greatly satisfied with one another, did not spare their mutual congratulations. Here, at the end of 1914, one could well believe that, thanks to their personalities, the conditions for good understanding had been reached between Germans and Austrians for the conduct of common operations, at the very least on the Eastern Front. The question of a unified command of the allied armies appeared soluble.

But that did not take Falkenhayn into account.

▄▄▄ IV

The defeats at Ypres and the Yser convinced Falkenhayn to abandon, for a long time, a decision in the West. But he was not at all certain about the intentions of the French and did not believe he was in a position to significantly reduce his forces on the Western Front. He accepted the necessity of doing something in the East, but he was resolved to send no more there than the necessary minimum.

However, if anything could crystallize Falkenhayn in his authoritarian and personal manner of seeing things, it was the opposition of Hindenburg. The latter made precisely this [opposition] manifest. From December onward, he categorically demanded that all large-scale efforts in France be abandoned, that the Western Front be amply reduced, even at the risk of losing some ground there, and that the center of gravity of German forces be transferred to the East. And Ludendorff added heavily that, without any doubt, such would have been the conception of the great Schlieffen, whom he himself had known and served, and whose spirit he claimed to be keeping alive.

That controversy, sustained by two individuals of Ludendorff's and Falkenhayn's character, quickly turned bitter. On both sides, ungracious judgments and malicious insinuations were mixed into it. At Posen (Hindenburg's headquarters), the war of the trenches with its microscopic measure of results was ridiculed. And the combatants in France affected to find mediocre the merits and the talents of the "men of the East," who having to fight only Russians, decked themselves out with easy victories and heaped up promotions and decorations.

Conrad, of course, was a partisan of the Eastern solution. In his conversations with Falkenhayn at Berlin in January, he portrayed the situation on the Russian front as very disturbing. It was so in fact, because the Grand Duke Nicholas was mounting an effort in the Carpathians, which the Austrians were resisting only with great difficulty. It was to be feared that the Russians might descend on Hungary before the spring.

Elsewhere, Conrad foresaw Italian intervention "by March at the latest." It is true that he had predicted it monthly since the beginning of the war. Already in 1907, on the occasion of grand maneuvers he directed in the Tyrol, he had proposed to Franz Joseph that, without a shot having been fired, they should invade Italy and attack this ally "as a preventive measure." But this time Conrad's apprehensions appeared to be justified; and one had to admit that in a very short time Austria would be forced to furnish and mightily equip a new front on the southwest. Obviously she could do that only if the Germans took over the major burdens of the Eastern Front.

Falkenhayn found it entirely natural that, to conserve the peace with Italy, Austria should cede Trente and Trieste, and told this to Conrad. The latter retorted "that on this reasoning Germany could disarm France by surrendering Alsace-Lorraine to her." Once this note was struck, the discussion could no longer modify either's opinion.

However, it was necessary to ward off the most pressing danger and to buttress the Austro-Hungarian front in the Carpathians, which threatened to collapse. At the request of the Austrians (who supported Hindenburg), Falkenhayn agreed to furnish them with four divisions. However, he imposed conditions on this cooperation that were literally humiliating for Conrad. He first required that a new army be formed with these four divisions and four Austro-Hungarian divisions, whose chief would be a German general—specifically, von Linsingen. This army would bear the title of the Imperial German Army of the Carpathians, although half of it was to be Austrian. Falkenhayn expressed his desire to personally designate the allied units that would make up Linsingen's army, under the pretext that many of the Austrian troops were unreliable. Finally, he absolutely refused to place the army of Linsingen under Conrad's orders—despite its being inserted in the Austrian front.[7]

Conrad, with a knife to his throat, was compelled to submit to these conditions, by the threat that he would not receive any German reinforcements. He did not forgive Falkenhayn for his disdainful severity; from this moment is to be dated that hostility between the two General Staffs—at first muffled, then openly declared—that resulted in the very gravest consequences for the Central Powers.

As to Hindenburg, Falkenhayn tried once more to deprive him of Ludendorff, who received orders to go and place himself at the disposition of Linsingen as chief of staff. But Hindenburg rebuffed him. He was now high enough in public esteem that he could not be taken so lightly. He wrote directly to the Kaiser in such a vein that it was necessary to give him satisfaction and return Ludendorff to him.

However, the counteroffensive executed by the Austrians, supported feebly by von Linsingen, yielded no other result than to complete the demoralization of Conrad's troops. The Czech and Romanian units refused to fight. In March, the Twenty-eighth Infantry regiment of Prague deserted as a whole to the Russians, after having literally negotiated its own surrender. A great number of Slavic units had to be dissolved, and their elements distributed among the Austrian and Hungarian corps, which were not strengthened thereby. The command was guilty of its typical lapses. Conrad excoriated his army chiefs in these terms: "The local defeat of a unit caused divisions and the entire army corps to abandon their positions, and the only response of the officers was to express their regrets. . . ."

All the efforts undertaken to raise the blockade of Przemysl failed, and the place was obliged to capitulate. The Russians immediately intensified the pressure. At the end of March, it was certain that Austrian resistance was at the point of collapsing suddenly.

Conrad had concealed nothing of this situation from Falkenhayn. For a long time he had proposed the measures for getting out of it. In March, in an interview he had in Berlin with the chief of the German General Staff, he demonstrated to him that an offensive executed by fresh troops against the Russian salient in Gorlice would have every chance of piercing the enemy front. He brought him Russian radio messages, deciphered in the normal way, which revealed that the dispositions of Grand Duke Nicholas offered a weak point precisely at the approaches to Gorlice. Finally, he showed him that this region lent itself particularly well to a surprise offensive, because of the density of railways that served it. Falkenhayn listened and took note of everything. He waited, before pronouncing on it, to see how the French attacks, just then being executed in Champagne, came out.

On April 1st Conrad, mortally anxious, sought out General von Cramon, the German delegate to his headquarters. He requested Cramon to telegraph Falkenhayn that Conrad demanded to be reinforced immediately and to be supported in the form he had recently proposed: a German and Austrian offensive against Gorlice.

What should the sentiments of the chief of the Austro-Hungarian General Staff have been the next day, when he received Falkenhayn's response? For he presented, as if it were his own invention, the project of an offensive against Gorlice, and pedantically explicated the reasons for it—those that Conrad had given him some days previously.[8]

Upon reading the dispatch from Falkenhayn, Conrad shrugged his shoulders and said to the head of the bureau of operations, General von Metzger, who had brought it to him: "They are going to take our maneuver away from us." And then, "After all, they are going to do what we want them to do, and that is what is essential."[9]

The penetration was to have been executed under the orders of Mackensen by an army of nine divisions, of which six were German. Mackensen, an able and successful leader, was appreciated for his flexibility by the Kaiser and Falkenhayn. The courtiers and those who were jealous liked to contrast him with Hindenburg. He excelled in such interallied commands and was to make a veritable specialty of them right up to the end of the war. In bringing his orders to Teschen,[i] he applied balm to Conrad's wounds, knowing that this in no way committed him; and insisted, during the course of the operations, that his headquarters report to Teschen as well as to Pless.[j] On June 2nd, having retaken Przemysl,

[i] The Austro-Hungarian General Headquarters had been at Teschen since the beginning of November 1914.
[j] German General Headquarters was (in part) at Pless from April 1915.

he telegraphed the Archduke Frederick, the nominal generalissimo of the Austro-Hungarian armies, "I ask your Imperial Majesty to announce to His Apostolic Majesty that the Second Army places Przemysl at his feet. . . ."

Mackensen's adroit methods, like the loyalty of Hindenburg previously, and the successes reaped together, had cleared the way for the complete coordination of German and Austrian efforts and for unified command. But this time again, the personality of the chief of the German General Staff would raise up obstacles.

▬▬ V

Falkenhayn had been at Pless since the end of April. There he was an hour away from Teschen by car, and his agitated activity drove him there continually.

"He would arrive like a meteor," noted General von Cramon, "seated beside his chauffeur, his eternal cigar in his mouth, leap to the ground before the vehicle had come to a stop, and greet Conrad with a quick word."[10]

The opposition between the two chiefs of the General Staff showed itself even in their very different outward demeanor. Falkenhayn was tall, of refined bearing, very well spoken; Conrad was short, taciturn, morose, never adorning his gray field-service jacket with any decoration. In their conversations, Falkenhayn rapidly warmed to his subject. His vivid imagination and facility with words gave him an advantage over his interlocutor, which Conrad tried to offset by making no reply.

The chief of the German General Staff would depart, persuaded that he had convinced the Austrian, and was annoyed when the next day he would receive a written note from Conrad, maintaining and clarifying the point of view of Teschen.[11] Conrad had his replies to the propositions from Pless drafted by Colonel Slamecka, "who possessed," von Cramon said, "a truly artistic ability to slide into the correspondence those disagreeable and repetitious points that envenom relations."[12] In short, from the month of May 1915, personal relations between the two great commanders had declined, and this state of things would soon render their divergence of views on the subject of the conduct of operations all the more acute.

Italy having decided to attack Austria, Conrad did not conceal the gravity of the situation; he even tended to exaggerate it. His bitter utterances about the perspicacity of Falkenhayn, who had never ceased to have confidence in the Bülow mission,[k] were not slow to be repeated at Pless. In other respects he experienced, on the occasion of this development, the melancholy pride proper to one who sees a misfortune he had ceaselessly predicted come to pass. More deeply sure than ever of the superiority of his judgment, he once again began to polish the projects for crushing Italy that he had kept in the forefront of his mind over the course of his whole career.

At the same time, the offensive in the East and even the war against the Russians appeared to him to be of secondary importance. At the beginning of June, at the height of Mackensen's success, he proposed straight out to Falkenhayn to interrupt the march toward the East and to mount immediately a decisive offensive against Italy. Simultaneously, he invited the Austrian chancellor, Berchtold, to negotiate a separate peace with Russia, which was to be purchased by ceding Galicia as far as the San, and by a promise to support the claims of Petersburg to Constantinople. It is true that he proposed equally to recoup the loss at the expense of Germany, from whom a part of Silesia was to be taken. . . . These suggestions of Conrad arrived in Berlin by way of Count Tisza and the Cabinet in Budapest, who were greatly frightened by them. The Magyars viewed the war only as a means of bringing the southern Slavs to heel once and for all and did not welcome a peace that would have made Russia stronger. Falkenhayn found new grounds, in these political schemes of Conrad, to oppose his military plans.

From the beginning of 1915, the German chief of staff nourished the intention of establishing a liaison with Constantinople, of raising Turkey up again, reinforcing her, and throwing her upon Russia in the Caucasus and upon England in Suez. Although he had been inspired with this plan by von der Goltz, by Enver or by Gantscheff,[1] he had made it his own. But if this was to be accomplished, the first condition was the inter-

[k] It will be recalled that Prince von Bülow was sent to Rome (as an ambassador at large) at the beginning of 1915, to attempt to maintain Italy's neutrality, by means of concessions from Austria that Berlin tried to extract from Vienna.
[1] Colonel Gantscheff, Bulgarian military attaché in Berlin, then at General Headquarters, was an active and ambitious man, very much devoted to Germany, who played a role of the first importance in the negotiations between Wilhelm II and Falkenhayn, on the one side, and Czar Ferdinand on the other.

vention of Bulgaria, which Falkenhayn pursued personally with ardor. In May 1915, Falkenhayn was in haste to exact a favorable decision from Czar Ferdinand.

The news from Gallipoli was more and more disturbing, and the taking of Constantinople by the Allies would have reduced Falkenhayn's whole project to nothing. But the Bulgarian High Command had no intention of engaging itself unless the outcome was certain. If Czar Ferdinand were to consider invading Serbia, he would need the assurance of a powerful German offensive on the Danube.

Falkenhayn had promised this cooperation. Sharply pressed by the French in Artois, he intended less than ever to reduce his forces in the West. It was thus from the Russian front that he planned to take away troops, even at the risk of limiting the offensive there.

It may appear astonishing, but it is certain, that with the Russian front pierced, Lemberg retaken, and Mackensen's success surpassing all hopes and offering magnificent prospects to be exploited, the two chiefs of staff of Germany and Austro-Hungary were both thinking of putting the brakes on their victory.

However, their motives were different, and each of them, seeing himself powerless to impose his own viewpoint, was at least going to succeed in ensuring the failure of the other's project. To Conrad, who asked for some German divisions to open the offensive in the Tyrol, Falkenhayn responded that Berlin was not at war with Rome. To Falkenhayn, who proposed the immediate concentration of an Austro-German army on the Danube, Conrad objected that he did not have troops available, and that furthermore operations in Serbia seemed to him neither opportune nor fruitful.

Hindenburg and Ludendorff concealed less than ever their contempt and their discontent with regard to the interallied strategy. They had never ceased to advocate the radical solution, which consisted in crushing Russia completely in the course of the year 1915.

Their plan was simple and grandiose. It consisted in enveloping, by a double maneuver of the wings, the great mass of Russian forces engaged in the Polish salient. Mackensen, victorious at Lemberg, would be repositioned toward the north in such a way as to take the Sarny-Kovel railroad. Hindenburg himself, suitably reinforced, would cross the Niemen between Kowno and Grodno and take Vilna; thereafter, he planned to fall back toward Minsk by Molodetchno. The armies of the Grand Duke Nicholas, crammed together in disorder to the west of the swamps of

Pinsk, would have found all their railway communications cut. Not being able to escape across the marshes of the Pripet, they would doubtless be brought to bay in a gigantic Sedan,[13] and the war with Russia could thus be brought to a sudden end.

Falkenhayn refused to adopt Hindenburg's project. He confined himself to the much more modest plan of a concentric offensive, executed on the Polish salient between Ossowietz and Rawaruska. He removed from Hindenburg the command of the whole front south of Novo-Giorgievk, constituting a new group of armies, the Leopold of Bavaria. He required the victor of Tannenberg to transfer the major part of his forces to the right, toward Lomsha and Ostrolenka, when Hindenburg's intention was to pursue by his own means the project of an offensive to the left, upon Vilna.

One must do justice to Conrad for lending to Hindenburg's plan his resolute, if somewhat tardy, cooperation. At the end of August, reassured on his Italian front and seeing clearly that it was too late in the season to commence preparation for an offensive in the mountains of the Tyrol, he understood that it was necessary to finish off tottering Russia in that year, 1915. He proposed to Falkenhayn to have the Austrians relieve a great part of the German divisions of the Leopold of Bavaria group. These latter would go to reinforce Hindenburg and would enable him to execute his offensive against Vilna under favorable conditions. In order to distract the attention of the Grand Duke Nicholas toward the south of the immense front, Conrad himself would attack in the region of Rovno. Falkenhayn refused.

In the month of August, with very few troops, Hindenburg nevertheless attempted to realize his great idea. He crossed the Niemen, took Vilna on September 9th, and pushed his cavalry as far as Smorgon, within a day's march of the principal railway junction of Molodetchno.

"It was still possible," the Field Marshal wrote, "to attain immense results in this direction. Hundreds of thousands of Russians could perhaps fall into our hands. If ever proud hope converged in men's souls with worried impatience, it was surely at that moment. . . . Would we arrive too late? Did we have sufficient forces? . . . Just a little farther, and our squadrons would have their hands on the vital artery of the Russians, and, that artery cut, the principal enemy mass would die. . . . But the enemy understood the terrible threat and made desperate efforts to avoid it. . . . Our cavalry divisions were obliged to retreat in face of his effort. . . . We have arrived too late. . . . We are exhausted."[14]

Despite grave losses, the Russians succeeded in executing their retreat. Historians will some day be in a position to assess the grounds for Falkenhayn's deadly obstinacy; it hardly seems probable that they will do honor to his character. To what degree was the clarity of his judgment obscured by jealousy of a rival's glory?

▬▬▬ VI

Meanwhile, Falkenhayn and Gantscheff had succeeded in persuading Czar Ferdinand and Radoslavov. At the end of August, Gantscheff arrived in Sofia, furnished with full powers to sign a military convention with the German and Austrian General Staffs. It was agreed that a common offensive would be undertaken immediately against Serbia, in which six German divisions, six Austro-Hungarian divisions, and the entire Bulgarian army would take part.

Difficulties arose when it became necessary to designate the leader who would conduct the operations. Conrad wanted an Austrian general to be chosen. He judged this to be a question of prestige for the double monarchy, since the execution of Serbia was politically an Austro-Hungarian matter. Falkenhayn, of course, demanded that the command be given to a German, and he proposed Mackensen. Conrad conceded, but on condition that Mackensen be placed under the orders of Teschen Headquarters; Falkenhayn pretended to agree, and they began to concentrate the troops.

That concentration was nearly completed when Gantscheff, obviously complicit with Falkenhayn, suddenly declared that there would be no military pact, nor Bulgarian intervention, unless the Bulgarian troops were assured they would fight under the orders of German Headquarters. To von Cramon, who brought him this news, Conrad responded calmly but firmly that, under these conditions, he would not provide troops.

"There are limits to everything," he added, "and I will not submit to new humiliations." And when his interlocutor repeated to him that his refusal would wreck the treaty with the Bulgarians, he concluded, "I regret that, but I have the duty, toward my emperor, my army, and my country, of protecting the prestige of Austria. . . ."

Falkenhayn rushed to Teschen and made a scene with Conrad, without result. He extricated himself from the affair, according to his custom, by a subterfuge, which was, to say the least, not brilliant. He promised Conrad that the orders would indeed be given to Mackensen by the

Austro-Hungarian General Staff and that nothing would be said of it to the Bulgarians. Then, when Mackensen, after having received the first directive from Conrad, passed to the stage of execution, Falkenhayn declared arrogantly that "before receiving the paper from Teschen, Field Marshal Mackensen had taken the orders from his Kaiser, as befitted a German officer."

During the whole Serbian campaign, conducted so vigorously and so successfully by Mackensen and the Bulgarians, the divergence of views between the two chiefs of the General Staffs became continuously more pronounced and their personal relations more embittered. Before long, the quarrels that agitated Pless and Teschen with regard to the organization of the interallied command against the Serbs focused on the conduct of operations itself. There were disputes with regard to the initial dispositions. Conrad wanted Mackensen's right on the upper Drina to be strong enough to carry out the encirclement of the enemy to the west while the Bulgarians accomplished it to the east. Falkenhayn, on the contrary, had Mackensen's only division on the upper Drina transferred from the right to the center. There is no doubt that this decision allowed the Serbian army to reach the mountains of Albania. It would have been cut off if Conrad had been heeded.

Consequently, when the broken Serbs withdrew upon the Adriatic, the chief of the Austro-Hungarian General Staff urged Mackensen to move his two armies obliquely in that direction, to cooperate with the Bulgarians in the definitive crushing of the enemy in Albania. But Falkenhayn ordered him to continue the march to the south. The German columns thus became entangled with the Bulgarian columns marching from east to west, which resulted in a halting of the pursuit, allowing 100,000 Serbs to take to the sea in the ships of the Entente.

Once Serbia was conquered, Conrad understood that it was necessary to take every possible advantage of the situation. He proposed to march immediately upon Salonica, so as to throw the few troops that the Entente had just landed there back into the sea, in order to discourage any inclination the Greeks might have had to intervene, and to frighten Romania. In October 1915, the Central Powers had ample forces at their disposition in the Balkans to take Salonica, and after the Russian defeat and the halting of the French offensive in September, they were at complete liberty in their movements. But already Falkenhayn thought differently, and cherished in his restless mind plans for an offensive on the Western Front.

Conrad immediately felt that there must be some change in the intentions of his [German] ally on this matter. Falkenhayn, however, took care not to tell him of it, continuing to employ toward Teschen his habitual method of dissimulation, which exasperated the Austrians. Conrad rushed to Pless on the 6th of November and bluntly invited the German chief of staff to explain himself. Falkenhayn replied that he had not changed his perspective and that he was in accord with Teschen on the necessity of marching toward Salonica. He even signed common instructions to this effect with Conrad, addressed to the military attachés in Athens so that Constantine would be warned.[15]

But the Austrian Chief of Staff had hardly returned to his Headquarters when he learned that out of the six German divisions of the Mackensen group, four had left Serbia and were going to recuperate in Hungary. And when he made his irritation clear at Pless, he was told that "this measure demonstrated in no way an intention to change the objective, but that one could not dream of marching across Serbia. And while waiting, it was logical to put the troops at ease, to preserve them from famine and typhus. . . ."

Looking through Falkenhayn's dilatory response, Conrad saw his about-face. He was outraged by it. On November 25th, he sent Pless a veritable ultimatum, declaring that he would instantly take back the Austro-Hungarian troops given to Mackensen if they did not march upon Salonica. Falkenhayn gained several days by speaking contrary to his thought once again. On the 27th he agreed to sign the following order with Conrad: "Marshal von Mackensen will continue the offensive against the enemy forces disembarked in Greece. He will cover his right, opposite Montenegro and Albania."

But at the same time he sent word to Mackensen not to budge, and to let the Bulgarians wage war alone upon the Vardar.

Conrad, outraged by the methods that had been employed toward him and conscious that he had in most circumstances judged situations better than his supercilious ally, finally convinced himself, after the Serbian campaign, of Falkenhayn's inferiority as a strategist and the mediocrity of his character. Henceforth, nothing could have persuaded the Austro-Hungarian chief of staff to accept Falkenhayn's directives. The question of unified command remained insoluble. What is more, no sincere collaboration would now be possible between the two great leaders. The Central Powers never learned to make use of the lessons of 1914 and 1915 in this connection. The particularly hard and perilous year that was beginning, found their strategies split and uncoordinated. They would pay dearly for this error.

▰▰ VII

Since the end of November, Falkenhayn had been silently preparing the offensive at Verdun. Out of mistrust and disdain, he had firmly decided to say nothing about it to Conrad. Even worse, when the chief of the Austro-Hungarian General Staff asked what his intentions were for the year 1916, he replied to him "that the chances of an offensive in the West were very slim." This system of dissimulation, adopted by Falkenhayn, would succeed in rendering impossible any collaboration between the two commands in the establishment of plans for common operations and in the distribution of their forces. The two Command Headquarters were going to prepare their efforts for 1916 each taking care not to let his ally know what he intended to do.

In December, seeing that Falkenhayn would definitely not agree to a march on Salonica to finish up the business in the Balkans, Conrad had resumed command over the Kovess army, which up to then had been under Mackensen's orders. And he warned Pless of his intention to utilize Kovess immediately, to conquer Montenegro and take possession of Albania. From the Austrian viewpoint, that intention was logical, but it did not square with Falkenhayn's. The German Chief of Staff desired from the bottom of his heart to see his allies remain everywhere on the defensive and to undertake the task—in Russia, in the Balkans, and against Italy—of holding these fronts over the greatest possible expanse. That would enable him to withdraw almost the totality of German troops and resources from there in order to engage them in the West. But he would have to explain himself unequivocally to Conrad. However, he did not want to do that at any price.

He therefore restricted himself to finding fault with the Montenegro expedition and to giving vent to his fury against Teschen when he saw the Kovess army abandon Mackensen, despite his protestations. From that point, and during the whole month of January, the two chiefs of staff did not see each other a single time, nor did they even write each other a letter.

While Falkenhayn worked to prepare the offensive in France, Conrad naturally turned back to his old project of crushing Italy. But he had a sufficiently high appreciation of the superiority of German troops to want to have them involved in it. Before the end of November, he had set in motion a plan for an April offensive. It was to be launched from the Tyrol, directed toward Asiago, and would eventually operate in the Venetian plain in such a way as to cut the communications of the main Italian striking force at the Isonzo. It was to be executed by sixteen divisions, of which eight were to be German. In the course of his conversations with Falkenhayn, and in various notes, he presented the project to him and requested his cooperation.

Falkenhayn naturally made every possible objection. It was too early to speak of a mountain operation; in the Tyrol there were not sufficient means of transport to concentrate rapidly the wedge for a breakthrough, and the element of surprise would be lost; the German troops were unfit for mountain warfare, etc. At bottom he was only trying to gain time, persuaded that the taking of Verdun would have the effect of a thunderclap and raise his own prestige so high that he could subsequently deal with Conrad as he pleased.

Conrad, discerning quite clearly that the main object was being concealed from him, resolved henceforth to match secrecy with secrecy, and pretended to renounce his project at the very time when he decided to execute it alone. He began preparations in secret for a great Austro-Hungarian effort in the Tyrol. Cramon himself was unaware of it.[16]

On February 8th, a dinner brought together at Pless the principal members of the two General Headquarters. Falkenhayn and Conrad were seated near one another and hardly spoke together. They rose from the table. The German marched toward the Austrian.

"I take leave of you. I depart imminently for Charleville with these gentlemen. We are going to attack Verdun. When? In a few days or a few hours . . . I wish you good luck." And each turned on his heel and walked off.[17]

Such was the "coalition" of the Central Powers. Germany and Austria commenced two divergent enterprises, separately and without a comprehensive plan. Between the leaders of their armies there was no trust and very little esteem. Nor were there any common reserves to parry a setback or exploit a success in concert. A fortiori, there was no unified command, no progress after 1914 along the road that could have led to one. The cannons of Brusilov in Galicia and those of Joffre and Haig on the Somme were going to avenge the logic of principles.

On June 4th, the Russians took the offensive on the Austro-Hungarian front, in the region of Rovno, then in Bukovina. They struck at sectors stripped of artillery and held by troops of very mediocre quality. All of Conrad's best infantry and cannon were in action near Asiago. The advance of the assailant was immediately quite rapid. The German reserves were also quite insignificant on the Eastern Front. Hindenburg alone had been able to compose a small reserve force, but he intended to conserve them.

And yet, despite the immediate gravity of the situation, neither of the two chiefs of the General Staff would agree at first to renounce his western project. There was an exchange of telegrams between Conrad and Falkenhayn on this subject; the violence of its language surpassed all imaginable limits.

Conrad alleged that he was on the point of seizing a complete victory in Italy. "To halt this offensive, after the success at Asiago, would be madness," he said. "Whereas the Central Powers would lose nothing, without doubt, if the ruinous attacks on Verdun were suspended." Therefore the task of reinforcing the southeastern front and of breaking Brusilov's offensive reverted to the Germans, according to him.

Upon receiving these propositions, Falkenhayn lost control of himself. He certainly did not expect, in June 1916, to carry off the decisive triumph in the West for which had hoped at first. But at the very least he wanted to take Verdun. Given his situation—which had been precarious within military opinion for a long time, and for a short time in the mind of the Kaiser—he made this a personal matter. To give way on Verdun, in order to engulf his divisions on the Stochod, would for him have been tantamount to a resignation; and for Germany it would be an avowal of resounding defeat.[18] He vented his anger against the Austrians in bitter and injurious terms, and initially responded to Conrad that he would have to extricate himself from the affair on his own.

However, on June 8th, the two chiefs of staff met again in Berlin. After a most violent scene, reason once again took hold. Conrad agreed to suspend the Tyrol offensive and to bring the mass of his divisions back toward Lemberg. Falkenhayn had all the German reserves in the East, notably those of Hindenburg, transported to the Stochod. A common counteroffensive was mounted on the northeast of Kovel, within Brusilov's northern flank.

But it quickly became apparent that these measures would not suffice to restore the situation. In twelve days of combat, the two Austro-Hungarian armies under attack had lost respectively 57 percent and 54 percent of their effective strength. By the 18th of June, it could be said that no organized resistance existed any longer in the regions of Brody, Tarnopol, and Stanislau. It was necessary to constitute a new front out of all remaining elements, under the threat of seeing the debris of the Austro-Hungarian army disappear completely. Furious and desolated, Falkenhayn was obliged to resign himself to reinforcing the southeast front with divisions from the west. That was to recognize the error of his vain western offensive. Now his personal disgrace could be postponed for only a matter of days.

In like manner, the situation of Conrad was also highly compromised. The innumerable enemies arrayed against the chief of the Austro-Hungarian General Staff—at court, in the political world, and in the army— joined their voices in unison to accuse him of incompetence and blindness.

The Hungarians did not like him, because they knew he accepted the ideas of the deceased Archduke Francis Ferdinand, the enemy of the dualist system and partisan of federation. Conrad had had sharp personal differences with Tisza. The Czechs hated him for his severity toward their deserters and their absentees and because he had publicly expressed his opposition to amnesty for their leaders. The high clergy fought him because he was a professed freethinker. Moreover, a recent incident had sharpened their hostility. At the time of the Tyrol offensive, Conrad had his intelligence service seize the correspondence of the bishop of Trent, a prelate of Italian sympathies, who was suspected of communicating with Rome by way of the Papal Nuncio in Vienna and the diplomatic pouch of the Vatican. Immediately the episcopate began to fulminate against "Conrad the sectarian."

The clergy and the ultramontanes, moreover, harbored resentment because the marshal had married a Jewess.[19] Conrad had committed the injustice of installing his family at Teschen. Although he personally lived in the most hardworking and reserved manner, he had not prevented the creation around the General Headquarters of a sort of worldly atmosphere, shaped by the wives of his subordinates, who rushed to imitate the example of his own wife—an unsuitable atmosphere under the circumstances. And the Viennese joked about "the life of the petticoats at Teschen."[20]

Finally, public opinion in Austria and Hungary, like that of all the belligerent nations at this time, was naturally driven, by suffering and anxiety, to turn away from the military and civilian leaders who had governed it up to this point. At Vienna, as in Paris, Berlin, and Petersburg, there was in 1916 an unreasoned desire for change.

All these circumstances, although unfavorable in themselves, could have been utilized by Germany to organize the interallied command at last and to seize effective direction of the war and operations. To succeed in this she enjoyed an exceptional advantage: the incomparable prestige of Hindenburg.

▄▄▄ VIII

Since the end of 1915, when he had witnessed, with rage in his heart, the unraveling of his hopes for the crushing of Russia, Hindenburg had been dwelling morosely at his headquarters in Kovno. He had categorically disapproved of the planned offensive in the West and declared on this matter that "Germany has been badly led." That phrase, immediately passed on, had naturally become popular. But it succeeded in antagonizing the Kaiser against the Field Marshal.

Wilhelm II did not like Hindenburg, and still less his chief of staff Ludendorff. His agitation dreaded their glacial severity; his ignorance feared the irony of their experience; his vanity took umbrage at their glory. He was, moreover, confirmed in his prejudices by the effort of an entourage that wanted to avoid, above all, the ascent to command of these two "iron Prussians." Bethman-Hollweg understood that their dictatorship would mean total war and the retreat of civilian power in the face of military authority. The people of the Kaiser's Cabinet were well aware that their personal influence would end with such an ascendancy, and that the uprightness of Hindenburg's character, and the imperious ambition of Ludendorff, would give them no room for intrigue. Finally, the general staff on the Western Front did not acknowledge the superiority of the "conquerors of the Russians" and had no desire to see the staffs of Mackensen, Gallwitz, Linsingen, and Woyrsch come with their officers to assume commands in France and overturn established routines and acquired positions.

Until now, all these objections prevented the reasonable solution.[21] The leader whose incontestable superiority in breadth of mind and character, whose brilliant record of services rendered had for a long time singled him out for the supreme command, had not been summoned to it. The opinion of the people and of the troops had long since been declared in his favor; and, most extraordinary, both were in agreement on this point with the opinion of the Junkers and the "Party of the Fatherland." The old Prussians of the right loved the warrior puritanism of Hindenburg and Ludendorff—their religion of effort; their unlimited contempt for all that was not Prussian, Lutheran, and soldierly; their inflexible confidence in the patriotic use of force and fraud, which had marked the character of their ancestors, in legend even more than in reality.[m]

Finally, the German industrialists had been captured by Ludendorff, who did not conceal his intention to carry out an immense program of manufactures in due time.

The failure of the Verdun offensive and the reawakening of the Russians brought the prestige of Hindenburg to a peak. A profound and general movement of opinion was unleashed in his favor. But, for the mediocre reasons that had so far kept him in a subordinate role, he was once again to be refused the supreme authority, despite the circumstances.

Falkenhayn thought for a moment that he had found a way to utilize Hindenburg's ability without increasing his glory. At the beginning of July [1916], he intended to name him commander of the Southeast Austro-Hungarian front, under the orders of Teschen. That would have been a sacrificial mission, on which the field marshal and his chief of staff would have used up their talents, and doubtless a part of their reputation, employing deteriorating resources to restore a situation that was repeatedly compromised. But Hindenburg and Ludendorff, sensing that their hour had come, categorically refused to comply. Falkenhayn— whose disgrace moved even closer with the commencement of Anglo-French attacks on the Somme—did not feel that he had the strength to compel them to obey.

Some days later, he tried to make concessions. He proposed to name Hindenburg commander in chief of the Eastern Austro-German front, from the Baltic down to the south of Brody. Thus the operations in the regions of Kovel and Brody could at last be conducted by one chief, and

[m] As is well known, these same pietistic and conservative people had no penchant whatever for the person of Wilhelm II and his son. They did not take them to be serious. They resented them for allowing into their entourage liberals and businessmen who wanted them to smile on Catholics and on Germans of the south. And they attributed their light weight, their inability to get to the bottom of things, to the Swabian origins of the Hohenzollern and their English marriages.

the exchanges and movements of troops between the field of battle and the quiet front to the north of Pripet would be regulated according to a uniform and coherent plan.

While awaiting a more radical organization, this disposition was logical. It was decreed on the 28th of July, in the course of a meeting in which Wilhelm II brought together Archduke Frederick, the two allied chiefs of staff, and the redoubtable field marshal. Conrad retained under his direct command only the front of the southern group of armies.[n] He nevertheless had it stipulated that he was to be consulted on all important measures that Hindenburg wished to take south of Pripet.

However, the Turks and Bulgarians, already much alarmed by the successes of Brusilov and by the dangerous situation on the Western Front, did not conceal their anxieties when they learned that the intervention of Romania was imminent. This new peril, which menaced them directly, gave them the audacity to exercise a salutary influence on their great allies. Czar Ferdinand and Enver-Pasha rushed to Pless to declare that it was urgent to establish a unified High Command for the Coalition forces, and that this command ought to be German. Ferdinand even proposed a plan according to which the German Kaiser would be charged with the supreme direction of the war, and the German chief of staff would in consequence conduct operations.

Conrad protested loudly. It was not at all because he failed to see the advantages of a unified command, but that he did not want at any price to be subordinate to Falkenhayn. The discussions and quarrels of the two chiefs of staff had been much too grave, their personal relations much too strained, for the Austrian thereafter to consider bending his ideas to those of the German. In addition, Conrad trusted less than ever Falkenhayn's perspicacity and strategic ability. The latter refused to acknowledge the possibility of a Romanian intervention, while Conrad was convinced of it.

The Austro-Hungarian chief of staff also distrusted Ferdinand, and this circumstance sufficed to condemn the Bulgarian plan in his eyes. He had not forgotten the affront Gantscheff had inflicted on him, during the Serbian campaign, in connection with the organization of the interallied command. In December, a true conflict arose between the Bulgarians and the Austrians on the subject of a delimitation of areas of responsibility in Serbia, and bloody skirmishes had taken place be-

[n] Then under the orders of the hereditary archduke.

tween the troops. Ferdinand, visiting Conrad to deal with this subject, had been subjected to severe treatment by the Marshal. Since then, the Czar had broken off relations with Teschen. In short, Conrad, hardly knowing what Ferdinand proposed, was resolved to make it fail. He immediately employed the heavy artillery, telegraphing to Franz Joseph that he was submitting his resignation.

The old emperor had very little liking for Conrad but held him in high esteem. He found him clumsy, stubborn, rude, and at times even insolent, but he appreciated his candor, his loyalty, his industry, and, all in all, despite the setbacks, he retained a solid confidence in his ability to lead. Moreover, Franz Joseph did not like to see new faces around him, and he was used to Conrad. In sum, the emperor of Vienna perhaps agreed intellectually that it would one day be necessary to subordinate his armies to a Prussian general, but he wanted to make such a sacrifice only very deliberately, and thought that Falkenhayn was not worth the trouble. He therefore rejected Conrad's resignation and invited him to draw up a project himself, "which would guarantee his sovereign rights, the dignity of the power of the Monarchy, and the authority of the Austrian General Staff."

But an event of the greatest gravity was finally to clear the way for logic, through the jealousies, the rancors, and the mistrust: on August 27th, Romania declared war on Austria-Hungary.

It was General von Cramon who telephoned this news to Falkenhayn from Teschen. The chief of the German General Staff at first refused to believe it. For him, it was the end, and a finale without beauty, for he had until the last moment denied the possibility of a Romanian intervention, and he was going to leave command with this proof of a new and weighty error.

Wilhelm could now no longer avoid Hindenburg. The latter, called to Pless on August 29th, was received while deboarding the train by the head of the military cabinet, who announced to him his nomination. Hindenburg and Ludendorff assumed a command the responsibilities of which they had long since taken the measure. For them, it was above all a question of establishing their uncontested authority over the allies.

Two days later, Archduke Frederick and Conrad were the hosts of the Kaiser at the German General Headquarters. Noticing the absence of Falkenhayn, Conrad asked Wilhelm II's aide-de-camp Plessen where the chief of staff might be. Plessen assumed a fitting expression: "Falkenhayn is not dining here; he does not feel well." Then: "Hindenburg has been named Chief of the General Staff of the German armies." Falkenhayn had been disgraced with the same offhandedness as Moltke before.[22]

Hindenburg and Ludendorff hurried to Conrad. They were not men to embarrass themselves with ambiguities and squarely proposed to him that he accept a shift to their command. Hindenburg was to secure, by delegation of the German Kaiser, "the conception and execution of a common program of operations, to fix, in particular, the objectives, the importance of the forces to employ, to resolve questions of command."

Conrad, knowing quite well that this was the prudent solution, was delighted to be rid of Falkenhayn. Full of esteem for the talent and personality of Hindenburg, greatly disturbed by the new situation created for the monarchy by the Romanian intervention, and seeing the need for a new German collaboration, he had the intelligence and the moral merit to accept the proposition. On September 6th, the agreement was signed. Nevertheless, Conrad had the following clause added to it, held secret between Germany and Austria:

> The German Kaiser commits himself, in military operations as in all negotiations concerning the conduct of the war, to ensure the same protection and integrity for Austria-Hungary as he does for the German Empire. In case the Austrian General Staff cannot accept the decisions of the Supreme Direction of the war, Kaiser Wilhelm is obliged to reach agreement with Emperor Franz Joseph.°

▬▬▬ Thus, more than two years after the beginning of their common efforts, the Central Powers had established unity of command for their forces. However, up until this point, they had carried the crushing weight of discord between their leaders; and for that reason they had wasted opportunities that would never come again. It was no longer possible to make full use of their resources, now finally joined—in a word, to conquer. Two years of badly repaired reverses, of catastrophes barely avoided, had weakened Austria-Hungary to the point that henceforth she could put at the disposal of a common leader only forces that were both materially and morally exhausted. By the time the critical situation created by Romanian intervention was restored, the monarchy of the Danube had reached such a state of weakness and discouragement

°It was on the basis of this clause that Emperor Charles could take back Austria-Hungary's freedom of action.

that her primary goal was no longer victory, but rather the end of the effort.

On 2 November 1916, Emperor Franz Joseph died at Schoenbrünn. With him died the spirit that had, until then, guaranteed Austrian fidelity to the German alliance. His death carried with it, a few days later, the disgrace of Marshal Conrad von Hötzendorf and the end of all serious military collaboration. The young emperor Charles shook off the strategic tutelage of Hindenburg and began to attempt, by secret paths, to break the political bonds that chained him to Germany. The unified command perished just after it was born.

4

The Fall of Chancellor Bethmann-Hollweg

I

The reverses of 1916 had gravely compromised the situation of the Central Powers. In the spring of 1917, Hindenburg and Ludendorff restored the situation in the West and in the East; they did not intend to end the war otherwise than by the decisive victory of their armies. The Russian Revolution and the defeat of the Franco-English offensive of April could only confirm them in their resolution and their confidence.

Nonetheless, they were well aware that the mass of the people had come to such a point of fatigue that successes no longer excited their enthusiasm. For a great number of Germans, from now on, it was only a question of ending it; and the most complete triumph, if promised for a distant future, appeared less desirable to them than peace of some kind, if it could be obtained immediately.

To convince the exhausted Empire to furnish the decisive efforts they envisioned, Hindenburg and Ludendorff judged it above all wholly necessary to restore its confidence. They believed that one could achieve this by constraining the press, by silencing the Left in the Reichstag, by suppressing the leaders of the "Independents,"[a] by securing a more just and regular distribution of food, and by terrorizing speculators. They thus required a government devoted to their cause. In other respects,

[a] In 1915, the German Social Democratic Party had split. The "Socialists of the Majority" intended to remain on patriotic ground, voting for the budget and following Scheidemann, Ebert, and David. The "Independents," or "Radicals," aspired to revolution and were under the direction of Ledebour and Haase.

they counted heavily on seizing the harvest when success was obtained and the moment came to gather its fruits, so as to make the most of the victory they anticipated. Therefore they prevented Chancellor Bethmann-Hollweg from throwing in his lot with Wilson's conception of a peace without victor or vanquished, established on the basis of the status quo ante bellum. And they insisted upon unrestricted submarine warfare.

From the moment when it became clear that the Petersburg Revolution was going to paralyze the combative force of the adversary in the East, what Ludendorff needed was a separate armistice and, if possible, a separate peace with the Russians. Furthermore, he firmly intended to enter negotiations only at the moment of his own choosing; and to impose the conditions he judged to be good.

Although Bethmann-Hollweg surrendered to the will and prestige of the military commanders in the question of the submarine war, he did so with death in his soul, and certainly did not acquiesce to it willingly.[1] Ludendorff sensed too well the chancellor's resistance to his projects and his ambitions, all the more since Bethmann, after his failure of nerve in January, had regained his composure. To be sure, he had let go Jagow, the undersecretary of state for foreign affairs. Jagow had been vilified by the military and the pan-Germanists because he intended to negotiate with the Entente, and because he had said openly, from 1915 on, that "we ought to consider ourselves fortunate, if we get out of this scot-free." But the chancellor had replaced him with Kühlmann, a diplomat after his own heart, who envisioned a neutral peace in the West and reconciliation with England. Bethmann had very liberally modified the project for a law of "obligatory auxiliary service." Ludendorff had called for the adoption and execution of that law to deliver the maximum military manpower to the front and to increase the labor force in war production. Bethmann had buried a proposal of the General Headquarters to set up a committee of military officers in Berlin, intended not only to censure but "to inspire" the entire press. Finally, he announced his intention to immediately institute universal suffrage for the Prussian Landtag elections and thereby to destroy the preponderant influence of the Junkers.[b]

[b] The elections for the Prussian Landtag were conducted by means of voting by class (with three classes), which gave agricultural proprietors — which is to say the owners of small, landed estates — a sure majority. Moreover, the House of

Furthermore, Bethmann and Kühlmann hoped to seize at last the occasion for a general peace, thanks to the Russian collapse, and they hardly concerned themselves with prolonging the war in quest of a hypothetical victory in the West. In any case, they relied on remaining in control of the negotiations if it became necessary to enter into particulars with the new government of Petersburg and to conduct the negotiations in their own manner without tutelage [from the military].

The General Headquarters wanted a chancellor of the Empire who was devoted to them and whose vigor on the home front could restore confidence, which threatened to collapse. Determined to end the war by arms, to prevent a general peace for the moment, and not to allow negotiations with the Russians except in a form they themselves chose, the General Headquarters resolved to provoke the fall of Bethmann-Hollweg.

From May [1917] onward, Hindenburg and Ludendorff no longer hid their hostility toward the chancellor and their intention to force him to resign power. In his daily reports to the Kaiser, Hindenburg alluded at every opportunity to the obstacles that the inertia of the government posed to the [Supreme] Command and called for "the strong man" who was lacking in the Chancellery of the Empire.

After three years of war, the policy and even the person of the chancellor were bitterly criticized in all quarters. The conservatives hated Bethmann for his domestic liberalism; the pan-Germans dreaded his moderation and his desire for reconciliation with Europe. The Socialists and Progressives found him too weak in relation to the military authority and blamed him for having been the chancellor of August 1914. No party forgave him for his attitude on the question of unlimited submarine warfare—the Right reproaching him for long opposing Tirpitz over it, the Left for having finally allowed it to be declared. Furthermore, in 1917 Germany was crushed with trials and privations, devoured with anguish and resentment, exhausted by strenuous domestic struggles. Feeling that its leaders did not measure up to its sacrifices, Germany showed itself instinctively disposed to retire the political personalities whose prestige had been worn bare in the course of these terrible days. Even those who did not expect the drama of German suffering to be ended by the replacement of Bethmann desired at least a change of decor.

Lords could wreck any reform that might happen to be voted by the Chamber of Deputies.

Nevertheless, Bethmann-Hollweg's position could still be powerful. Above all, the Kaiser valued this chancellor. Moderate without being soft, industrious without ostentation, respectful without servility, Bethmann was the very model of a good servant, and that character pleased Wilhelm II, whose superficial authoritarianism and easily offended prestige Bethmann never vexed. Moreover, Bethmann had none of the starchy and insolent manners that the Prussians—newcomers to authority—willfully affected, even toward the Kaiser, and which so exasperated him in the likes of Tirpitz, Ludendorff, and Helfferich. And when the maladroit cried out around him, "It is a Bismarck we need!" they only confirmed Wilhelm II in his attachment to Bethmann-Hollweg. For the sovereign had begun his reign by discharging the Iron Chancellor; and at the deepest level of his wounded pride, he harbored the burning memory of the humiliations that Prince von Bülow had inflicted upon him.[2]

Moreover, the Kaiser labored under no delusion regarding the general situation, despite the systematic optimism that his habitual entourage affected in his presence. The defeats acted profoundly upon his nervous nature and periodically threw him into crises of discouragement, in which he cherished dreams of peace and the reconciliation of peoples. Then, it pleased him to think that he had by his side a chancellor who sought a way to end the war honorably. Finally, for what it was worth, Bethmann was a counterweight to the dictatorship of Hindenburg and Ludendorff, which Wilhelm II found very difficult to endure.

If the Conservatives and National Liberals passed up no opportunity to attack the chancellor in the Reichstag, and even to insult him, the Catholic Center, the Progressive Left, and the Social Democrats accommodated themselves well enough to his policy. In general, the democratic parties approved his inclinations toward a general peace; indeed, the Socialists found that he pushed too timidly in this direction. Erzberger, Gothein, and Scheidemann expected electoral reform in Prussia from him and the establishment of a parliamentary regime in the Empire. Above all, they defended him out of hatred toward the pan-Germanists, who dragged him through the mud, and for fear of seeing him replaced by a puppet of the High Command.

However, it was precisely in this majority that Ludendorff was to discover the ally whom he needed to provoke the fall of Bethmann-Hollweg. He found there an active, insinuating, eloquent man, one possessed above all by the frenetic desire to push himself up to the first rank, devoured by the thirst for power. Ludendorff saw how to put the passion of Erzberger into play, so as not to disclose himself too fully and too soon. By exploiting this parliamentary ambition, the extraordinary soldier was going to turn public opinion suddenly around, throw his enemy to the ground, and then, despising and neglecting his accomplice, to abandon him, furious and desolated, before the ruins he had made.

II

Erzberger was a man of ambition, but not of a low grade. Since the opening of the war, this Silesian, one of the leaders of the Catholic Center, had deployed his intelligent and varied capacities in the service of Germany. In 1915 he had built up a great propaganda service abroad, despite the skepticism of the Wilhelmstrasse and the cantankerous distrust of the military authorities. In this capacity, he had traveled throughout Europe, wherever the state of war allowed him access. He was often seen in Bern, having a word with such and such a person among the cosmopolitan mass that lived there more or less on the margin of the laws of the belligerent countries. He had on several occasions filled Vienna with his adroit agitation, now in favor with Burian, then with Czernin. He enjoyed the confidence of the episcopate (notably of Cardinal Piffl of Vienna) and was very closely tied to the Prince of Liechtenstein and his great Christian Social Party. He was even able, after the death of Franz Joseph, to get himself introduced to the "Ladies of Parma."[3]

At the beginning of 1915, he had hurried to Rome to lend Prince von Bülow the support of his Vatican connections and his parliamentary experience. There he had put himself in the limelight, cooling his heels in the waiting rooms of Salandra, Orlando, Giolitti; gaining Wiegand an audience with Pope Benedictus XV; getting Bertram, the archbishop of Breslau, named cardinal; obtaining, through the intervention of the Holy Father, the liberation of certain French and German civilian prisoners, and the exchange of wounded prisoners of war; and above all, speaking to the Curia about the possible restoration of a pontifical state with a section of Rome, a bit of countryside, and a port.[4]

In February 1916, he had stayed in Constantinople. There, with the support and subsidies of the "German Association of the Holy Places," whose president was Cardinal Hauptmann, he quickly sought to take over, on behalf of the Catholics of the Empire, everything left behind by the expelled French monks in the way of schools, charitable foundations, and churches. He did his utmost to obtain the transference to Germany of the French protectorate over the Christians of the East, which had been denounced by the Turkish government. And he proposed to the sultan to transfer guardianship over a part of the Holy Places[c] to the King of Bavaria, in exchange for the baton of a Prussian field marshal.[5]

At Bucharest in the spring of 1916, received by King Ferdinand, he had tried to frighten him with the prospect of a [combined] German, Hungarian, and Bulgarian invasion if he did not recall Bratianu and follow a policy of benevolent neutrality toward the Central Powers.[6] And Erzberger tried to seduce him by the eventual offer of Bessarabia.[7]

Sofia had welcomed him with pleasure. He founded a German newspaper there, organized a visit of Bulgarian parliamentarians to Berlin, obtained fellowships to German universities for Macedonian students, and took it upon himself to transmit to Rome the desire of Czar Ferdinand to have a nunciature in Sofia.

Erzberger communicated regularly with Petersburg. He had been to Warsaw, to Copenhagen, to Stockholm, introducing himself into every circle, talking to each and all, astounding everyone by his activity and his resources, linking together broad and particular interests with one another, making of all the affairs in which he got involved—and he got involved in everything—a sort of huge speculation in politics.

Traversing Europe in this way had placed Erzberger in a position to know both the big picture and the details of international politics, to listen to and provoke the complaints of German diplomats about the mediocrity of the government in Berlin, to pack his memory full of the [self-]interested suggestions of neutrals and the laments of allies, to measure the cruel difference between the resources of the Central Powers and those of their enemies, and to escape very early the tumultuous illusion that at once encouraged and clouded the minds of the Germans. Since 1916, he had been convinced of the necessity to achieve a general peace as soon as possible, without haggling over the conditions. Moreover, he was persuaded that one man in Germany was capable of negotiating it: himself. Erzberger was determined to become the chancellor of the peace.

In the spring of 1917, when the Russian revolutionary regime announced its intention of ending the war as soon as possible, he thought his hour had come. It was the moment for Germany to enter directly into

[c]The Coenaculum.

negotiations, first with Petersburg, then with London, and finally with Paris.

From that moment on, understanding with the Russians was possible. In April, the Lvov-Kerensky government had declared that it renounced all conquest and that it fought only for the integrity of Russian territory. That was to open the way for all [the] arrangements concerning Poland and even Courland. An advantageous peace in the East could be seized if one were moderate. What is more, the Vatican, doubtless under instruction, had never ceased to let the German government and Erzberger know that peace was possible with London if Berlin completely and forthrightly renounced claims on Belgium. With its allies thus satisfied, France would be obliged, under their pressure, to stop the war. The autonomy accorded to Alsace-Lorraine would give her some consolation.

Such was Erzberger's plan. But above all he wanted to accomplish it himself. Already, in the month of May, unable to keep still, he had been to Stockholm to make contact with the official delegates of the Russian government. Bethmann, who was not sorry to have exact information as to the true intentions of Petersburg, had let him go. Erzberger, triumphant, had returned with a project of an immediate armistice. But Ludendorff, warned immediately by a telegram from the military attaché in Sweden, protested vigorously to the Chancellery, declaring that an armistice was a military matter that concerned him exclusively.

Moreover, Ludendorff was pursuing his own scheme for a separate peace with Russia outside the [German] government and without its knowledge, in order to be in a position soon to open a decisive offensive in the West. He brought about an exchange of communications with Petersburg, across the front, by means of members of Parliament. The Russians sent delegates, to whom Ludendorff had handed over the preliminaries of the peace as he understood it, along with the conditions of an armistice. But upon receiving that communication, the delegates had fled in terror and did not reappear.

Erzberger came to understand that to negotiate a general peace in his fashion, it would not be sufficient for him to become chancellor. He would have to come into it carried by a movement of opinion powerful enough to make the prestige of Hindenburg pale before his own, a movement that would enable him to impose his will on Ludendorff. Bethmann-Hollweg would have to cede his place as a result of some grandiose parliamentary demonstration in favor of peace, a demonstration instigated by Erzberger and managed so that it made him the necessary chancellor. Thus Erzberger conceived it: he would personally inaugurate the parliamentary regime in Germany. He would be sustained in the Reichstag by an unshakable majority of the Center and Left; backed up domestically by the frenetic desire of the people to make an end to it as quickly as possible, and externally, by the action of Vatican diplomacy (promised in advance). He would exploit the magnificent opportunity of the Russian Revolution and the momentary depression of the French. To please Wilson, he would put a stop to the submarine war, which he had never ceased to combat. He would open negotiations with the Entente and would be able to bring them to a conclusion by his force of address, flexibility, and intrigue.

But how could he throw himself wholeheartedly into the enterprise, without at least the tacit agreement of the all-powerful military commanders? Erzberger knew well that without Ludendorff's approval, no eloquence, no parliamentary ability, could make the Reichstag decide, or constrain the Kaiser. Suddenly he was given to believe that he had obtained this approval.

▰▰ III

On 10 June, Colonel Bauer, the trusted officer of Ludendorff, presented himself at Erzberger's quarters. Colonel Bauer, who was responsible at High Command for transmitting to the home front all demands for materiel and with supervising its fabrication, was in contact with everyone considered to be an important personality by politicians, the press, industry, finance, and the worker's unions. He was often seen in the corridors of the Reichstag; he was listened to in the committees. There he served as the messenger and echo of the quartermaster. Whatever he said was considered as said by Ludendorff; whatever he heard was conveyed to the High Command.

Erzberger was stupefied by Bauer's discouraged tone. "I share absolutely," the Colonel declared, "your way of judging the general situation. I am much astonished by the entirely unwarranted optimism that rules in Berlin, on the subject of the way the war will end. The German people do not see it clearly! Today more than ever, what is in order is anxiety. . . . At this moment, the enemy has four times more munitions than we do. In the spring, it will have at least six times more, and if this disproportion is not to be sharpened still further, everything will have to go exceedingly well for us, and exceedingly badly for the enemy! We have been able to maintain ourselves up to now on the Western Front. Will we be able to do so in the future? It is most doubtful. . . . In any case, one surely must count on a new winter of war. . . ."[8]

Bauer departed from Erzberger, leaving him convinced that the High Command, contrary to appearances, desired a general peace as much as he did. Probably the officer had other proposals for the deputy. Later events make one think that a true agreement was reached between Ludendorff and Erzberger, through the mediation of Bauer. The soldier wanted right away to break down the obstacle that the chancellor posed for his conceptions of the war and the peace, conceptions that he concealed for a time. The deputy judged that the (at least tacit) approval of the High Command was an unexpected and decisive support for the campaign that he was planning to conduct. Each of these two men of vaulting ambition, who quietly hated each other, voluntarily accepted the alliance of the other, in the hope he could better dominate him after the success of their common enterprise. Together they went to work—with what ardor and what activity!—to overthrow Chancellor Bethmann-Hollweg.

On the day right after the negotiation with Bauer, each of them started to campaign. Erzberger wrote to the chancellor on June 11th to reproach him for not opening negotiations with Russia without losing a day. He had a copy of his letter sent to each deputy. Then, he declared to everyone, notably to Dr. Solf, a member of the government, that he would put himself at the head of the opposition.

On 19 June, Hindenburg in his turn expedited to Bethmann-Hollweg a bitter and morose letter. "The hopes of the enemy," he wrote, "are founded above all on our lack of foodstuffs and primary materials, on the divisions between Germans, their discontent, the victory of the radical Social Democracy. The enemy's hopes are founded on the weakening of our morale, the internationalist currents that flow through the country . . . ; upon the desire for peace, which we publish, alas, loudly and everywhere!"[9]

Then, when Bethmann responded on the 25th that "he did not share the High Command's way of seeing things, and that it was a matter of bringing about a peace of conciliation as quickly as possible,"[10] Hindenburg wrote to the Kaiser, "Our gravest worry, at the moment, is the weakness of the country's morale. It is necessary to galvanize morale; otherwise the war is lost. . . . Therefore it is a question of resolving the very difficult economic questions and those which, at home, have a capital importance for the future. . . . Is the chancellor capable of resolving these questions? . . . That is doubtful. . . . And nevertheless, it is absolutely necessary to resolve them; otherwise, we are lost. . . ."[11]

The inventive mind and ardor of Erzberger were presently going to exploit a favorable political incident in order to open the decisive parliamentary campaign against Bethmann.

■ IV

The Reichstag was obliged to reconvene in the first days of July, to vote the trimester credits. At the end of June, the Social Democrats —echoing the discontent that was rapidly growing among the people, under the effects of their anguish and privations—had declared that they would refuse to vote the credits for the first time in the war. That decision would be grave if it were irrevocable. Since it denied the Government the means of continuing the war, it would be an affirmation, proclaimed by the largest and most popular German party, that the war had to be ended immediately. It would moreover have grave parliamentary consequences. The Social Democrats occupied almost a third of the seats in the Reichstag.[d] They usually carried the Progressive Party with them in their wake. In order to govern without the Left, henceforth, it would be necessary for the chancellor, whoever he might be, to put himself into the hands of Count Westarp and his conservative pan-Germanists. But the Catholic Center would not agree to that at any price, and the people still less. The menacing opposition of the Social Democrats, displayed so clearly and at such a moment, threatened to precipitate an insoluble parliamentary deadlock and a dangerous crisis in public opinion.

Did the Social Democrats in fact want to refuse the credits for national defense? Several times before they had worked this sort of extortion on the government, to push them toward democratic concessions and to compromise them for good in relation to the Right. This time, once again, it appeared that Bethmann-Hollweg would in the end obtain the vote of credits from Ebert, Scheidemann, and Noske, by means of a further promise—that of universal suffrage in Prussia, for example. Furthermore, at bottom the Socialists did not care to burn their bridges behind them. They greatly dreaded a military dictatorship, because to respond to that they would have had to unleash the revolution. Now they did not want that at all—out of patriotic sentiment, surely, but also from fear

[d]This includes the Independents, already in opposition.

they would see such a revolution escape them immediately and pass first to Ledebour and Haase, then to Liebknecht, and to Rosa Luxemburg.[e]

Nevertheless, Erzberger had no sooner learned of the threat from the Social Democrats than he made use of it to send a gale of panic through the political world. He set himself up in the corridors of the Reichstag and began to throw fuel on the fire, clamoring that the decision of the Socialists was sparking a dreadful crisis, that it was going to deliver Germany to the pan-Germanists, and that the feeble government of Bethmann was incapable of preventing these developments. Then, there would be war to the bitter end and without limit, the peace with Russia lost, growing poverty at home, and forced labor for all. It would mean the isolation of Germany, her allies would refuse to follow her into the abyss, and the last neutral powers would take sides against her. One could believe it coming from him, Erzberger, who had gone in the month of March to the International Catholic Congress in Berne and who had just returned from Stockholm.

On July 3rd, gathering around him those members of the Center who were part of the "Principal Committee," he sought to draw over reasonable men, some of whom, like Spahn or Groeber, were terrified at the thought of mounting an opposition, of overthrowing a chancellor, of upsetting the Kaiser and the General Staff. He recounted to them his interview with Colonel Bauer and portrayed Hindenburg and Ludendorff as devoured by unacknowledged misgivings. "What is needed," he said, "is to unify the Center, the Progressives, and the Social Democrats, in a bloc. The bond of this bloc should be a solemn proclamation by these parties, who are a majority of the Reichstag, affirming that the aim of the German war effort is the reconciliation of the nations." The adroit deputy added, "Moreover, such was indeed the intention of the Kaiser, on 4 August 1914, when he declared in his manifesto, 'We are not driven by the desire for conquests, we want only to defend the national territory against the foreigner.'"[12]

The next day, Erzberger took the floor in the Principal Committee, convened to examine and discuss the war credits before they were put to a vote in the Reichstag. He vigorously attacked the government, which had declared intensified submarine warfare and had sworn that it would lead within six months to the capitulation of England. "These six months

[e] Liebknecht and Luxemburg were then in prison.

it has lasted," cried the interpellator, "and today we no longer dare fix the term for its success. A totally unjustified optimism has been promoted among the people on this score. . . . The Reichstag can no longer be optimistic. . . . Now this question is posed to it, this terribly grave question: How to leave the war? . . . We were told that we could dictate the peace, thanks to our sword. That is false! None of our enemies has yet agreed to submit to our terms, none will ever accept them. . . . Since the sword cannot end the war, politics and diplomacy must reach it. . . . Alas! The most capable diplomacy in the world can never repair the wrongs that the submarine war has done to us everywhere politically. . . ."[13] Then he declared that the official statistics published each day by the chief of the Naval General Staff, giving the tonnage of the commercial vessels of the Entente sunk by the submarines, were false and compared them to the figures of the British Admiralty. Finally, he concluded, "The great national duty of the hour is to restore, without losing a day, the moral unity and the cohesion of the German people. At all costs we must put a stop to our domestic quarrels, notably the battle over war aims, for in this lies the grave weakness of the fatherland. To pursue these quarrels, is to impose on Germany more trials, and renewed sacrifices."[14]

Some explanations were heard from the vice chancellor, Helfferich, and from the minister of the Navy, Admiral von Capelle. They reverted to their habitual reasoning. "England has 15 million tons of commercial ships. It requires 7 million tons for the army; 8 millions therefore remain for feeding its people. Now this provisioning is impossible with less than 5 million tons. But we are sinking at least 500,000 tons a month, which is to say, 3 million tons in six months. . . ."[15] "And, nevertheless," Erzberger repeated, "England does not capitulate. Therefore your figures must be false, and you have deceived us."

The deputies parted in consternation, while Noske and Hoch cried out, on behalf of the Socialists, "Under these conditions, we cannot possibly vote the credits. . . . The government has no program except to hold on. That is not enough for us." Finally, by threatening to reconcile themselves with the socialist "Independents," and speaking of revolution, they succeeded in alarming the bourgeois of the Left.

The Progressives, greatly moved, met again within the hour and decided to enter right away into discussions with the Social Democrats, the Center and even the National Liberals, in order "to seek a solution." But to seek a solution at such a moment meant to open a crisis.

Chancellor Bethmann-Hollweg was astonished to receive the news of this sudden parliamentary agitation. He found it all the more embarrassing to quell it because he was fundamentally in agreement with those who provoked it. He had long condemned the unrestricted submarine war. And if, from weakness, he had adjusted to tolerating it, his good sense and his conscience had not ceased to suffer from it. He thought only of negotiating a rapid peace, and to achieve it, he would gladly have borne the pan-Germanist frenzies. Perhaps, had he suddenly exploited this political turmoil for his own benefit, Bethmann-Hollweg could have succeeded in retaining power, by placing himself resolutely on the ground of peace without conquests and of the democratic transformation of the Empire; dismissing from the government the likes of Helfferich, Stein, and Capelle; grouping behind him the majority of the Left and Center in the Reichstag; and appealing to public opinion against the pan-Germanists. But for that he would have had to talk frankly and firmly to the Kaiser, break Ludendorff, silence Tirpitz and Reventlow, form a parliamentary ministry, order the submarines to return to their ports, proclaim before the world that he was ready, without conditions, to evacuate Belgium and Northern France. From the bottom of his soul, the chancellor wished to see Germany follow this path; but he lacked the energy to open it for her. Not with impunity had he bowed his convictions and his conscience, on terrible occasions, before the will of the warriors, accepting the invasion of Belgium, tolerating "unrestricted warfare," and allowing the drowning of civilian passengers. A character abased, a heart made vile, refused to serve with courage a mind that remained lucid.

At first he believed he could extricate himself from the affair, and rally the disorganized Left at a stroke, by announcing that the granting of the Prussian electoral reform by the Kaiser was imminent. In fact, that promise did restore a passing calm in the souls of certain democrats in the Reichstag.

But, on the morning of July 6th, before the Principal Committee, Erzberger resumed his offensive and focused it by delivering the address of a minister-to-be. He began by painting for the deputies the exceptional importance of the vote they were about to take.

> Since the beginning of the war, a vote of credits has never taken on such significance. If we do not accompany it with a political action of grand scope, we vote at the same stroke the campaign for the autumn. The winter campaign would follow necessarily, and next would come

the offensive of the spring. Now, do you want a new year of war? Yes or no? If yes, it will cost at least 50 billions in new expenses for Germany; and who can measure the extent of the irreparable losses in men, which that year will cost the fatherland? . . . To all these questions, the government has only one response: hold on. But to hold on, one must first be convinced that the coming year of war will bring us a more advantageous peace. Now, I see no such possibility. . . . The enemy war machine is becoming more and more powerful, while on our side the scarcity of men and primary materials makes itself felt more cruelly each day.

Then, returning once more to the question of submarine war, he showed by what errors and by what willful exaggerations the minister of the Navy had rendered himself culpable, and by extension, the government.

A government that is so grossly deceived can no longer count on the confidence of the Parliament. . . . If it is necessary to conduct the war with energy, it is no less necessary to work with vigor and method to achieve peace. The best means at the moment is to muster an immense majority in the Reichstag, to declare that Germany wants a peace of conciliation, to reject every idea of oppressing peoples by modifying frontiers. We can disregard the uproar that such a resolution will draw forth from the pan-Germanists; and even if it is necessary to lead 25,000 of them to the cold showers, that will be much less costly than to pursue the war."

He concluded by affirming that the moment had come to move to a parliamentary regime.

The Kaiser keeps all the deputies of the Reichstag at a distance, and everywhere it is said that he is badly informed about what the people of Germany think. . . . Coldly, inexorably, one must know how to draw from present circumstances the political consequences that reason imposes. Our entire system of domestic politics must be changed; whether it is a question of the mode of suffrage or of the collaboration of government and Parliament. . . . May the Reichstag never have to hear the people cry to it, "It is too late!"[16]

Erzberger's speech produced an immense impression. The Principal Commission of the Reichstag had occasionally heard philippics as bitter.

But they had never been delivered by anyone except the Independent Socialists. This time, a considerable figure, known to be a patriot, held to be well-informed, whose ambitions were recognized, the moral leader of a great party that was at once popular and moderate, had affirmed publicly, without mincing words, what so many Germans thought. He had compressed all the just criticisms that filled their minds into an eloquent and impassioned discourse. And, above all, he had shown the route that could lead Germany out of anguish and misery, toward peace and hope.

Amidst a glacial silence, Helfferich, the vice chancellor, tried in vain to give the deputies a little confidence in the results of the submarine war. Then von Stein, the minister of war, provoked a thousand ironic interruptions, by painting in an optimistic light the current and future military situation. Erzberger, who had again in mind the declarations of Colonel Bauer, made the minister of war fall silent, by replying that such was not the opinion of the High Command and that they would be happy to hear Hindenburg himself give explanations to Parliament. They departed from the place in the middle of a great commotion. In the midst of it, Ebert proclaimed, in the name of the Social Democrats, the adoption of Erzberger's idea of a great manifesto of the Reichstag; and General von Stein, beside himself, ran to call Hindenburg by telephone, to plead with him to come to Berlin to respond to the deputies himself. A few moments later, the rumor spread through the corridors, that the Kaiser would be back again in the capital the next day, in anticipation of the development of the growing crisis.

The afternoon passed in secret meetings, Erzberger making great efforts to draw the National Liberals over to his point of view. He counted greatly, in fact, on uniting a crushing majority behind his proposition. The old party of Bismarck, representing heavy industry and banking, counting among them in the Reichstag men of worth like Stresemann and Richthofen, would have a decisive weight in the balance. Moreover, if one wished to constitute a parliamentary cabinet, one would be obliged to turn to the National Liberals, the only party that could provide ministers who had the technical aptitude for finance, provisioning, transportation, and industry. Erzberger, who already saw himself as chancellor, was well aware while using the Socialists that he could not remain dependent on them once in power; he secured for himself in advance the means of governing, if necessary, without their cooperation. Finally, he recognized that many deputies in his own party feared an exclusive alliance with the Social Democrats and that he could without difficulty draw them along if he could range the National Liberals to their right in the battle.

Stresemann and Richthofen were very reluctant to enroll themselves under the Silesian's banner. Although they generally disapproved of the pan-Germanist exaggerations in July 1917, they were by no means resigned to seeing the war end in a peace without gains; and if they too hated Bethmann, it was for his moderation. Furthermore, they had reason to think that if the Kaiser one day agreed to take a chancellor from the seats of the Reichstag, he would be tempted to choose among them; and they did not wish to appear beforehand to be placing themselves in tow behind someone else. Finally, and above all, they were determined to act only in accord with General Headquarters, bound to it by a thousand ties that united heavy industry, which they represented, with the war. They claimed to be waiting until Hindenburg had made his opinion in the matter known clearly.

As to the Conservatives, they observed with profound joy the battle undertaken by the Left against the chancellor, whom they detested and despised. They took great care not to intervene, for fear they would see the combatants come to immediate agreement. They expected a dictatorship, of Tirpitz or of Ludendorff, to emerge from the confusion they were witnessing.

Bethmann-Hollweg, learning of what had transpired at the Principal Commission, had the naïveté to think that he could disarm the opposition by persuading Erzberger. He invited him to visit him and expressed to him the surprise his unforeseen hostility had caused. "You attacked my back," he declared, "like Zieten coming from the woods without a moment's warning!"[17] Erzberger replied that he had announced his opposition in advance. Then, the chancellor read to him the speech that he had written for the coming plenary session of the Reichstag, calling him to witness that on the whole he found himself entirely in agreement with him. Erzberger was obliged to concur that aside from some nuances he himself could have given the speech. Moreover, it was not in his interest to excite the active resistance of the chancellor. He took leave of Bethmann-Hollweg, leaving him convinced that all this parliamentary agitation was essentially superficial; that it would fall off as quickly as it had begun; and that to make himself its master, Bethmann-Hollweg had only to give some satisfaction ceremoniously to the Left—such as the proclamation of universal suffrage in Prussia.

V

From Kreuznach, Ludendorff followed the progress of the offensive against Bethmann with even more attention because his own name was constantly mentioned during the brawl.[f] Every party drew its clinching arguments from the declarations of the High Command. A letter that Hindenburg had written to his wife in May, in which he announced that the war would end in August, was leaked out by Helfferich, to be passed around the corridors of the Reichstag and reported in the newspapers. The marshal's wife had immediately shown the letter to her friends in Hanover; they had not kept the secret. General von Stein, the minister of war, again repeated Ludendorff's assertion "that it was simply necessary to hold out until the imminent moment when the submarines will have brought England to its knees." Erzberger, from his side, made much of his conversation with Colonel Bauer. He repeated what the industrialist Röchling had just told him upon returning from the High Command: Röchling had represented the opinion of Kreuznach as pessimistic.[g] He concluded that, overall, the military commanders viewed the coming of a new year of war with anxiety.

The need felt by these ministers and deputies to appear in agreement with him gave Ludendorff the measure of his prestige among the politicians and inspired in him the desire to make personal use of it. In addition, he knew that German morale was in an unstable state of equilibrium; and he feared that a parliamentary crisis, if it were prolonged to excess or took on too demagogic a character, could suddenly set off profound and irreparable repercussions. Thus on July 6th, when following the famous session of the Principal Committee the minister of war

[f] The German General Staff Headquarters had been transferred from Pless to Kreuznach in February 1917. The liquidation of the Russian offensive of 1916, the finishing off of Romania, the threatening tension on the Western Front, the displacement of the Austrian High Command from Teschen to Baden, had determined this change. [Ed. note: Mackensen's forces had decisively defeated the Romanian Army by February, although it was not completely destroyed.]

[g] Röchling, director and proprietor of the great iron and steelworks of Völklingen near Sarre-Louis, was under particular obligations to Erzberger. In 1915, through the efforts of the Holy See, the Catholic Deputy had obtained the liberation of this Saarland industrialist, who had been interned in France. Arrested a second time in France, after the armistice, and found guilty of common law crimes and misdemeanors committed during the war, this same Röchling was liberated again in 1919, in circumstances that remain mysterious.

telephoned Hindenburg to plead with him to come instantly to Berlin, Ludendorff worked fervently to convince the old marshal. Hindenburg was loath to dilute his glory with these parliamentary intrigues. Nevertheless, he gave way to the urging of his quartermaster, and they set out together for Berlin.

Their arrival made Bethmann-Hollweg understand, at a stroke, the gravity of the crisis that threatened him. Had the head of the government come to such a low point that generals would come to intrigue against him in the middle of the Reichstag? In this circumstance the chancellor showed himself capable of dignity and address. Upon the arrival of the Kaiser on the 7th, he calmly said to him that it was no more than a matter of a passing excitement among the deputies, over whom he, Bethmann, would very rapidly make himself the master; and that, on Monday the 9th, he would obtain a vote of confidence in the plenary session of the Reichstag. The Kaiser was very happy to hear from his chancellor that things were going to be set in order. He dreaded political tempests, fearing, with good reason, that in these times of trouble they would carry the Empire toward revolution. Then, Bethmann again told Wilhelm II that the moment had come to grant universal suffrage for the Prussian elections, which would appease the Left and would permit them to await the development of the general situation, without too many shocks on the domestic front. The Kaiser sided with this advice and charged him to prepare a decree to this effect. Finally, the chancellor announced to his sovereign the arrival of Hindenburg and Ludendorff and told him firmly that he could not tolerate it and was asking him categorically to intervene.

The initiative of his generals roused the Kaiser's ire. He considered their authority already quite sufficient. Their role was already so extensive that they need not attempt to add to it the dismissal and choice of chancellors of the Empire. Constantly humiliated by their military prestige and their superiority in strategy, often discomfited by their puritanical rigidity, he was profoundly gratified to catch them at fault and make them feel his displeasure. He called them in immediately and declared to them straight out that "there could be no justification for their presence in Berlin" and advised them "to return in haste to Headquarters, where they would certainly be much better occupied." Hindenburg and Ludendorff, who had barely detrained, at once started back on the road to Kreuznach. And for that day, Bethmann-Hollweg remained master of the battlefield.

Erzberger had counted on the arrival of the generals to strike the final blow. He was now in possession of the text of the famous peace resolution, on which he wished to obtain a near-unanimous vote from the Reichstag, thereby becoming the obvious successor to Bethmann. Richthofen, Gothein, David, and he himself[h] had drafted this text, and the Silesian proposed to submit it that very evening to Hindenburg and Ludendorff. On the basis of what he thought he knew about their true intentions, he had no doubt they would assent, and expected to be in a position then, with supporting evidence, to proclaim himself in accord with the High Command. A dinner had been arranged that would bring together the generals and the candidates among the deputies for ministerial positions: Erzberger, Spahn, Stresemann, Richthofen, Payer, etc. Soldiers and politicians would there be able to break the ice. They would inform each other, without holding back, on the present and future military situation and on the moral condition of the German people. The details were to be decided there for the decisive attack that would overthrow Chancellor Bethmann-Hollweg. Thus, when Erzberger learned that Hindenburg and Ludendorff, sent back by the Kaiser, were again heading toward Kreuznach, he could not contain his disappointment and his fury. He spent the whole of Sunday the 8th making it known everywhere, especially in the press, that Bethmann-Hollweg had insulted the glorious soldiers; that he had chased them out of Berlin, because at all costs he wanted to prevent the representatives of the people from being instructed by the generals on the true military situation.

This incident, skillfully exploited by Erzberger, produced an enormous impression. From every part of Germany, telegrams streamed into the High Command, assuring Hindenburg of the nation's unlimited confidence in him. They urged him to seize the dictatorship, and ended by persuading him that in reality there existed no authority other than his own, and that his will would undoubtedly triumph if he would merely take the trouble to express it clearly.

▰▰▰ VI

On Monday, July 9th, the members of the Principal Committee of the Reichstag returned to their seats. The deputies arrived there

---

[h] Respectively for the National Liberals, the Progressives, the Social Democrats, and the Catholic Center.

highly agitated. This time, the chancellor believed it wise to come in person to the Committee.

His entry was greeted with cries and exclamations. He had hardly seated himself when Stresemann, the leader of the National Liberals—outraged, like his entire party, at the treatment inflicted upon Hindenburg two days before and personally vexed at having been unable to participate in the famous conspiratorial dinner—called Bethmann to account with the utmost violence. From his seat, he demanded of Bethmann, amidst the applause of all the deputies, "What could he be coming to do at the Reichstag?"—and summoned him to go immediately to submit his resignation to the Kaiser. Bethmann-Hollweg was stupefied by this welcome. Seeing that Erzberger was preparing to take the floor, Bethmann pushed him into a corner of the room and demanded that he answer, yes or no, whether the Center was of the opinion that he should remain in power. "Mr. Chancellor," Erzberger responded, "a great number of my political friends desire that you should leave."

Then, the Silesian reiterated his speech of the previous days, painting in somber colors the perils that Germany faced if the Socialists left the majority. He waxed indignant that Count Westarp had declared, in the name of the Conservatives, that he would reject a status quo ante peace. He added:

> Such proposals chill the blood, when one reflects that the fourth winter of war is at our doors. . . . The Swiss Stegemann,[i] who is perhaps as favorable as possible to our cause, recently said to me, "The military situation of the Central Powers is good as a whole, but do not fool yourself, it in no way corresponds to the general situation, and if you consult only the map of war in deliberating your decisions, you will be committing an error." . . . There we have the exact truth![18]

He then returned to the declaration of peace "without annexations and without indemnities," which he proposed to the Reichstag, and concluded:

> To realize at last the fertile accord between the government and the Reichstag, it is necessary to establish a parliamentary regime, and to begin with, to allow into the ministry deputies having the confidence of the political parties. In every case, it is necessary to make contact

[i] Stegemann was director of the *New Zurich Daily*.

between the Reichstag, on the one hand, and the Kaiser and the command of the armies, on the other.[19]

In the afternoon, the chancellor sent word to Erzberger that he had taken the decision to leave power, once he had settled the question of universal suffrage in Prussia and some others of the same order. He called upon the Catholic Center to take a clear position on him. The governing committee of the party sent him the following resolution:

"The Center Party of the Reichstag judges that Chancellor Bethmann-Hollweg's maintaining power would aggravate the difficulties of eventual peace negotiations. Consequently, it leaves to his conscience the task of fixing the date of his resignation."[20]

The National Liberals and the Progressives, consulted on the same terms, addressed to Bethmann analogous orders of the day, and the chancellor made it known "that he understood the consequences to be drawn from this lack of confidence of the moderate parties of the Reichstag." The Principal Committee, considering the crisis still open, decided to suspend its sessions and throughout the day of the 10th, Erzberger expended great effort to organize a ministerial combination "of national defense," of which he would be the head. However, he did not succeed in this: the Socialists refused to enter a cabinet where they would find Richthofen and Stresemann, and these two were unable to tolerate governing together with Scheidemann, Ebert, and David.

All Berlin was bubbling; the most extraordinary rumors flew through the streets. The press freely reproduced the declarations made in the Reichstag and added commentaries of a violence and a precision unknown since the outbreak of the war. For the military censors (whether from stupor or by calculation) permitted the journals to publish everything they would have harshly prohibited at other times.

On Wednesday the 11th, emotion rose still further, when it was learned that the chancellor had transmitted to the Prussian Council of Ministers the imperial proclamation ordering the electoral reform and that five ministers, among them the minister of war, had immediately submitted their resignations, under the pretext that the chancellor no longer possessed the authority required to undertake such a reform.

However, despite the growing gravity of the crisis and the now generally manifested opposition against the person of Bethmann-Hollweg, the Kaiser remained immovable and refused to accept the chancellor's resignation. He did not wish to consult further with the heads of the parties and thereby make a moral concession that would certainly have appeased them. At the very most, the head of his civil cabinet, von Valentini, would summon Erzberger to declare to him on behalf of the sovereign, "that he would not under any pretext discharge Bethmann-Hollweg until the war was ended; that it was an irrevocable decision in his mind; and that there was nothing more for Erzberger and his friends to do but to get used to it." Then, Valentini had the cruelty to add that "if the Kaiser kept Bethmann, it was for lack of men capable of replacing him." He enumerated a certain number of possible candidates, among whom Erzberger did not figure, and explained the reasons that disqualified each of them from the Kaiser's choice.[21] The ambitious deputy was bitter to learn that the military command's candidate was Herr von Bülow. If the Kaiser did not want Bülow, it was because the ambassador of Austria, Hohenlohe, had come to say that his sovereign and his government would consider that nomination as an unfriendly act.[j]

▬▬ VII

Hindenburg and Ludendorff had returned to their headquarters at Kreuznach furious and humiliated by the treatment to which the Kaiser had made them submit in Berlin. They attributed its rigor, not without reason, to the influence of Bethmann-Hollweg. There they remained for four days without reacting, persuaded that the parliamentary assault would suffice to overwhelm the chancellor. They thought they could await the end of the crisis without engaging themselves further, satisfied to read the mass of telegrams of confidence and respect coming to them from every quarter in the country, and to pass a great number of these on to the press. But on July 11th, Ludendorff learned that the Kaiser had refused to accept the resignation of Bethmann-Hollweg; that the chancellor had announced to the Prussian Ministry the granting of universal suffrage; and that, as a result of this concession, the opposition of a part of the left was beginning to weaken. Ludendorff understood that he was going to lose the battle if he did not resolve to commit himself to it personally and completely. He proposed to Marshal Hindenburg that

[j] Austrian opinion, above all the opinion of the Court, had not forgiven the Prince von Bülow for his insistence on bringing Vienna to make territorial concessions in order to disarm Sonnino and prevent Italy from entering the war.

he immediately send his resignation to the Kaiser and declared that he himself demanded to be relieved of his functions as first quartermaster and be given a command without delay. Hindenburg concurred in his opinion and telegraphed Wilhelm II that he requested to be relieved if Chancellor Bethmann-Hollweg remained in office. At the same time, the quartermaster saw to it that the press was alerted to this countermove.

The day of July 12th unfolded in a frenzied and incredibly tense atmosphere. The resignation of the generals, announced by the newspapers in the morning and already known by informed circles the previous evening, provoked an immense and profound popular emotion. This was the day after the victorious defensive at the Chemin des Dames and in Artois, just when the Russian army was beginning to disintegrate; the prestige of Hindenburg and Ludendorff was heavy, not only with the weight of services rendered and the moral greatness of the Marshal, but also with all the frenetic hope that Germany, crushed by ordeals, attached to his person. This romantic people, sick with anguish, invested that hope with a religious character.

Thus, once rumors of Hindenburg's departure had begun to fly, the crisis took on a popular and national cast that it had never displayed prior to this point. In Berlin it was immediately recognized that a solution had to be found quickly, under the threat of extremely grave consequences.

The German crown prince, who had also rushed to the capital, was the first to comprehend this. This clarity doubtless came to him, in the first instance, from his desire that his future crown should be preserved. It also arose from the spirit of opposition by the eldest son of the Kaiser, a tradition within his family, and from the counsels of an entourage inspired by the ambition of von Maltzahn.[22]

The prince learned of Hindenburg's resignation on the evening of July 11th. He immediately decided that the moment had come, if he wished to play a useful and advantageous role, for him to intervene by serving as negotiator between Wilhelm II, his Parliament, and his generals. He meant to prevent popular commotions that could bring the Hohenzollern throne tumbling down. He decided to consult at once the heads of the Reichstag parties—a concession the Kaiser refused to make to them—and to present their views to the sovereign.

The deputies, called to meet at the residence of the crown prince, replied in different ways to the questions he put to them. They were, however, agreed on one point: Conservatives, National Liberals, Catholics, Progressives, Socialists—all declared unanimously that, in the present state of things, the chancellor would have to leave power.

Erzberger made a long exposition to the prince about his policy and spoke to him of Bethmann-Hollweg. "Throw him out the door to the Reichstag!" cried the crown prince. This violence made an impression on the Silesian, who, envisioning himself already chancellor, thought it politic now to spare his predecessor. He responded coldly, "The Parliament cannot so treat a head of government who is about to obtain universal suffrage for Prussia."

Then, Erzberger made his way to the meeting of the Center Party, which awaited him. With Spahn presiding, they disputed bitterly over Hindenburg and the famous peace resolution. Many of the Catholic deputies were now loath to vote for it. The resignation of the marshal had convinced them that the true reason for the conflict between the soldiers and Bethmann-Hollweg was the chancellor's peace policy. Hence they feared to participate in a demonstration that would weaken the High Command in the eyes of the public. Spahn himself proved to be quite eager to scuttle the resolution proposed by Erzberger. He revealed a conversation that he had just had with the vice chancellor, Helfferich. "Helfferich tells me that Hindenburg declared to him on his way to Berlin last Saturday: 'I am quite hopeful of making peace myself within the month.' In these conditions, our resolution for a peace without annexations or indemnities would be an error."[23]

Erzberger rushed to find Helfferich. Hearing Spahn reiterate his declarations, Helfferich responded sharply, "I never said anything like that, and Hindenburg said nothing of the kind. All this is an incomprehensible misunderstanding. . . ."[24] Amidst Erzberger's cries of triumph and the general uproar, Spahn fell from his seat, choking with astonishment and indignation, struck down by apoplexy.

Nevertheless, the crown prince, after his consultation with the parliamentarians, had gone to the Kaiser, to inform him of it and to plead with him, for his sake, to dismiss Bethmann-Hollweg. He found the sovereign in a deep depression caused by the resignation of Hindenburg and Ludendorff. Little as he cared for them, he recognized their indisputable superiority. He believed, as did all Germany, that they were indispensable. He was therefore prepared to sacrifice Bethmann to them, however much that would cost his pride. But he judged that his imperial prestige was at stake in the matter. Having declared to the world his intention to keep Bethmann, despite the contrary opinion of everyone, it would be disastrous suddenly to accept his resignation. The subtle mind of von Maltzahn found a way to inspire the crown prince with an adroit solution, one that preserved the sovereign's dignity as much as possible. That solution was adopted.

Wilhelm II began by telegraphing Hindenburg that he refused to accept his resignation and that he invited him to come discuss it in Berlin. The stay in the capital, that had recently been denied the field marshal was therefore granted. This time, however, it would be by order of the Kaiser. As regards Bethmann, they had it rumored about that the Kaiser had refused to permit him to resign because he did not want to concede to the demands of the Left. Thus it was left in suspense what might happen if the Right equally demonstrated its hostility. Von Maltzahn hurried to ask the Conservatives, the National Liberals, and the Center, to provide him at once with a statement on this subject. Count Westarp, Stresemann, and Erzberger were only too happy to satisfy him, each for different motives. And during this same evening of the 12th, the Kaiser, who was in possession of the motions of No Confidence voted against his chancellor by the most monarchist parties in the Reichstag, announced his acceptance of Bethmann-Hollweg's resignation.

▰▰▰ VIII

Ludendorff and Erzberger had thus triumphed together. But while the soldier's success was to be complete and prolonged, the politician's had no tomorrow. On the evening of July 13th, it was learned that the nominee to the post of chancellor was Michaelis, heretofore high commissioner of provisioning, an experienced and conscientious functionary, but without distinction. The military had chosen him, judging that if the Kaiser refused to call the one statesman that Germany possessed, Prince von Bülow, they could desire nothing better than a personage of second rank, who would have no desire for initiatives on a grand scale and would be entirely disposed to make himself the executor, in the government, of their wishes.

Erzberger then grasped—with what bitterness!—that he had been working for precisely the man he had thought to dominate. For the present, a calm followed this acute crisis. The new chancellor would benefit from it in every way, and it would no longer be possible, for several months, to gather together again the Center and the Left in a comparable operation. Thus the possibility of Erzberger's becoming chancellor receded to the horizon. It would never again reappear under such favorable conditions for the general peace of conciliation, which the Silesian had dreamed of negotiating.

Ludendorff did not wait long, moreover, to inflict the cruelest wounds on the pride of his accomplice and to demonstrate crassly that he had deceived him. As early as the afternoon of the 13th, the meeting that had been so harshly demanded, between Hindenburg and the leaders of the Reichstag parties, took place.

The generals declared that they looked forward to the future with the greatest confidence. When Erzberger cited statistics to prove the failure of the submarine war, Ludendorff pretended to ignore them and to consider the question secondary. And when the Silesian produced his famous proposal for a peace resolution, the quartermaster responded that this demonstration hardly interested him. At the very most, he advised him to use the expression "peace of equilibrium" rather than "peace of conciliation," because the term "equilibrium" could be more useful. Hindenburg found it necessary to put "a little more pepper" in the text of this pale proclamation. And the two soldiers demanded that it should end with a phrase in which the Reichstag pronounced itself entirely in accord with them and expressed its admiration for and confidence in the army. The deputies complied forthwith.

On July 19th, the Reichstag adopted the resolution. The result of the voting had scarcely been declared when Michaelis read a dispatch from the High Command. It announced the launching of the victorious offensive, begun in the East to respond to the futile assaults ordered by Kerensky; it predicted the rapid and complete collapse of the Russian army.

Then, profiting from the effect produced by this news, Michaelis began a speech in which he indicated that he would interpret the peace resolution adopted by the Reichstag "in his own fashion" and that he wished to govern only in full and constant agreement with the High Command. Moreover, he obtained (from a Left still in disorder) a vote for the famous war credits.

The next day the Kaiser, his calm restored, convoked the principal deputies of all the Reichstag parties, judging that granting this favor would no longer bind him in any way, now that the crisis was resolved. They presented themselves in good order, arranged by the Chancellor Michaelis and Helfferich, still vice chancellor. The proposals the Kaiser put to them threw them into the most profound bewilderment. Wilhelm II congratulated the Reichstag for declaring that it desired "a peace of equilibrium." However, in fact, despite Ludendorff's insistence, the resolution spoke only of "conciliation." "The term 'equilibrium' is very well chosen," said the Kaiser. "Moreover, that does not surprise me, for it is he who chose it!" and he pointed to Helfferich who was offering him a cigarette. "Equilibrium will consist in what we take from the enemy in money, primary materials, cotton, minerals, petroleum. Yes, it is a capital word!"

The amazement of the deputies knew no bounds when they heard Wilhelm II announce to them that England and America had concluded an alliance to strike Japan after the war and that he had it from an absolutely dependable source that Japan and Russia had agreed to parry the blow. "Evidently," he said, "the present war cannot be ended by the defeat of England. But we will come soon to an understanding with France, and then, the war properly so-called will begin: the whole continent, organized under my command, against England. That will be the second Punic War. . . ." Then, he began speaking of the offensive going on against the Russians and the exploits of his son, Eitel-Frederic, who commanded a guard division. "He nicely kicked up their democratic dust! Besides, where my guard appears, there is no more democracy. . . ."

He turned toward Erzberger, who was listening, devastated, and told him that he had been quite wrong to doubt the success of the submarine war. "The east coast of England is now no more than a field of wrecked ships. Two or three months from now, England will be done for. . . . Imagine that there are 4 million tons of cereals in Australia ready to embark, and England no longer has ships to carry them! . . . Besides, the officers of our submarines inform me that they no longer encounter, so to speak, any enemy ships on the high seas. . . ."

Erzberger valiantly responded that "this appears incomprehensible to me, since our Admiralty announces every month that we have sunk 600,000 more tons of shipping." The Kaiser turned away from him, and launched himself into considerations on the future of riverways. "We are going to divert the lower Danube, at Cernavoda, directly toward Constanza, along the Trajan Wall. Thus Romania will no longer have the Danube, and that will be her punishment."k

kThe Dobroudja, occupied by the Germans and Bulgarians following their victories of 1916, was to be taken from Romania by the Treaty of Bucharest. [Ed. note: However, as de Gaulle notes in the next chapter, it was not given to the Bulgarians, contrary to what they had expected.]

Erzberger had some words of pity for the unfortunate Romanian people. "There are many people down there who have nothing more than the shirts on their backs." The Kaiser then told them, "When I was the heir-apparent, I worked for some time at the ministry of foreign affairs. One day, the Prince von Bismarck said to me, 'In Eastern Europe, there are two kinds of people: those who carry their shirts outside their breeches, who are good devils; and those who tuck their shirts into their pants and carry decorations on their chests, who are all swine. . . .'"[25] Thus ended the consultation with the parliamentarians.

An ironic conclusion to an impassioned crisis, during which, under the ferment of Erzberger's ambitions, Germany, weighed down by suffering, had confusedly sought the end of the trial in the direction of moderation and democracy. The powerful will of Ludendorff had been able to bring this crisis to birth, to exploit it, and bring it to an end in a fashion that served his designs. Now, the decisive point passed, all obstacles overthrown, the quartermaster had expanded the boundaries of his power and his prestige. He had stabilized his dictatorship and given it definition, gained the time (which threatened to run out on him) for the pursuit of his grandiose undertaking. But he had, with the same blow, cut down the required authority of the imperial government; and his success untuned the instrument from which he intended to draw a better performance.

Henceforth, Germany would docilely allow herself to be directed by Ludendorff, so long as he could blind her with victories and dazzle her with hopes. But when, overtaken by reverses, she suddenly staggered into an irreparable disequilibrium, deprived of the supports indispensable for righting herself, she sensed, in her mortal fever, that she had at her head a failing government, without independence and without credit, just at the moment when she was wrenched by an irresistible need to see her civil and military leaders in their places and to feel the edifice of their authority solidly on its foundations and in its proper proportions. The sudden collapse of a strong and valiant people was going to testify to the vengeance of violated principles.

5

The Debacle of the German People

In the moral crisis[1] that causes the disaster of an army, it is customary to study first the loss of confidence in victory; then, the surprise, resulting from a brutal manifestation of the enemy's will and carrying with it stupor and discouragement; then the panic, following upon some incident of battle; and finally, the debacle or capitulation. These phases of moral breakdown are to be found again in a nutshell, in the history of German opinion during the course of 1918.

I

At the beginning of the year, Germany was seized as if by vertigo with victory; Russia and Romania had given up the fight.[2] Never since the famous days of August 1914 had the whole of Germany been found more united in hope, more resolved to conquer. It truly seemed, in the weeks that preceded the great offensive, that this people was drawing new strength from all the sacrifices it had accepted, from all the privations it had suffered, from all the disappointments it had endured.

The Kaiser had been silent for months on end, and had even taken it upon himself, during his voyage in Courland, to say nothing that had any color. In the month of February, he turned back solemnly toward the West. Announcing that he would take up residence at General Headquarters, he began to visit the training camps of the assault troops who were being prepared there.[3] Passing a division of the Guard in review, he delivered a speech in which, by way of a peroration, he cried, drawing his sword, "And now, we are going to break down the doors of those who do not want our peace!"

Some days before the offensive, the King of Bavaria said to the young soldiers of Ratisbonne, "Germany has pushed her frontiers toward the East. She needs new ones toward the West as well, further off and stronger."

The government of Count Hertling had been unable to disguise its internal dissensions over the course of the winter, despite the political ruses of the chancellor, whom Ledebour characterized as "the old parliamentary fox." We know in what circumstances this government had been formed. In November 1917, Michaelis was obliged to withdraw before the open hostility of the Reichstag. Fundamentally, this was because he did not want to adopt as his policy the July resolution for a peace "without annexations and without indemnities," and because he did not agree to support universal suffrage energetically before the Prussian Chambers.

Hertling, until that point president of the Bavarian Council, had taken power, and his task was not easy. Internally, he had to make concessions in order to calm the irritability of the Left, [yet] without abandoning any serious prerogatives of the Crown, and without upsetting the High Command. Externally, he had to make peace with Russia, taking from her as much territory, money, and economic advantage as possible. But for the moment, this had to be done without displaying an excessive appetite. It was also necessary not to vex the exhausted and groaning Austrians, nor to obstruct the campaign of the pacifists in France and England, before the day when the offensive was begun. Moreover, it was necessary to treat the United States and Wilson carefully, so that they would not hurry their conscription and armaments programs.

The views of the collaborators Hertling had chosen corresponded to these necessities. To calm the Left, they were given as vice chancellor Herr von Payer, who was the head of the Progressive Party in the Reichstag and had replaced the famous Helfferich, the "Ludendorff in sheep's clothing." To satisfy Austria, and so as not unmask himself too soon before Europe and America, he kept at Foreign Affairs Herr von Kühlmann. Kühlmann was a skeptical and subtle career diplomat from the old school of Count von Arnim.[4] In the eyes of liberal Germany, Kühlmann was considered a great man, because he had once said, "There is more than mere force at the foundation of politics; there is right as well. . . ." And the pan-Germanist Right secretly dragged him through the mud.

The winter had been rough for this cobbled-together ministry. The brutal peace treaties of Brest-Litovsk and Bucharest and the imperious protests of the Social Democrats about universal suffrage had led to many skirmishes within the ministry and to serious conflicts with the military command—that is to say, with Ludendorff. The will of the military and of the pan-Germanists had prevailed, as always. Von Payer no longer opened his mouth; Kühlmann was waiting for a favorable opportunity to send him packing—

Suddenly, an understanding came about as if by magic. The same hope united the formerly quarrelsome ministers. The great offensive in the West having been decided, they all set to work to make it victorious; the General Staff vouched for its success. Immediately, Count Hertling, heretofore unctuous and conciliating in his speech, raised his voice. In the response he delivered in February to the famous Fourteen Points of President Wilson, he assumed a haughty and ironic tone, that no one was accustomed to hearing from him. Herr von Payer, supposedly ill in Stuttgart, recovered immediately and returned to occupy his post. Kühlmann, voluntarily in exile in Bucharest, returned to Berlin with a smile on his lips. Their differences, poorly hidden yesterday, when victory seemed distant, suddenly ceased abruptly today, when they saw it approaching. If Ludendorff triumphed in the West, Hertling, von Payer, and Kühlmann would immediately unite to crush the fallen enemy without restraint.[5]

In that case, they would find the political world remarkably docile. The Reichstag had fought bitterly, all through 1917, over the question of peace. We recall that, in July, the Left and the Center had apparently carried the Reichstag by obtaining passage of the famous resolution for "no annexations and no indemnities." But the great military and political successes at the end of the year had turned the situation around. The easy and overwhelming Italian defeat in October 1917 and, above all, the triumph of Maximalism in Russia, the fall of Kerensky, and the signing of the peace treaties of Brest-Litovsk and Bucharest had sufficed to give back to the annexationists all their prestige.[6] The Conservatives and the National Liberals resumed their insolence. The Catholic Center, which appeared for a moment to have gone over to moderation under the leadership of the ambitious Erzberger, played turncoat again and embraced pan-Germanism.[a] Erzberger himself did not hesitate to affirm

[a] Since the fall of Bethmann-Hollweg, Ludendorff had severely persecuted Erzberger. He was refused passports to Hungary in September 1917. He was prohibited from publishing a speech he gave in October in his electoral district. He was prevented from speaking in Ulm. He was threatened with prosecution for high

"that the peace of Brest-Litovsk was completely within the framework of the Reichstag resolution: no annexations and no indemnities" and that, after all, he ought to know, since he was its author.

The Progressive and Radical left, altogether ashamed of its recent defeatism, tried to exculpate itself by protests of patriotism and hatred of the enemy. The great man of German liberalism, Friedrich Naumann, set the tone. After having so long celebrated the German conception of liberty, in opposition to that of the Latins and Anglo-Saxons, he now acclaimed German force.[7]

Lastly, the Socialists, confounded and repentant, confined themselves to a humiliated silence. They allowed the dismemberment of Russia at Brest-Litovsk and of Romania at Bucharest to pass without serious protest. And when the revolutionary Russian newspapers appealed to Scheidemann, [reminding him] that he had sworn two months before in Stockholm "that the German people would be sure to prevent its governors from carrying out any annexation," he replied to them with that species of candor that is a quite characteristic trait of this people: "Is it our fault, we Socialists, if the Russians, since Stockholm, have thrown down their arms before the German soldiers?"

Some sincere extremists, who wanted to prevent at any cost the coming hecatombs, tried in January to organize strikes in the arms factories. The repression by the military authorities was brutal and swift and was moreover openly approved by the immense majority of the population. The Socialist leaders in the Reichstag disavowed the movement, and Ebert pompously affirmed in the Principal Committee that "one must look somewhere other than here for those who would induce the working people to deny arms to the men in the trenches!"

The press was once again unanimous in exciting the public, with a view to the formidable strains of the coming offensive. The pan-German organs—the *German Daily News,* the *Gazette of the Cross,* the *Cologne Gazette,* the *Gazette of the Rhine and Westphalia,* the *Local Reporter,* etc.— unleashed their war cries, especially against Wilson. They held up before the eyes of the public the hope of immense annexations and enormous indemnities. In all their columns, it was a question [of keeping] the Flemish coast; of the Flemish movement in Belgium; of the Briey

---

treason, under the pretext that he had, during a meeting, indicated the number of German submarines. [Reichsfinanzminister Matthias Erzberger, *Erlebnisse im Weltkrieg* (Stuttgart: Deutsche Verlags-Anstalt, 1920), 268–69.]

basin; of the French colonies—notably Morocco; of the economic market of Western Europe, on the point of being conquered like that of Eastern Europe. In these columns Austria, and notably the Emperor Charles and Empress Zita, were continually abused—even insulted—because of their known hostility against the anticipated offensive and their desire for a rapid peace by any means.

The liberal newspapers—the *Frankfurt Gazette,* the *Berlin Daily,* the *Munich Late News,* etc.—expressed profound sadness that the German peace offers of 1916 and 1917 had not been accepted by the Entente.

"But now," they added immediately, "it is too late. It is Hindenburg and Ludendorff who are going to make peace triumph." Imprecations against Clemenceau's address were constantly repeated; great pains were taken to persuade the people that this statesman's future hung only by a thread, that a single reverse would suffice to overthrow him and M. Poincaré with him.[8] And a crowd of articles appeared about France:Poor France!—exhausted, incapable of a serious effort, stripped of men, of courage, of economic resources, famished. Why had she not lowered her weapons when there was still time, when the Kaiser held out his generous hand to her? Now she would have to be pillaged, held for ransom, stripped of her colonies, thrown into revolution and economic upheaval.

As to the Socialist press, with unflagging tenacity it resumed its habitual chant, the hymn of peace. It took pains to protest that there was only one obstacle to a peace settlement: the obstinacy of the Entente governments, in particular those of M. Clemenceau and Mr. Lloyd George. And in bulky articles in *Vorwärts,* the Socialist leaders of the Entente were entreated to meet in Holland with Scheidemann to discuss methods to shorten the war. Meanwhile, during these very days, majorities in the Reichstag were voting the trimester war credits.[9]

Public opinion, thus stirred in its greed by the pan-Germanist press, was assured by the liberal dailies that the enemy was at its last gasp and that, furthermore, the German government had done everything to arrange a peace of understanding. It was convinced by the Socialist journals that the imperialists were on the side of France and England and that Wilson was nothing more than a liar. Thus persuaded, public opinion accepted the prospect of the imminent offensive with the docility natural to this people and soon anticipated it resolutely.

In addition, public opinion accepted the offensive all the more willingly because the High Command of the army, then in all the éclat of its glory and prestige, immediately put before the public the need for it and guaranteed its success. Marshal von Hindenburg, convening the war correspondents in February at Headquarters, made the most explicit declarations to them: "The Eastern Front," he said, "has ceased to exist. For the first time since the beginning of the war, we can concentrate our forces on one front, the principal front, in such a way as to end the campaign by the decisive action." Then, reviewing the adversaries who would have to be encountered, he added, "The English have acquired considerable tactical skill, but they are ignorant of strategy, and strategy is what bestows victory. . . . The Americans are brave, but poorly trained and moreover not very numerous, because our submarines have done good work. . . . The French," he concluded, "are, as always, the most valiant of our adversaries, and (if they did not mistreat our prisoners of war in the most inhumane fashion), one would have to render them the fullest homage. But their losses are now beyond their capacity to endure. They have fallen to the rank of a second-class army. I just cannot understand, speaking strictly from a professional viewpoint, how their commanders could possibly have dared to impose such terrible losses on their troops for the sake of insignificant results."

And General Ludendorff, taking the floor in his turn, added, "We are prepared for everything; we have everything: trained men, artillery, provisions, tanks. . . . Our superiority in numbers and resources is not considerable, but it is notable." And he concluded, "I promise you, gentlemen, a rapid and complete victory."

Thus, when the great offensive of the spring began, Germany found herself as united, resolute, and fierce, as she had been in the first days of the war.

Aroused covetousness, the will to escape at whatever cost from suffering and sorrow, an able and many-sided propaganda, and, finally, a national spirit of discipline that made the masses think like the leaders — all this shaped the wills and hopes of men into a formidable quiver. With all its soul and all its élan, the German Empire pressed its armies to the attack.

"The army groups of Crown Prince Rupprecht of Bavaria and of the Crown Prince of Germany, under the orders of His Majesty the Kaiser and King, have begun the assault on the English positions," announced the communiqué of March 22nd.[10]

During these four months of furious offensive, the majority of the German people let themselves be carried along by enthusiasm. And besides, they were encouraged in this direction by almost all that could count as authority in the country, deploying every resource. The Kaiser had the newspapers distribute long accounts of his deeds and gestures, his role in the battle, his absolute confidence of success; and the magazines [carried] thousands of supporting photographs or drawings. Every day Hertling published heaps of brassy telegrams, sent to him by all the pan-Germanic associations of the Empire. The Reichstag, including the Left, redoubled its demonstrations of recognition and enthusiasm for Hindenburg. The "Party of the Fatherland," directed by Grand Admiral von Tirpitz, had organized everyone whom the pan-Germanists considered to be the purest and most resolute among the retired officers, the gun merchants, ruined shipowners, imperiously categorical professors. They conducted a relentless propaganda campaign, aimed at public opinion, calling for annexations and merciless indemnities in the West and in the colonies, as well as against statesmen like Herr von Kühlmann, who were suspected of "impurity."[b] The press, which the Wolf Agency stuffed every day with long communiqués drafted by General Headquarters, outdid itself in hosannas of enthusiasm for the High Command, of confidence in victory, of hope for a quick, glorious, and advantageous peace.

The popular masses at first showed themselves relatively reserved, so long as the successes won were only against the English. Many said very quietly (or in any case thought) that the harshest adversary would be the French army and that so long as it had not entered the fight, nothing decisive had been accomplished. The nomination of General Foch to the post of commander in chief of the Allied armies caused heads to shake, because the authorities, and the press, had repeated endlessly that the British would never consent to a unified command.[11]

But, at the beginning of June, when the Chemin des Dames was taken by assault, and German troops had rushed up to the Marne, there were no longer any doubters. The French themselves were beaten! The strongest positions of their front had been taken in record time and with mini-

---

[b]In April, Ludendorff tried to repeat against Kühlmann, with Erzberger's co-operation, the maneuver that had been so successful against Bethmann. In April 1918 he sent to Erzberger a trusted officer to pressure him to attack Kühlmann and to make him believe that the High Command wanted very much to see him become minister for foreign affairs. This time, Erzberger showed the tempter the door. [Erzberger, *Erlebnisse im Weltkrieg*, 269; see also the account of the maneuver in Chapter 4, section III.]

mal losses! And, with one voice, the press, both Right and Left, intoned the song of triumph: the High Command of Ludendorff deserved total confidence; the élan of the troops had made them irresistible; the Allied soldiers had lost courage; and Foch had no more reserves. The approaching blow would catch him empty-handed, and this blow would be decisive; it would carry the armies up to Paris, already bombarded by the miraculous canons invented by formidable German technology.[12]

▬ II

A German public stretched to the limit with hope watched the June offensive between Montdidier and Noyon. The attack was directed against Compiègne, and from there against Paris. Each could look at his map and measure the scant distance separating the armies from their goal. Their relative defeat, which the newspapers made great efforts to conceal, produced a profound impression. From this day signs began to appear—first of nervousness, then malaise, then anxiety—that revealed cracks in confidence and lapses of will.

Several other pieces of information, moreover, coming unexpectedly, blow upon blow, contributed to reestablishing skepticism.

The peace treaty of Bucharest, which had not given northern Doubroudja to Bulgaria but had promised Andrinople to the Turks, had gravely disappointed the already nervous and exhausted Bulgarians. Radoslavov, the man of the German alliance, had been obliged to step down from office, and Malinov formed a cabinet. Everyone knew that Malinov had always been the brilliant second to Danev, the man of the Entente, who was currently in safe custody.[13]

Elsewhere, the position of Austria gave rise to very serious anxieties. The cabinet of von Seidler in Vienna was quite unable to pass its budget; and in Budapest, grave labor disturbances had broken out with armed support. The Austro-Hungarian press sharply scolded Herr von Payer, who had spoken, in all innocence, "of thoroughly investigating the economy of the alliance." And Count Tisza, the most substantial political man in Hungary, and to that point the most faithful to Berlin, summoned in a journalist in order to tell him that he found the words of Herr von Payer "essentially regrettable."

Thereupon the great Austro-Hungarian offensive on the Piava was launched; it was impatiently awaited, and no one doubted that it would inflict on Italy a disaster comparable to that of the preceding October.

From the first news, one could see that it was a failure; and the withdrawal behind the Piava River of Austrian troops, who had crossed it, showed that this defeat was decisive.[14] Henceforth in Germany the conviction was general that one could no longer count on any aid whatever from the Allies in Vienna and Budapest. And the opinion that Foch would be forced to divert the last divisions still thought to be at his disposal, in order to limit an Italian rout—an opinion heretofore widely held—vanished abruptly.

The people had nourished great hopes of an easing of the food situation, thanks to the harvest in the Ukraine. Everywhere it had been said by the most authoritative sources that the Ukraine was the most grain-rich country in the world and that substantial relief supplies were expected to be drawn from there. But now very bad news was announced from this quarter: the harvest would be mediocre; moreover, the Ukrainian peasants were restive; and lastly, means of transport were lacking to carry appreciable stocks of grain. Suddenly it was announced that the bread ration of 250 grams could well fall to 200 grams in a short time.

The official figures of tonnage sunk by submarines throughout the month of May were much lower even than those for the two preceding months. How could that be? This formidable weapon, from which so much was expected, was it going to quit working just at the moment when troops from the United States were arriving on the continent in substantial numbers?

Germany again began to doubt. The press on the Left welcomed with characteristic acidity a frenzied speech by the Kaiser at General Headquarters, in which he declared, "With these battles we are going to decide which conception must prevail: the Prussian-Germanic conception of Right, of Liberty, of Morality; or instead, the Anglo-Saxon conception of Money. One of the two must destroy the other."

The *Frankfurt Gazette* protested, "The German people do not want to fight on until that point [is reached]."

And a socialist paper wrote sententiously, "Each man should measure his words [before speaking], in high places as well as low, on the throne as well as in the workshop."

Herr von Kühlmann had passed some very bad moments during the last three months. The pan-Germanists no longer accused him merely of "understanding nothing of the interests of the fatherland," and of "having nothing of a Bismarck about him." Dominated by anxiety and the onset of disillusionment, they took to condemning him for his private life, stirring up against him the empress—a good person who was particularly austere and merciless toward sin.

Sensing that his position was untenable, he resolved to depart abruptly on his own terms. He did so on June 24th by delivering a speech to the Reichstag that produced an immense effect in Germany. Kühlmann took up a proposition advanced by Marshal von Moltke in 1885, which affirmed that the war of the future could well last seven years, even thirty years. He declared that the future war predicted by the marshal was under way and that, moreover, it seemed to him improbable that a solution would ever be reached by arms.

The pan-Germanists immediately went berserk. And although the aging Hertling came the next day to make honorable amends at the podium, Ludendorff no longer hesitated to demand the resignation of Herr von Kühlmann. He did not fail to obtain it.

But the blow had been effective. Among the masses, confidence in victory rapidly disappeared, and they began again to complain and grumble. In the political world, bitter and cunning quarreling again resumed, worse than ever. In the press, gall flowed in full columns. The left-wing newspapers accused the pan-Germanists, the "Party of the Fatherland," and Admiral von Tirpitz of stupidities and mistakes—notably in their calculations and their promises of success with unlimited submarine warfare. And the right-wing journals threw their thunderbolts against the defeatist Liberals and Socialists, who had corroded the confidence of the German people just at the moment when they were most imperatively in need of it.

The Socialists had observed the popular enthusiasm of the last three months in silence, ready to take advantage of it to benefit their party, in case the offensive succeeded. But when the hoped-for success did not come, they felt a growing bitterness rise among the people; and they saw the enemy more resolute than ever. They then decided to take a new attitude, exploiting the doubts of the masses and simultaneously attempting to excite comparable sentiments in France and England. Herr Scheidemann made his return to the stage after a long silence. He did so first, with great pomp, in Holland, meeting with Troëlstra, the leader of the Netherlands Socialists, and giving him instructions for the delegates from Paris and London, whom he could not see in person. Then he returned to Berlin; and on July 2nd, in the Reichstag, on the occasion of the discussion over the third reading of the budget, he announced point-blank that neither he nor his party would vote for war credits—this for the first time during the war. He explained his attitude in a speech full of bitterness, in which he announced to the government that it hardly governed and that the policy of the Empire was made at military head-quarters. He asserted that the peace of the world could not be attained through arms, and that the German people wanted the war ended as rapidly as possible.

It was done! Despite the considerable successes achieved since the opening of the offensive; despite the repeated assertions of the High Command that victory was assured; despite the innumerable articles in all the news-sheets, written to prove that the reserves of the Entente were irrevocably exhausted; despite the caricatures in the satiric journals representing the Eiffel Tower fleeing from the shells or a French railroad engineer hooking up a freight train of commodities to a single railcar containing all Foch's reserves; despite the maps published by the pan-Germanist organizations, plastered up everywhere and marking the stages on the road to peace by the advances of [German] troops toward the West; despite the war exhibitions organized in Berlin, Munich, Hamburg, and Breslau, where cannons, machine guns, and tanks, taken from the enemy, were displayed in heaps—[despite all this,] Germany was plunged into doubt, just when it was about to deliver the final blow. Germany no longer believed in victory.

On the 15th of July, the Champagne offensive failed completely. No one was seriously surprised. They were resigned to defeat in advance.

And yet, no longer hoping for victory, Germany could not imagine defeat. No one believed that her commanders could find themselves flagrantly caught in error; that her troops could, moreover, be significantly thrown back; that the enemy might, in its turn, be capable of attacking. On the 16th of July, the officious *Gazette of Northern Germany* articulated the unanimous sentiment when it wrote: "The question is now resolved. The French—we are certain of this—no longer have either the material force, or the initiative, or the capacity for decision, which would be necessary to undertake a counteroffensive. . . ."

Two days later, between the Aisne and the Marne, the thunderous attack of the Fayolle army group began.[15]

III

The 18th of July will remain a day forever memorable in the history of the war.[16] And by no means only because it marked both the retaking of the offensive by the troops of the Entente and the beginning of an uninterrupted series of victories up to the final triumph. For it also manifested, in this war between peoples, the will of one group suddenly imposing itself on its adversary, by virtue of surprise. It was not only the German army and its commanders who were taken unawares by the French counteroffensive led by General Pétain. It was the whole German nation that was suddenly taken by surprise, and remained so right up to the final collapse, as if they had been stunned.[17]

A sort of moral stupor all at once gripped a proud and authoritarian sovereign, a formerly tenacious government, a docile political world, a confident and resolute military command, an obedient and courageous soldiery. At a blow, as by the fatal stroke of a magic wand, that stupor annihilated the warlike qualities of the German people and suddenly enlarged their faults. Thus in battle the very best army, taken by surprise, suddenly finds itself without valor.

This should have been the moment for this imperiled people to galvanize itself for effort. In order to round the difficult cape, in order to reorganize its resources, to recover from its surprise, to adapt itself to the new phase of the war, it was essential that the nation be capable of pulling itself together with a concerted effort around firm and resolute leaders.

But bitter and damaging quarrels and impassioned intrigues had degraded the civilian leaders of Germany, both in their own eyes and in the eyes of the public.

Furthermore, the military chiefs, taking advantage of the weakness of their sovereign and abusing their prestige, had taken authority and credit away from the government. Germany found with dismay that the logical and necessary harmony of powers in the State had been untuned.[18] Staggering in the night, the colossus groped in vain for the support that would have enabled it to right itself. Unable to find that support, a valiant people suddenly despaired of its strength. Henceforth, it would react to the redoubled hammer blows of Destiny only with an incurable resignation, a moral lassitude that will remain the astonishment and the lesson of History.

The Kaiser had heretofore been so prolix, so friendly to photographers and to the illustrators of the *Illustrated Times,* so well situated in the battle, according to the articles of the *Local Reporter.* Now he did not open his mouth, made no more gestures, and vanished into the secrecy of General Headquarters. Only on September 12th, when the general offensive of the Allies was fully under way did he decide to speak, before the factory workers of Essen.

This speech, instead of comforting everyone as it ought to have done, added to the general anxiety by its tone: at once sad, humble, and seemingly detached from earthly things — things to which it was however high time to pay attention.

The government, instead of quickly adopting a stance and a policy suited to the circumstances, presented at the outset a spectacle of disarray, which steadily increased. The day after our victory between the Aisne and the Marne, on July 22nd, Hertling felt himself obliged to take the floor. At this moment, the reversal still appeared remediable; indeed, its repair was being announced. This would have been a cleverly chosen occasion, at the beginning of the defensive, to affirm Germany's lack of interest in Belgium. Hertling preferred to launch into tumultuous explanations, declaring that Belgium would serve as the "proof of [German] strength."[19] This simultaneously exasperated the Left, which wanted him to renounce Belgium immediately in order to deprive the enemy of its principal argument for unity and resolution; and the Right, which demanded the Flemish coast and Brussels.

Admiral von Hintze, a personal friend of Ludendorff, had replaced the unfortunate Kühlmann at Foreign Affairs. The next day, he sent Helfferich, the former finance minister and vice chancellor, to Moscow as ambassador. It may be recalled that the ambassador of the Empire to Russia, Count Mirbach, had just been assassinated. The nomination of Helfferich was, at least, the assertion of a program. For this economist-financier was a convinced pan-Germanist; and among the statesmen of that time, his brain was one of the best organized. He had in mind a plan for the total subjugation of Russia (economically at first and politically thereafter); and he made no secret of it. Exactly eight days later, Helferrich gave way to a panic terror, the causes of which can never be precisely determined. But the principal cause appeared to be fear of death. He fled his post in great haste and returned directly to Berlin. As no one replaced him, this flight produced the most deplorable effect on public opinion, all the more so because one could see quite clearly that the government was powerless, either to send Helfferich back to Moscow, or to replace him, or even to take a part in the business.

For informed minds, one other occasion underscored just as clearly the disarray of the government. While Ludendorff's offensive lasted, Austria was satisfied to whine about the misfortunes of the times. But when she beheld the offensive checked and then replaced by an attack by Foch, Austria stampeded. In her terror she found something like energy. The Emperor Charles and his ministers were seen disembarking to the German Headquarters. There they were heard speaking firmly, demanding to be consoled with Polish compensations for the new sacrifices that the Monarchy of the Danube would be obliged to make. The Habsburg Emperor openly demanded the crown of Poland for himself.

The Poles, represented by Prince Janus Radziwill, exploited the opportunity to demand an immediate solution in what concerned them.[c] There again, the governors of Germany were incapable of deciding anything. They sent both away empty-handed, the Austrians furious and frightened, the Poles exasperated.

On August 20th, however, it seemed that the Hertling government had decided on a definite political line. Dr. Solf, the minister for the colonies, delivered a clever and moderate speech to the "German Association." Without completely committing himself, Solf let it be clearly understood that Germany renounced all conquests in the West; that it would fully evacuate Belgium and Northern France on condition that its colonies be returned and some others be added to them. Already the Liberals were congratulating each other; already Austria was smiling; already ears were listening for some encouraging words from Wilson.

Eight days later, a complete about-face. The text of a "supplementary" treaty signed with the Moscow Bolsheviks was published; it was a monument of imperialism.

Estonia and Livonia were to be detached from Russia. The frontiers of the Ukraine, which were under German control, were to be extended toward the East. Some territories of the Don and of Georgia were reserved for occupation and a protectorate. Batoum was left to the Turks. At the same time, the political oppression of Finland was redoubled. The Finnish Parliament, two-thirds purged, voted for the monarchic principle, and the Grand Duke of Hesse, the Kaiser's brother-in-law, let it be known everywhere that he was ready to accept the crown. The Duke of Urach journeyed through Lithuania like the sovereign-to-be; and the German landowners in Courland were allowed to publish their supplica-

[c]After proclaiming the Kingdom of Poland in November 1916 and forming an "activist" government in Warsaw, the Central Powers had never been able to reach agreement on what to do with the new state, what sovereign to give it, or what frontiers to trace for it.

tions to the Kaiser, imploring the favor of being made part of the Kingdom of Prussia.[20]

At the same time, the Berlin government allowed the military to unveil in its full amplitude a gigantic plan for the resurrection of Islam by Turkey, to benefit Germany. The former Khedive of Egypt, Abbas-Hilmi, who had been deposed by the English, was received in great pomp at General Headquarters by the Kaiser, who promised to restore him. The leaders of Turkestan were allowed to solicit the protection of the [German] Empire for a Muslim Republic of Turkestan. The Muslim rajahs of India addressed letters of homage to Wilhelm II. The head of the Tripolitan Sudanese arrived in Constantinople, where he was received as a sovereign. In exchange, Prince Fuad-Bey was sent by the Sultan to organize the Sudanese war on the Upper Nile, in Tripolitania, and in Cyrenaica.

In short, everything was done to heighten the exasperation and will to conquer of the enemies in general, and of England in particular, [and] to definitively discourage German opinion, stunned by continuous defeats in the West and stupefied by the new and undefined tasks that were being set out for it.

Every day Bulgaria sharpened its tone. It wanted the whole of the Dobroudja. It wanted to see the Turks definitively renounce claims to the Maritsa line and to Andrinople.[21] Response was made in some bitter journal articles, claiming that Germany had given Bulgaria everything she had acquired during the war. "Where would she be, at present," she was asked, "if she had followed the policy of Romania or Serbia? Without doubt at the same point as these powers."

Thrown into confusion by these reverses, the Berlin government showed itself incapable of establishing and following the moderate, clear, definite policy that might perhaps have allowed it to group popular masses around itself, to reassure the Allies, and to dampen the élan of its enemies. To the contrary, it emerged from its sterile hesitations only to provoke the whole world.

The political parties remained confounded in the same stupor. Whereas in the past, while things were going well, the great political associations multiplied their gatherings and conferences, exposing the questions of the day to the popular masses, encouraging them to hold on, thus glorifying German strength, throughout the course of this critical period they remained completely inactive. In the Reichstag, all parliamentary life stopped cold: no more "Principal Committee," no more conferences of the party leaders. Each kept a malicious eye on the other. Then, angry passions and divisions appeared in full view. The Right heaped blame upon the Socialists and Progressives, who had weakened the courage of the people by their defeatism and diminished confidence in the High Command. The Left threw all fault back upon the Conservatives, who had pushed Germany into imperialism, who had been the cause of unlimited submarine war, of American intervention, of the 1918 offensive—instead of the brilliant peace that could have been signed during the winter, by being moderate.

"Furthermore," cried the Progressives, "where is the universal suffrage promised to Prussia for more than a year?" The Catholic Center, itself profoundly divided between Groeber and Erzberger, exposed a thousand scandals in the war industries. In the midst of the general tumult, The Socialists saw the approach of the time when they could enter the government, and they did everything possible to augment the disarray, protesting against the wretched food supplies available to the people. . . . The Independent Socialist extremists worked now with joyous hearts, proclaiming openly the coming revolution.

In the month of September, everyone was in agreement, but only in demanding the resignation of Hertling. The old chancellor, just recently heaped with unanimous praise, suddenly found himself surrounded by enemies. "We need a Bismarck," cried the people on the Right. "This Bavarian dotard can do nothing for us."

"Hertling is definitively compromised," the Left clamored. "He was neither able to resist the pan-Germanists, nor to impose his policy on General Headquarters, nor to bring universal suffrage to a vote."

Thus, in the hour of peril, the political parties redoubled their tumults and exacerbated their passions.

The press no longer displayed skill or firmness; it must be said that they felt cruelly embarrassed. Having demonstrated for such a long time, and so pompously, that Ludendorff was the greatest warrior of modern times, that Foch had no more reserves, that victory was near and certain, it was difficult suddenly to assert the contrary. The press had until recently taken all its doctrine from the Wolf Agency and its communiqués. Now it sought to excuse itself by tarring that agency with contemptuous remarks. The left-wing press moved suddenly from the most absolute confidence to the most explicit defeatism, under the pretext that the people ought to know the truth, in order to elevate its resolutions to the height of the peril. "Yes, we have been deceived," they said. "Yes, our High Command has lost the initiative, and it looks like that will be permanent. Yes, the French are an heroic people, the English are determined to conquer, the Americans more numerous than the sands of the sea." Foch is a proven master of battles. He has formidable reserves, "an immense number of divisions" wrote the *Frankfurt Gazette*. "He has artillery quite superior to our own. He has tanks; we have none of them. Our armies ceaselessly withdraw. It is true that the enemy cannot break through our lines in this way, but there is no reason to bring our elastic retreat to a halt."

The right-wing press was no more inspired, in its adjurations to courage. As Theodore Wolf said in the *Berlin Daily,* they were literally howling for death. "Universal conscription must be proclaimed," it said. "Set up dictatorship, have all the defeatists arrested, and especially the socialist leaders; we must die magnificently."

Count Reventlow, in the *German Daily News,* believed he had hit upon a masterstroke: every day, he published a pompous eulogy of Clemenceau: "There is a head of government who knows what he wants, and who shows it!—That is what Germany needs!—That is what she does not have!"

Thus the German press—which had previously been remarkable for its political sense and timing, which had always managed to strike the tone that was needed at the time when it was needed, to sustain public opinion by means of every truth and every lie—suddenly lost all its usefulness, just at the moment when it became indispensable. And instead of preaching unity, setting an example, reanimating confidence and propagating sangfroid, it spread confusion everywhere, augmenting exasperation, anguish, and discouragement.

Public opinion, which no longer felt itself guided as it was accustomed to and needed to be, forthwith displayed the most complete moral confusion. From the day after July 18th, dizzying rumors began to fly and to find credence everywhere. "Hindenburg has committed suicide, Ludendorff has just been arrested as a traitor by General von Böhm. The French have taken 140,000 prisoners at the Marne," etc.

The old leaven of discord between the different Germanic peoples, notably between North and South, inspired mutual malevolence. In Prussia it was said that Crown Prince Rupprecht of Bavaria had been deprived of his command because he had proposed to the Entente a separate peace for the southern [German] states. In Bavaria it was said that Ludendorff had just had an entire Bavarian division shot because they had torn the Kaiser's crest from their peaked hats. A printed tract was distributed everywhere, in which a certain major, who had no qualms about signing his name, asserted that the Bavarians had given up at the attack of Debeney on August 8th, on the Ancre, and that they had surrendered en masse to Mangin's troops, on the Ailette.

This got to the point that Hindenburg himself was roused. The old marshal published several harsh and morose warnings in which he heaped reproaches on those who spread such rumors or lent them an ear. It had no effect.

In the great cities, the food situation suddenly worsened because the public authorities, who until then had fought energetically against speculation and smuggling, were now overwhelmed and discouraged and suddenly displayed the greatest laxity. At night, armed bands of thieves, for the most part deserters, began to roam the streets, even in Berlin, ransacking here, assaulting there, rifling shop cash registers, smashing windows, stealing luggage in the train stations. The sleep of the city dwellers was continually broken by gunshots exchanged between these gangs and the police.

In Berlin, during September, eighty policemen were killed or wounded, and troops had to come to the assistance of the guardians of the peace, with posts and patrols.

There was a terrible outbreak of Spanish influenza at this time, which struck down numerous victims, notably among women and young people. In Berlin, 2,000 people a week died of influenza.

As always in times of trouble and anxiety, the mad pursuit of pleasure broke loose. Everywhere the cinemas, the concert halls, the theaters had to turn people away. New ones were opening all over. Every café had its orchestra that began playing in the morning. Germany flaunted vice in broad daylight. Venereal diseases, whose spread had been contained by Draconian measures, suddenly multiplied infinitely, when these measures were no long applied. A physician from Munich wrote that "in the month of August, the number of syphilitics in Bavaria has doubled." Incredible as it seemed, in this month of September, at the height of the national anguish, the promoters of public balls chose to demand with a great clamor that the ban on dancing, imposed by the police since the start of the war, should be lifted.

In the midst of the general stupor it would have been a great thing for Germany if the High Command of the armies had shown poise and demonstrated its confidence. In fact, however, it did nothing of the sort. On

July 30th, General Ludendorff thought himself obliged to declare publicly "that his whole strategic plan for the year had failed, that he had been mistaken in his estimate of the enemy." And Hindenburg tried to restore the morale of the country by announcing that he was bringing the troops back to the rear in order to spare the blood of the soldiers, because, he said, "too much of this blood has flowed." Everyone immediately drew the conclusion that the High Command had found its master in the enemy;[22] that the retreat was going to continue without respite, since it was a matter of limiting losses; and that these losses were frightful.

A measure taken by the General Headquarters in this same period contributed to terrifying the people. Toward the end of August, the High Command saw the retreat intensifying all along the front, and sensed that they were no longer able to contain it. They ordered the immediate evacuation, to the interior of the Empire, of all the wounded who until then had been cared for in medical units in Northern France, Belgium, and Alsace-Lorraine. And for two weeks, the public could see the jam-packed train stations, the railway lines encumbered with innumerable hospital trains, and horse-drawn wagons crammed with the wounded. One could only conclude from this that the losses surpassed imagining; and this deepened the national stupor even further.

Thus, overwhelmed beyond remedy since the surprise of July 18th and incapable of regaining their self-control, the Kaiser, the ministers, the political parties, the newspapers, the people, and the German military leaders, all abandoned themselves to fate. They were vanquished, before the battle, in their hearts. From the end of August, everyone in this discouraged country felt that the first grave military or political event would lead decisively to an insurmountable national panic. The incident took place in the last days of September: it was the capitulation of Bulgaria. At once the crisis unleashed itself.

▓▓▓ IV

To tell the truth, the news from the Macedonian front had been bad for more than a week.

The Allied army of General Franchet d'Esperey had launched its offensive. It was known that the Serbs (whose entire destruction had been decreed long since) had taken part in it with vigor; that the Greeks (who had been represented in Germany as oppressed by the Entente, waiting only for an opportunity to throw themselves upon the French and the

English) had, in actuality, thrown themselves upon the Bulgarians; that the latter had lost ground. But no one expected the thunderclap that suddenly exploded. Malinov asked for an armistice from the Allied commander in chief for the East, and straightway signed the capitulation demanded by the conqueror.

The authorities tried at first to veil the catastrophe, or at least to attenuate its effects. The Wolf Agency released optimistic communiqués about it: "Czar Ferdinand disapproved of Malinov; the Sobranie[23] has disavowed his policy; the Bulgarian High Command refused to lay down their arms. Furthermore, massive reinforcements, German, Hungarian, and Turkish, were en route to Macedonia; Mackensen in person was taking command of the operations. . . ."

But soon it was necessary to yield to the evidence. Bulgaria rendered up its arms and opened its territory to the enemy. Turkey was isolated and was moreover herself beaten in Palestine at this moment; she could not continue the war for long. The southern frontier of Austria was about to be opened, and the troops of Franchet d'Esperey were going to drag in Romania, against the Central Powers, once again.[24]

The government of Hertling was overthrown at once, amidst a hue and cry of curses from all the [political] parties. Prince Max von Baden was named chancellor. He formed an extraordinary ministry. In it, seated around this hereditary prince of a royal house, one could behold the old Catholic ultramontane Groeber; the ambitious Silesian leader of the Center, Erzberger; a radical skeptic, von Payer; the most conservative of the Prussian officers, General von Scheuch; and above all, Scheidemann. In the name of Social Democracy, he had forced his entry into the government of the Empire. In order to bring his party definitively into power, Scheidemann had resolved to promote defeatism and panic.

The parties vied with each other in railing. Count Westarp, in the name of the Right, and Herr von Richthofen, for the National Liberals, demanded mass mobilization. The Catholic Center and the Progressives solemnly demanded universal suffrage in Prussia and ministerial responsibility to parliament. The Majority Socialists summoned the government to decree the subordination of the military to civil authority and to strip Ludendorff of his functions. The Independents held forth with the utmost violence, insolently demanding that Liebknecht be set free, which moreover was immediately accorded to them.[25]

Hindenburg and Ludendorff, who had always, up to that point, exhibited a solid character and absolute resoluteness, abruptly lost their heads. On September 30th, they hurried to Berlin, and announced brutally to Max von Baden that they were no longer answerable for anything; there had to be an immediate armistice or they would suffer a dreadful military catastrophe. The chancellor had decided to open peace negotiations; he preferred to do it without at the same time begging for an armistice, which would be a public avowal of despair.

But Ludendorff, beside himself, demanded the request for an armistice. This suddenly revealed to the Allies the extent of German panic, [thereby] multiplying tenfold their will to fight to the finish and confirming their resolution not to set down their weapons prior to a complete capitulation of the enemy.[26] After long discussions, the famous note addressed to Wilson was dispatched. Germany started irrevocably down the path toward disaster and humiliation.[27]

Each day the panic now intensified. On the Western Front, the Allied advance rushed forward headlong. The communiqués of the Entente, which all the newspapers published prominently, proclaimed to Germany that every day she was abandoning thousands of prisoners and hundreds of cannons to the enemy. Turkey gave up the fight and opened separate negotiations. Austria began to dissolve. The optimists had invented for themselves the hope of seeing Wilson separate himself from France and England, in order to impose the armistice before capitulation. This hope now evaporated in its turn. Germany understood that she was not going to escape her destiny. And consequently, each began, at first in the secrecy of his heart, then in a whisper, then loud and clear, to demand the end, no matter how, at whatever price it could be had, but immediately. "Enough suffering!" they said.

The Kaiser, despite the urging of his ministers, refused to come to Berlin. He remained prostrate at General Headquarters, no longer involved himself in anything, made no decisions. He was incapable of trying anything to revive the morale of his panic-stricken people. Every day, the journals of the Right might recall the heroic epoch of Frederick the Great, when, seeing the State in danger, the territory invaded, when all seemed lost for the fatherland, the greatest King of Prussia saved his country by dint of his energy, cunning and activity. But Wilhelm II kept silent. The *German Daily News* and the *Gazette of the Cross* urged him to proclaim his dictatorship, to take their power away from the lawyers and chatterers who were destroying Germany. He still kept silent. He did not emerge from his silence until the end of October, in order to write the chancellor a letter full of humility. It was an acknowledgment of the imminent disaster; it announced he would submit himself to the new laws, adopted or being prepared, that would take away his powers and leave him only the shadow of his authority.

The government, more agitated than active, piled up projects for constitutional laws, administrative and social legislation. It released all the political convicts from prison as well as those who, without being convicted, had been detained as suspects.

Scheidemann posed the question of the Kaiser categorically, presenting a memorandum to Prince Max von Baden in which he threatened to quit the cabinet if Wilhelm II remained on the throne.

The parties, already resigned to the disgrace, or seeing it as inevitable, sought only to come out of the brawl advantageously. The Conservatives, perceiving that all was lost, and foreseeing that the battle would end any day in a rout, wished at least to give themselves the prestige of pure patriotism and an indomitable spirit of sacrifice. "Everyone to the front!" Count Westarp kept saying. But it was clear to everyone that this was pure posturing and that, far from being able to conduct everyone to the front, the Command was beginning to question whether it could much longer maintain at the front those who were already there. The Center and the Progressives clamored "I told you so"—that people ought to have listened to them when they demanded a frank policy renouncing all annexations and all indemnities. As for the Socialists, they could no longer contain their joy, seeing that their hour had come, by virtue of the disaster; and they now loudly demanded the most rapid capitulation possible and the abdication of the Kaiser.

The press did everything to precipitate the rout. The pan-Germanist newspapers, burdened with a heavy conscience, sought to revive in the public the courage of despair; and to do so, playing the role of Cassandra, they clamored that the territory was going to be invaded, the cities of the Rhine torched, the countryside devastated forever. The illustrated journals published terrifying drawings, representing what the German lands would look like after the enemy had passed by, making readers imagine the inhabitants of the country famished, falling with exhaustion, driven, by French Spahis with whips in their hands, to rebuild the ravaged North of France.[28] The pan-Germanist associations, with the cooperation of the military authorities, mass-produced and put up posters in the railroad stations, the barracks, and the large cafés. They portrayed the formidable canons of the Entente firing over the Rhine, at German cities in flames, with the legend, "This is what will happen to us, if the enemy succeeds in invading us." These frightening pictures produced no effect, however, other than to increase the panic. They confirmed people in their resolve, now firmly fixed, to have peace at any price, before an invasion.

As for the left-wing journals, their voices swelled, openly accusing the Kaiser, the crown prince, the High Command, and the Conservatives, of having brought on the disaster. The Kaiser above all was disgraced. The *Frankfurt Gazette* brutally invited him to draw the consequences of the note from Wilson, which declared his firm wish not to deal with the Hohenzollerns. The Socialist papers encouraged despair and fury. On October 20th, the *Vorwärts* declared, remarkably, that "prolonged resistance can only make the peace heavier and more difficult." It insulted the Kaiser daily. On November 2nd, it wrote, in regard to him: "As for this man—who, under the pretext of being the leader, has managed to return from the most terrible of wars, carried on for his glory—may he disappear uninjured with his six sons!"

The High Command, recovering a bit from its panic on September 30th, appeared to have gotten control of itself somewhat, and it now conveyed a more optimistic impression. But on October 25th, General Ludendorff—under the howls of the left, abandoned by the Kaiser, fundamentally discouraged, furious, humiliated to see the military authority subordinated to the civil power (which meant, in the last resort, to Scheidemann)—quit his position. It was serious enough in itself that the military command should be disorganized, at the most critical time, by a resignation. But in this particular case, it was irreparable, because Ludendorff had concentrated in himself all power and all initiative. With him gone, the General Headquarters lost all direction. Moreover, the imperious and ambitious quartermaster had taken care to arrest the ascent, in succession, of all those who might have counterbalanced his prestige. He had kept in the shadows men like Falkenhayn, von Hutter, von Böhm, von Gallwitz, von Bülow, and Groener. None of them could impress themselves sufficiently on the army and the country to give them confidence.

Furthermore, public opinion, at present, had given up the siege.

Nothing and no one could rally the public, nor persuade it to make supreme sacrifices. Popular demonstrations, demanding the ending of the war, broke out here, there, and everywhere, spontaneously at first, then organized by the leaders of the Independents. Liebknecht, released from prison, was carried in triumph through Berlin by a delirious crowd of soldiers and men and women of the people. He delivered a frenzied speech at the Siegesallee, which he capped with the cry, "Long live the Revolution!"[29]

In many places, reinforcements destined for the front were prevented from departing, by popular action. The innumerable deserters now in the great cities showed themselves in public with impunity, jeering at the impotent police forces. Armed robberies and assaults redoubled. Remarkably, the food situation in the cities eased because the speculators and hoarders believed that peace was at hand and that Germany would soon be provisioned; so they hastened to liquidate their stocks of merchandise. But the authorities were incapable of taking advantage of the situation to restock their reserves. Herr von Batocki, implored by the government to resume his position as director of rationing, categorically refused, declaring "that he could not organize chaos."[d]

The life of pleasure became yet more ardent. During the war a great many people had amassed notes of the Reichsbank—industrialists, large and small merchants, working men and women. Now they all hurried to spend them; for the rumor circulated that the State was going to declare bankruptcy, and that these notes would be worth nothing in peacetime.

The whole of Germany—military, political, social, and administrative—snapped at a single blow, like an overextended spring. Now everywhere people spoke openly of capitulation. Austria had just set an example, on November 1st, and, by opening its territory to the enemy, completed the moral panic of Southern Germany, which suddenly found itself directly threatened. The president of the Bavarian Council, Herr von Dandl, departed for Berlin, bearing an ultimatum threatening a separate peace. And tracts were circulated throughout Bavaria, calling upon the king to break with Prussia, to make peace in his own interest or risk facing revolution within three days.

During the first days of November 1918, Germany entered into revolution, like a routed army, driven mad by terror and suffering, that begins to slaughter its leaders and to surrender itself to every exaction.

Already for several days, tumultuous demonstrations had taken place in Berlin, Hamburg, Munich, Stuttgart, and Breslau, in which the soldiers took part. Then, on November 5th, the uprising of the fleet at Kiel broke out, unleashed by the rumor of a planned sortie and an imminent naval battle.[30] The uprising spread to the ports of Hamburg, Bre-

[d]He had exercised that function in 1915 and 1916.

men, and Lubeck. Committees of workers and soldiers, prepared long in advance by the leaders, suddenly took over direction of the movement. During the night from the 7th to the 8th, the Bavarian Republic was proclaimed.[e] The riot spread to the cities of the Rhine. Everywhere it assumed the character of an insurrection of soldiers against their officers.

In Berlin, after three days of confusion, the revolution gained the victory.

In the midst of this hurricane, the government of Max von Baden (abandoned just in time by Scheidemann, who ran to follow the insurgents, since he was their leader) was blown about like a blade of straw. Ebert succeeded him, while the Kaiser fled to Holland. And the Reichstag, the only constituted body that had the right to speak then in the name of the country, dared not even convene itself.

The news from the front was disastrous. Bands of disarmed soldiers, furious, flowed back toward the interior. They were storming trains, using threats to force the engineers to drive them; striking, wounding, and killing the officers. They were selling everything at trifling prices: their weapons, their equipment, their boots, horses, machine guns, bicycles, wagons. Everywhere, soldier's committees were being set up, above all in the places where the troops halted.

The prisons, opened by the riots, had expelled onto the public highways all the common outlaws—murderers, thieves, etc. Great numbers of prisoners of war, having escaped a collapsing security, roamed through the countryside, looking for adventure. They even traveled to the cities, adding to the general confusion. The passenger or freight trains, chock-full of all sorts of people, notably of soldiers who had demobilized themselves, no longer ran on time, and the number of accidents involving loss of life, already conspicuous during the first week of November, rose to sixty-six. Pillage, violence, disorder everywhere. It was finished.

Before his dismissal, Prince Max von Baden urgently sent German plenipotentiaries to Marshal Foch; but they represented only a people

[e] In the proclamations of Kurt Eisner, plastered on the walls of Munich on the morning of the 8th, the new Bavarian government announced that "it was immediately sending delegates to Bern with full powers to sign a separate peace with the Entente." [Kurt Eisner, theater critic for the *Münchener Post,* was a follower of Lenin; he had declared the establishment of a Revolutionary Soviet Republic in Munich, on 7 November 1918, with himself as its head of government.]

in flight. They signed everything that was demanded. Fehrenbach, the former president of the Reichstag, and then of the National Assembly, recounted the way in which the Ebert government sanctioned the conditions of the armistice accepted by General von Winterfeldt and Erzberger:

> We were assembled at the Palace of the Chancery with Ebert and some others. The text of the armistice was brought to us. We looked at ourselves, overwhelmed. "This is incredibly harsh!" said someone. "Yes, it is harsh," Ebert responded. "But is there anyone here whose opinion would be to refuse?" There was a long, terrible silence. For the rest of my life, I shall remember this silence . . .

Documentation

Editor's Note: What follows is a translation in its entirety of the list of sources provided by de Gaulle. For a more detailed, chronological list of the sources shown below and a list of relevant works available in English, see the Appendix.

WORKS	AUTHORS
Memoirs	Kaiser Wilhelm II
Memoirs	German Crown Prince
My Life	Field Marshal von Hindenburg
My Memories of War	General Ludendorff
Documents of the German GHQ	Ibid.
Considerations on the World War	Chancellor Bethmann-Hollweg
Memoirs	Chancellor Michaelis
The War As I Experienced It	Erzberger
Recollections	Grand Admiral von Tirpitz
Wartime Letters	Ibid.
Letters and Documents	Left by Colonel General von Moltke
The Supreme Command, 1914–1916	Colonel General Falkenhayn
Four Years at the Austro-Hungarian GHQ	General von Cramon
The War of Lost Occasions	General Hoffmann
The March on Paris	Colonel General von Kluck
My Report on the Battle of the Marne	General von Bülow

Works that treat the operations of August–September 1914 in France and Belgium and on their preparation:	Generals von Kuhl, von Tappen, von Hausen, etc.
Memoirs	Gerard
The Road to Catastrophe	Doctor Nowak
Private Memoir	Princess Blücher
Ludendorff Painted by Himself	Hans Delbrück

The German press during the war
Proceedings of the plenary sessions of the Reichstag
Proceedings of the sessions of the "Principal Committee of the Reichstag"
Etc., etc.

Appendix Augmented Version of Documentation

Organized by year of publication, the first section of this list includes sources from de Gaulle's documentation list and others available to him at the time he wrote *La Discorde chez l'ennemi*. The second section lists relevant works available in English.

WORKS USED BY DE GAULLE

1917

Gerard, James W., Late Ambassador to the German Imperial Court. *My Four Years in Germany.* New York: George H. Doran Co., 1917.

1918

Gerard, James W. *Face to Face with Kaiserism.* New York: George H. Doran Co., 1918.

1919

Bülow, Generalfeldmarschall Karl von. *Mein Bericht zur Marneschlacht.* Berlin: Verlag August Scherl, 1919.

Hindenburg, Generalfeldmarschall Paul von. *Aus meinem Leben.* Leipzig: S. Hirzel Verlag, 1919 or 1920.

Ludendorff, Erich. *Meine Kriegs-Erinnerungen, 1914–1918.* Berlin: E. S. Mittler und Sohn, 1919.

Nowak, Karl Friedrich. *Der Weg zur Katastrophe,* 20 Auflage. Berlin: Erich Reiá Verlag, 1919. [In place of a preface, this volume begins with a letter to Dr. Nowak from Feldmarschal Conrad datelined Vienna, 18 March 1919. This was evidently de Gaulle's primary source of information on Conrad's activities and viewpoint.]

Tirpitz, Alfred von. *Erinnerungen.* Leipzig: Verlag K. F. Köhler, 1919.

1920

Cramon, A. von. *Unser Österreich-Ungarischer Bundesgenosse im Weltkriege.* Berlin: Ernst S. Mittler und Sohn, 1920.

Erzberger, Reichsfinanzminister Matthias. *Erlebnisse im Weltkrieg.* Stuttgart: Deutsche Verlags-Anstalt, 1920.

Falkenhayn, Erich von. *Die Oberste Heeresleitung 1914–1916 in ihren wichtigsten Entschliessungen.* Berlin: Ernst S. Mittler und Sohn, 1920.

Hausen, Generalobersten Freiherrn von. *Erinnerungen an den Marnefeldzug 1914,* mit einer einleitenden kritischen Studie herausgegeben von Friedrich M. Kircheisen. Leipzig: K. F. Köhler, 1920.

Kluck, Generaloberst Alexander von. *Der Marsch auf Paris und die Marneschlacht 1914.* Berlin, Verlag E. S. Mittler & Sohn, 1920.

Ludendorff, Erich, ed. *Urkunden der obersten Heeresleitung Über ihre Tätigkeit 1916–1918.* Berlin: E. S. Mittler und Sohn, 1920.

Tappen, Generalleutnant z.D. von, Kriegsbeginn bis Herbst 1916 Chef der Operations-Abteilung beim Chef des Generalstabes des Feldheeres, Bis zur Marne 1914. *Beiträge zur Beurteilung der Kriegführung bis zum Abschluss der Marne-Schlacht,* 2.Auflage. Berlin: Verlag Gerhard Stalling, 1920.

1921

Bethmann Hollweg, Th. von. *Betrachtungen zum Weltkriege 2.Teil, Während des Krieges.* Berlin: Verlag von Reimar Hobbing, 1921.

Kuhl, H. von, General der Infanterie a.D. 1914 Chef des Generalstabes der 1.Armee. *Der Marnefeldzug 1914.* Berlin: Verlag Ernst Siegfried Mittler & Sohn, 1921.

Michaelis, Georg. *Für Staat und Volk: Eine Lebensgeschichte.* Berlin: Furche Verlag, 1922.

Wahlstatt, Evelyn Mary (Stapleton-Bretherton) von. *Une Anglaise à Berlin: Notes intimes de la Princesse Blücher, sur les événements, la politique et la vie quotidienne en Allemagne, au course de la guerre et de la révolution sociale de 1918.* Traduit par Mlle. Cavaignac. Paris: Payot, 1921. [In the original English edition, listed under "Works Available in English," the author is identified as Evelyn, Princess Blücher.]

1922

Delbrück, Hans. *Ludendorffs Selbstporträt.* Berlin: Verlag für Politik und Wirtschaft, 1922.

Kaiser Wilhelm II. *Ereignisse und Gestalten aus den Jahren 1878–1918.* Leipzig: Verlag K. F. Köhler, 1922.

Kronprinz Wilhelm. *Meine Erinnerungen aus Deutschlands Heldenkampf.* Berlin, S. Mittler & Sohn, 1922.

Moltke, Generaloberst Helmuth von. *Erinnerungen Briefe Dockumente 1877–1916: Ein Bild vom Kriegsausbruch, erster Kriegführung und Persönlichkeit des ersten militärischen Führers des Krieges.* Stuttgart: Der Kommende Tag A.-G. Verlag, 1922.

1923

Hoffman, Max. *Der Krieg der versäumten Gelegenheiten.* Originally published
1923 (228 pp.). In *Die Aufzeichnungen des Generalmajors Max Hoffmann,*
2 vols., edited by Karl Friedrich Nowak, 5–232. Berlin: Verlag für
Kulturpolitik, 1929.

WORKS AVAILABLE IN ENGLISH

Evelyn, Princess Blücher. *An English Wife in Berlin: A Private Memoir of Events,
Politics, and Daily Life in Germany throughout the War and the Social
Revolution of 1918.* New York: E. P. Dutton, 1920. [In the French translation
of this work, which de Gaulle cites, the author is identified as Evelyn Mary
(Stapleton-Bretherton) von Wahlstatt.]

Ex-Kaiser William II. *My Memoirs: 1878–1918.* London: Cassell & Co., 1922.

Hindenburg, Marshal Paul von. *Out of My Life,* 2 vols. Translated by F. A. Holt.
New York: Harper & Brothers, 1921.

Hoffmann, General Max von. *The War of Lost Opportunities.* Translated by A. E.
Chamot. London: Kegan Paul, 1924.

Kuhl, Hermann Joseph von, Chief of Staff of the First Army, 1914. *The Marne
Campaign 1914.* Fort Leavenworth, Kans.: Command and General Staff
School Press, 1936.

Ludendorff, General Erich von. *The General Staff and Its Problems: The History
of the Relations between the High Command and the German Imperial
Government as Revealed by Official Documents.* 2 vols. Translated by F. A.
Holt. New York: E. P. Dutton, 1920.

———. *Ludendorff's Own Story, August 1914–November 1918: The Great War
from the Siege of Liege to the Signing of the Armistice as Viewed from the
Grand Headquarters of the German Army.* 2 vols. New York: Harper and
Brothers, 1920.

Lutz, Ralph Haswell, ed. *The Causes of the German Collapse in 1918: Sections of
the Officially Authorized Report of the Commission of the German Constituent
Assembly and of the German Reichstag, 1919–1928, the Selection and the
Translation Officially Approved by the Commission.* Translated by W. L.
Campbell. London: Oxford University Press; Stanford, Calif.: Stanford
University Press, 1934.

———. *Fall of the German Empire, 1914–1918.* 2 vols. Translated by David G.
Rempel and Gertrude Rendtorff. London: Oxford University Press; Stanford,
Calif.: Stanford University Press, 1932.

Tirpitz, Grand Admiral Alfred von. *My Memoirs.* 2 vols. 1919; reprint, New York:
AMS, 1970.

Translator's Notes

INTRODUCTION

Unless otherwise indicated, translations from French and German sources are by the editor.

1. Perhaps the best way to introduce *la querelle de l'homme* (the argument or strife over humanity) as a theme of de Gaulle's thought is to show how it unfolds in his first book, as we do below. Provisionally, the reader may find useful the following summary by Daniel J. Mahoney:

   > Great nations must concern themselves not only with protecting their interests and maintaining their independence, and not only with sustaining their national honor and self-respect, but also with serving the cause of civilization and humankind. De Gaulle called this most elevated and rare dimension of statesmanship the *"querrelle de l'homme."* He truly believed, and in a most realistic way, that nations like Britain and France could provide important and at times indispensable service to the cause of humanity. . . . de Gaulle believed that the most sublime task for modern statesmanship was the protection of a "certain conception of man" threatened by the general evolution of modern society.

   Daniel J. Mahoney, *De Gaulle: Statesmanship, Grandeur, and Modern Democracy,* foreword by Pierre Manent (Westport, Conn.: Praeger, 1996), 100.

2. Jean Lacouture, *De Gaulle,* Vol. 1: *The Rebel, 1890–1944,* trans. Patrick O'Brian (New York: Norton, 1993), 50.

3. De Gaulle later commented, "I believe that I would have died if I had not been able to recall the lines of my favorite poets." Georges Cattaui, *Charles de Gaulle, l'homme et son destin* (Paris: Fayard, 1960), 33.

4. Charles de Gaulle, *Lettres, Notes, et Carnets,* Vol. 1: *1905–1918* (Paris: Plon, 1980), cited hereafter as *Carnets 1.* On Pascal, see 338, 370; Balzac, 329, 373; Bourget, 376; Chamfort, 332, 369; Fontenelle, 357; d'Aguesseau, 373; Flaubert, 388. For de Gaulle's own aphorisms, see 332, 343, 344, 371, 372, 378, 380, 395.

5. Letter to his mother, 21 March 1917, in de Gaulle, *Carnets 1,* 400.

6. *Carnets 1,* 401. In his novella *The Shadow-line,* Joseph Conrad offers an almost identically worded account of a comparable experience, from the captain's finding himself in "conditions of moral isolation" (249) to his bitter conclusion, "I am no good" (251). Conrad, *The Shadow-line, Typhoon, The Secret Sharer,* ed. Morton D. Zabel (New York: Doubleday, 1959). In his au-

thor's note, Conrad underscores the moral analogy between this story and what men at the front experienced during the Great War.

7. Letter to his mother, 1 November 1918, *Carnets 1,* 525.

8. Jean Lacouture, *De Gaulle,* Vol. 1: *Le Rebelle, 1890–1944* (Paris: Editions du Seuil, 1984), 70. De Gaulle fell on 2 March 1916.

9. Jean Pouget, *Un certaine capitaine de Gaulle* (Paris: Fayard, 1973), 102–3.

10. Ibid., 103.

11. Ibid.

12. Lacouture, *Le Rebelle,* 83.

13. See Charles de Gaulle, *Mémoires de guerre,* 3 vols. (Paris: Librairie Plon, 1959) for numerous passages that speak to this point:

> But as for me, with such a hill to climb, I had nothing. (1:70)

> But there is no France without a sword. The most important thing, first of all, was to constitute a combat force. (1:74)

> . . . faced with America's enormous resources and the ambition of Roosevelt to make law and dictate rights throughout the world, I felt that independence was well and truly at stake. In sum, while I wished to try to reach an understanding with Washington, we had to do so on a practical basis but standing on our own feet. (1:82)

> We spoke of Roosevelt and of his attitude toward me.
> "Don't rush things," said Churchill. "Look at the way I yield and rise up again, turn and turn about."
> "You can," I remarked, "because you are seated on a solid state, an assembled nation, a united Empire, large armies. But I! Where are my resources? And yet I, as you know, am responsible for the interests and destiny of France. It is too heavy a burden, and I am too poor to be able to bow." (2:52)

> During the five days I passed in the federal capital, I witnessed with admiration the flowing torrent of confidence that was carrying away the American elite, and I observed that optimism goes well with those who have the means for it. (2:237)

14. See this edition, Chapter 1, section I.

15. Pouget, *Un certaine capitaine,* 103.

16. Charles de Gaulle, *Le Fil de l'épée,* presentation par Alain Peyrefitte (Paris: Plon, 1996), 55.

17. Ibid., 122. As this passage attests, de Gaulle was much concerned after the war with the fetish of strategic "doctrine" in the French officer corps. But I do not believe that he ascribed the slaughterhouse offensives to which officers reverted during the war to the systematic inculcation of a doctrine of the offensive. Nor should one take his analysis of German failings, in *The*

Enemy's House Divided as a covert, indirect critique of the French military. He would probably agree with Porch's assessment: "In the final analysis, the tactical offensive was not the product of a system, but of the lack of one. It was the very disorganization of the army which was responsible for its popularity. The high command, composed largely of timid old men, looked on helplessly as young, dynamic officers eager for a doctrine, any doctrine, took the offensive." Douglas Porch, "The Spirit of the Offensive," chap. 11 in *The March to the Marne: The French Army, 1871–1914* (Cambridge: Cambridge University Press, 1981), 213–31; quote on 231.

18. *Le Fil de l'épée,* 56.

19. See this edition, Chapter 1, last sentence of opening section.

20. For notes on "Faire la philosophie de l'action," see *Carnets 1:* 333–35, 367–68, 380, 387; on lectures by General Foch, 382, 386–87; on the work by le Bon on crowds, 391; on other subjects treated in *Le Fil de l'épée,* 394.

21. See this 1924 entry in Charles de Gaulle, *Lettres, Notes, et Carnets,* Vol. 2: *1919–June 1940* (Paris: Plon, 1975), 215: "Partout où la canaille vient boire, les sources sont empoisonnées (Nietzsche)." Compare this entry from 1919: "'Le dédain,' dit Vigny, 'basse monnaie pour payer les choses humaines,'"—that is, "Disdain," says Vigny, "is base coin to pay in return for human things." Ibid., 11.

22. *Carnets 1,* 336–37.

23. De Gaulle wrote: "At bottom, men cannot do without being directed, any more than without eating, drinking, and sleeping. These political animals have need of organization, that is to say, of order and of chiefs." *Le Fil de l'épée,* 87. Larcan has this passage in mind when he says, "It is perhaps the most widely-known thought of Aristotle that comes from de Gaulle's pen in *The Edge of the Sword.*" Alain Larcan, *Charles de Gaulle: Itinéraires Intellectuels et Spirituels* (Presses univérsitaires de Nancy, 1993), 90.

24. *Le Fil de l'épée,* 91.

25. Ibid. Lazare Hoche was perhaps the ablest general of the French Revolution, prior to Napoleon. See also de Gaulle, *France and Her Army,* trans. F. L. Dash (London: Hutchinson, 1946), 43–45.

26. Max Weber makes a similar point: "This is the decisive psychological quality of the politician: his ability to let realities work upon him with inner concentration and calmness." Max Weber, "Politics as a Vocation," in *From Max Weber: Essays in Sociology,* trans. and ed. Hans H. Gerth and C. Wright Mills (New York: Oxford University Press, 1946), 115.

27. See this edition, Chapter 5, section II.

28. "Thus," Pouget concludes, "de Gaulle again received the nickname that his first captain had instinctively bestowed on him in 1910." Pouget, *Un certain capitaine,* 103–4.

29. See Wolfgang J. Mommsen, *Max Weber and German Politics, 1890–1920* (Chi-

cago: University of Chicago Press, 1984), 190–203, 227–44, 257–66, 273–78, 286–96, 311–31; Max Weber, *Gesammelte Politische Schriften* (Tübingen: J. C. B. Mohr, 1958), 432–92; Marianne Weber, *Max Weber: A Biography*, trans. Harry Zohn (New York: John Wiley, 1975), 590–94, 617–38.

30. Will Morrisey, *Reflections on De Gaulle: Political Founding in Modernity* (Lanham, Md.: University Presses of America, 1983), 8.

31. See the brief but quite remarkable 1921 article by this title ("Préparer la guerre, c'est préparer les chefs,") in de Gaulle, *Articles et Ecrits* (Paris: Plon, 1975), 59–66.

32. For a judicious assessment of de Gaulle's realism and a correction of the view that he was simply a Machiavellian, see Mahoney, *De Gaulle*, 6–7, 58–61, and the section "The Problem of Machiavellianism," 62–66.

33. Lacouture, *Le Rebelle*, 83.

34. Ibid. For these lectures, see *Carnets 1*: 413–97.

35. Leo Strauss, "German Nihilism: Lecture Delivered on February 26, 1941," *Interpretation: A Journal of Political Philosophy* 26, no. 3 (Spring 1999): 365.

36. In 1918 Georges Catroux, then a major, was a fellow prisoner with de Gaulle at Ludwigshafen. In June 1940, General Catroux was in charge of French Indochina. A fortnight after the Vichy government declared de Gaulle a rebel and ordered him to return to France for a court martial, Catroux was dismissed, for "crossing the Rubicon" to de Gaulle's Free France. Gaston Bonheur claims (1) that de Gaulle began to write *The Enemy's House Divided* in the aniline factory prison in Ludwigshafen in 1918, and (2) that his first reader was Catroux. He also claims (3) that de Gaulle had begun to assemble the materials for it at this time. Since none of the German memoirs on which the book is explicitly based was published before 1919, I think these claims are untenable. See Gaston Bonheur, *Le glaive nu: Charles de Gaulle et son destin* (Geneva: Trois Collines, 1945), 38. De Gaulle's biographer Lacouture repeats the second claim, in *Le Rebelle*, 123. However, Catroux's most recent biographer makes no mention of Catroux's having read *La Discorde* in any draft. He quotes Catroux's precise recollections of de Gaulle at Ludwigshafen:

> A man who meditated, who had done a great deal of work, in the sense that he read many German newspapers and reviews treating the development of the war; and that he analyzed, correctly and in advance, the successive states of mind of the German command, of the German people and the course of the war, such that the German defeat seemed to him to be certain in the near future. Catroux divined in the young twenty-six year old officer the force of character and the prophetic intuition he demonstrated in the inferences he deduced from events; and Catroux was all the more aware of this kind of prescience because circumstances often confirmed his predictions. He also appreciated "the capacity for exegesis"

in de Gaulle, as well as "the maturity of a mind that had reflected not only on the strategic problems of the war, but about strategy in general, with what was required to mobilize for combat all the resources and all the means of a country."

Henri Lerner, *Catroux* (Paris: Albin Michel, 1990), 69.

37. Jean Gaulmier, *Charles de Gaulle, écrivain* (Paris: Editions Charlot, 1946), 8–10.

38. Fritz Stern, "Historians and the Great War: Private Experience and Public Explication," *Yale Review* 82, no. 1 (January 1994): 48.

39. As discussed below, there is evidence that Chapter 5 was composed, in its earliest version, during de Gaulle's service in Poland, toward the end of 1919 or the beginning of 1920. It is also the chapter that owes least to the memoirs of the German generals and statesmen.

40. See the Appendix for an augmented version of de Gaulle's documentation. Of the twenty-three titles in de Gaulle's list, one (by the American ambassador to Germany, James Gerard) was published in 1917; another by Gerard in 1918; five in 1919; seven in 1920; four in 1921; four in 1922; and one in 1923. The only reference to his study of the German memoirs in de Gaulle's published notebooks is this entry, dated April 1920:

> The Memoirs of the Crown Prince recount the tragic scene in the course of which Wilhelm determined to abdicate without bringing himself to do it . . . Groener said to him that the gatherings of rebels had formed at Louvain and Verviers in order to march against the Supreme Command Headquarters. Hindenburg added that he could respond only with one thing: to withdraw the troops into the fatherland, but on condition that Wilhelm himself should go (8 November).
>
> And we signed the armistice three days later!

Carnets 2, 76.

41. Jacques Vendroux, "Introduction," in Charles de Gaulle, *La Discorde chez l'ennemi* (Paris: Plon, 1972), xxx.

42. Perhaps its most distinguished rival for this honor would be Gerhard Ritter's *The Sword and the Sceptre,* 4 vols. (Coral Gables, Fla.: University of Miami Press, 1969). In his Documentation section, de Gaulle cites a careful reading of some of these memoirs, Hans Delbrück's *Ludendorffs Selbstporträt,* a long review article on the books by Bauer, Bethmann-Hollweg, and Ludendorff.

43. Verisimilitude would rule out seminar-style teaching; but de Gaulle's scholarly standards were in certain respects closer to the German seminar form than to the lecture format adopted at St.-Cyr.

44. Cf. *Carnets 1,* 337: "Descartes says: 'The supreme end of our studies ought to be to render ourselves capable of judging solidly and truly, not only regarding scientific matters, but in every kind of event.'"

45. Mahoney, *De Gaulle,* 7–8. I would add only that this summary of de Gaulle's judgment applies to the memoirs of the civilian authorities no less than to those of the military officials—that is, to Kaiser Wilhelm II and the Crown Prince, to Erzberger and many other party leaders, no less than to Ludendorff and Tirpitz.

46. Charles de Gaulle, "La défaite, question morale," in *Articles et Ecrits* (Paris: Plon, 1975), 127. The chief differences between this lecture and Chapter 5 of *The Enemy's House Divided* are that de Gaulle has deleted almost all exclamation marks and all comparisons between Germany and France.

47. Lacouture, *Le Rebelle,* 103. This passage was omitted from the English translation by O'Brian (cited in note 2 above), at 57. From Lacouture's French edition, it would appear that Medvecki's remarks refer to the end of 1919 or the beginning of 1920.

48. De Gaulle, "La défaite, question morale," 127.

49. As Lutz observes:

> The winter of 1918–1919 was filled with violent discussions by representatives of almost all political parties concerning the questions of responsibility for the dramatic military and internal collapse. Indeed, these problems had so penetrated the national consciousness that a rational solution was promptly demanded by the majority of the newly elected National Assembly. Specifically, the nation demanded answers to these questions: "Were we defeated in battle? Did the submarine warfare fail? Did the Supreme Army Command really deceive us and impose upon us in its daily reports? In the fall of 1918 were we still able to continue fighting? Why did the Navy mutiny? Did those at home really stab the fighting armies in the back with the dagger of revolution? Did the Pan-Germans and the Fatherland Party really prolong the war for selfish purposes?"

Ralph Haswell Lutz, "Foreword," in Lutz, ed., *The Causes of the German Collapse in 1918: Sections of the Officially Authorized Report of the Commission of the German Constituent Assembly and of the German Reichstag, 1919-1928, the Selection and the Translation Officially Approved by the Commission,* trans. W. L. Campbell (London: Oxford University Press, and Stanford, Calif.: Stanford University Press, 1934), v.

50. Alan Bullock, *Hitler: A Study in Tyranny* (New York: Harper, 1964), 115–20.

51. Weber, *Politische Schriften,* 476–85, 490–92, 551–66; Weber, "Politics as a Vocation," 117–18.

52. Lacouture reports that de Gaulle intended the final volume of his *Memoirs of Hope* to be a tour de force, taking this genre to its acme and submitting his actions to the judgment of the most serious critics:

> He was working hard on the second volume, revising the second chapter that he had already read to his son. He planned to complete that volume, which would deal largely with his foreign policy, by a series of dialogues

in which he would speak in turn with Clovis and Charlemagne, Philippe-Auguste and Colbert, Napoleon and Clemenceau on the theme of "What would you have done in my place?" It was a fearsome undertaking, both for the statesman and for the writer.

Jean Lacouture, *De Gaulle,* Vol 2: *The Ruler, 1945–1970,* trans. Alan Sheridan (New York: Norton, 1993), 589.

53. One entry, from the end of his last prison notebook, adumbrates a standard that de Gaulle later sought to meet in writing his own memoirs:

Read the Memoirs of M. de Freycinet for the period from 1848 to 1878.

I savoured these. They are written by a man many of whose ideas are not my own, but whose elevation of mind and political sense are indisputable. Their tone is deliberately very calm, stripped of political passion and oratorical contrivances. The style is excellent, the content richly nuanced.

Read with particular interest what he says about his role in the delegation of Tours and Bourdeaux. He is able to judge serenely while letting us see clearly the services he has rendered, conveying a satisfying impression of modesty . . . in every case he puts the sincerity and uprightness of his character and intentions beyond question.

Carnets 1, 397.

54. See Mahoney, *De Gaulle,* 2–8. To my knowledge, the only philosophical commentary on *The Enemy's House Divided* appears in Will Morrisey's *Reflections on de Gaulle: Political Founding in Modernity* (Lanham, Md.: University Presses of America, 1983), 1–39, esp. 5. It is appropriately focused on this theme. As Morrisey says, for his purposes the Foreword "is the most important part of the book, containing some of the most instructive pages de Gaulle wrote." In interpreting de Gaulle's statecraft and writing, Morrisey has the advantage of a wide acquaintance with the books de Gaulle read and with modern French literature; see also his companion study, *Reflections on Malraux: Cultural Founding in Modernity* (Lanham, Md.: University Presses of America, 1983).

55. Yves Rey-Herme, *Mémoires de Guerre: de Gaulle écrivain* (Paris: Hatier, 1978), 9.

56. On *la querelle de l'homme* as a theme of de Gaulle's thought, see Mahoney, *De Gaulle,* 100, 106.

57. Apart from the indirect evidence supplied by his modes of writing, we know very little about de Gaulle's study of Nietzsche, except for this recollection of Jacques Vendroux:

The memory comes back to me of a shaded corner on the terrace of Seven Fountains, on a beautiful August morning: for a moment he interrupts his reading to give amused support to the still-wobbly steps of his infant son. He puts an open volume down on the garden table as he leaves it. A glance reveals its title: *Thus Spake Zarathustra.* It is undoubtedly his rejection of the Nietzschean Overman, so dear to the Prussians, that dictated to him the concatenation of his first work, and inspired its philosophy. Vendroux, "Introduction," x.

58. On this fundamental problem, consider these quotations, which de Gaulle paired in his prison notebooks: "Fontenelle says: 'One would lose courage if one were not sustained by false ideas.' Rivarol says: 'Bad luck to the one who unsettles the foundation of a nation. There is no century of enlightenment for the populace.'" *Carnets 1*, 337.

59. This edition, Foreword.

60. The subtitle of Nietzsche's *Ecce Homo* was *How One Becomes What One Is*.

61. See Robert Eden, *Political Leadership and Nihilism: A Study of Weber and Nietzsche* (Gainesville: University Presses of Florida, 1984), 98–133.

62. Friedrich Nietzsche, *Beyond Good and Evil*, trans. Walter Kaufmann (New York: Vintage, 1965), Aphorism 19, 201.

63. Although de Gaulle's insight here should be obvious even to the least introspective of Nietzsche's readers, the point has not been taken by intellectual historians, in part because this dimension of Nietzsche's influence is harder to document than his impact on artists and writers. Thus Aschheim makes no effort to trace Nietzsche's influence in German military circles. See Steven E. Aschheim, *The Nietzsche Legacy in Germany, 1890–1990* (Berkeley: University of California Press, 1992).

64. In striking contrast to Paul Valéry's widely read and much-republished essay "A Conquest by Method," de Gaulle shows that Moltke the elder's system was far from a model of Cartesian rationalism applied to military practice.

65. Chapter 2, footnote i.

66. See Ritter, *Sword and the Sceptre*, which is also a study of German World War I memoirs. Ritter was evidently unaware of de Gaulle's book; he considers neither the kinds of evidence de Gaulle adduces for Nietzsche's influence nor de Gaulle's subtle analysis of the Moltke system, summarized below. Ritter argues that Bernhardi was unique and that Nietzsche's impact was confined to Ludendorff's circle, Colonel Bauer in particular. De Gaulle's wartime prison notebooks contain roughly sixteen pages of outline notes summarizing his reading of Friedrich von Bernhardi's *Deutschland und die nächste Krieg* (1912). See *Carnets 1*, 354–66, 378–86.

67. This edition, Chapter 1, section II.

68. A glance at Churchill may be useful here. In volume 1 of *The World Crisis*, 6 vols. (1923–1931; reprint, New York: Charles Scribner's, 1951), Churchill treated the First Battle of the Marne as a confirmation of his own early prediction that the Germans were bound to become overextended as they got close to Paris (see 1:261–65, 271–77, 329–31); whereas De Gaulle argues that the Germans were not overextended and could well have won. Volume 6 of *World Crisis*, entitled *The Eastern Front*, was published in 1931, seven years

after de Gaulle's work appeared, but it is evident that Churchill did not yet appreciate the questions raised by de Gaulle. In reviewing the victory at Tannenberg, Churchill centers attention on a sequence of conflicts between Headquarters and a commander in the field, General François. He applauds François's insubordination and cheers him for defying Ludendorff. This episode obviously repeats the pattern to which de Gaulle draws attention in his account of the German defeat in the first Battle of the Marne. Churchill's approach conforms very closely to the judgments of the German military historians, whom de Gaulle faults as irresponsible, for their unwillingness to criticize a foolhardy procedure that led in one instance to glorious results. Cf. Churchill, *World Crisis,* 6:196–207.

69. De Gaulle was mistaken in the view that Tirpitz was one of the "old Prussians." Born in Prussia in 1849 to parents who were not Junkers, he was made a noble only in 1900.

70. See de Gaulle's statement comparing Hindenburg with Ludendorff, quoted above in this Introduction, at note 65.

71. This edition, Chapter 1, section II.

72. This edition, Chapter 3, section II beginning and section III. Churchill's assessment of Conrad von Hötzendorf is diametrically opposed to de Gaulle's. See Churchill, *World Crisis,* 6:28–30.

73. See this edition, Chapter 3, section I; Chapter 2, de Gaulle footnote i.

74. See this edition, Chapter 4, section II end, section III, section V end, section VIII beginning.

75. This edition, Foreword.

76. Ibid.

77. Ibid.

78. De Gaulle, *France and Her Army,* 23.

79. See Aristotle, *Politics,* 1276b16–19, 32–36; 1277a2–6, 13–16.

80. "In truth, the military spirit, the art of the soldiers, their virtues, are an integral part of the capital of humanity. . . . Moreover, this abnegation of individuals for the good of the whole, this glorified suffrance—to which the troops give themselves up—corresponds preeminently to our aesthetic and moral concepts: the highest philosophic and religious doctrines have chosen no other ideal." De Gaulle, *Fil de l'épée,* 51.

81. "Returning after a long war to his homeland Ithaca, Ulysses had himself bound to the mast of his boat, to avoid surrender to the seductions of the Sirens and shipwreck in the watery abyss. May French military thought resist the secular lures of the a priori, of dogmatism and the absolute! So as not to succumb to these lures, may it bind itself to the classical order! From this order it could draw that taste for the concrete, that gift of measure, that feel for realities, which clarifies audacity, inspires maneuver, and makes action fruitful." De Gaulle, *Fil de l'épée,* 122.

82. Charles de Gaulle, *The Complete War Memoirs,* trans. Jonathan Griffin and Richard Howard (New York: Carroll and Graf, 1998), 3.

83. Cf. Pierre Manent, *The City of Man* (Princeton, N.J.: Princeton University Press, 1997), 164.

84. This edition, Chapter 4, section IV, after callout for note 15.

85. Charles Williams, *The Last Great Frenchman: A Life of General de Gaulle* (New York: Wiley, 1993), 337.

86. This edition, Foreword, final paragraph.

87. I have taken the liberty of putting de Gaulle's subject in place of Scott's:

> This is the story of a rape, of the events that led up to it and followed it and of the place in which it happened. There are the action, the people, and the place; all of which are interrelated but in their totality incommunicable in isolation from the moral continuum of human affairs.
>
> In the Bibighar gardens case there were several arrests and an investigation. There was no trial in the judicial sense. Since then people have said there was a trial of sorts going on. In fact, such people say, the affair that began on the evening of August 9th, 1942, in Mayapore, ended with the spectacle of two nations in violent opposition, not for the first time nor as yet for the last because they were then still locked in an imperial embrace of such long standing and subtlety it was no longer possible for them to know whether they hated or loved one another, or what it was that held them together and seemed to have confused the image of their separate destinies.

Paul Scott, *The Jewel in the Crown* (New York: William Morrow, 1966), 3.

FOREWORD TO THE FIRST EDITION

1. The term *péripéties* commonly means incidents or events, but de Gaulle's use of it here may have an additional resonance in the five acts of this "drama." The word derives from the ancient Greek *peripeteia,* meaning a reversal of the normal order, or, in a more specific use, a sudden change of condition, fortune, or circumstances on which the plot in a tragedy hinges, such as Oedipus's discovery of his parentage. See Aristotle, *Poetics* 1452a22,34. On de Gaulle's acquaintance with ancient Greek tragedy, see Alain Larcan, *Charles de Gaulle: itinéraires intellectuels et spirituels* (Nancy, Fr.: Presses universitaires de Nancy, 1993). On liberation day, August 25, 1944, de Gaulle reportedly recited ten of his favorite lines in Greek, from Euripides' *Hippolytus.* Claude Guy, *En écoutante de Gaulle, Journal 1946–1949* (Paris: Editions Grasset & Fasquelle, 1996), 34. Another favorite line, which we also find in de Gaulle's prison notebooks, bears particularly on this book: "Pride, child of happiness, who devours his father" (from Aeschylus's *The Persians,* a tragedy on the fallen enemy of Athens). See de Gaulle, *Lettres, Notes, et Carnets,* Vol. 1 (Paris: Plon, 1980), 215.

1. De Gaulle uses the French term *empereur;* in future instances, we shall follow the custom of using the German term, Kaiser.

2. Wilhelm I (1797–1888) became King of Prussia in January 1861. When the War of 1870 began, Prussia stood at the head of the Northern German Confederation. The ultimatum from France that precipitated the war put the Northern Confederation on the defensive, and thus activated the defensive alliance between the Northern and Southern German Confederations. As the North and South fought together under Prussian leadership in this victorious campaign, public opinion in favor of union grew mightily, enabling Wilhelm's minister-president Bismarck to negotiate a lasting union of the German states even before the end of the war. During the siege of Paris, on January 18, 1871, Wilhelm I was proclaimed Kaiser of a newly united Germany, in the Hall of Mirrors at Versailles. He opened the first imperial parliament of Germany on 21 March. Wilhelm I entered Berlin at the head of his troops on 16 June 1871, when DeGaulle's narrative begins.

3. Helmuth Carl Bernhard von Moltke (1800–1891), Prussian field marshal, was for thirty years chief of staff of the Prussian Army, the greatest strategist of the latter half of the nineteenth century, and the creator of the modern method of directing armies in the field.

4. *Manière* has an exact English equivalent in "manner," but it does not convey de Gaulle's thought to the contemporary reader. Here he means to underscore the role of imitation and example in professional military training, perhaps by analogy to art. A *tableau à la manière de Degas* is a painting recognizably in the style or manner of Degas; and De Gaulle argues that German commanders consciously modeled their conduct and thinking on the impressive *manière* of von Moltke senior. The obstacle to our understanding the term lies in our democratic resistance to the moral reality in question—i.e., subordination to an authority or master—a resistance that De Gaulle amply justifies here, albeit in his own manner.

5. Wilhelm II (1859–1941) became Kaiser of Germany on June 15, 1888, upon the death of his father, Frederick Wilhelm; Frederick Wilhelm had reigned for only ninety-nine days, having succeeded the aged Wilhelm I a few months before he himself passed away on March 9, 1888.

6. Helmuth Johannes Ludwig von Moltke (1848–1916) was made quartermaster general in 1904 and became chief of staff of the German army in 1906, at the age of sixty-six and in failing health.

7. The first of these two dates, 1 July 1866, marked the opening of the campaign that decided the war between Prussia and the Habsburg Empire of Austria and Hungary. The second, 15 August 1870, was the starting date of the campaign that decided the war between Prussia and France and that

was the catalyst for the unification of all the German states into an empire, under the hegemony of Prussia.

8. Alexander von Kluck (1846–1934) took part in the Austro-Prussian War of 1866 and the Franco-Prussian War of 1870, and was twice wounded at the battle of Colombey-Neuilly. In 1906 he was promoted to the rank of general of infantry; at the outbreak of the Great War he was inspector-general of the Eighth Army Inspection.

9. On July 3, 1866, at Königgrätz, in the greatest battle of the nineteenth century, the Austrian army was defeated, leaving the road to Vienna open to the Prussian armies under von Moltke. The Austrian emperor then sued for peace, ending the war of 1866. In the decisive action of the Franco-Prussian war, on August 18, 1870, Moltke attacked the French under Bazaine and drove him into the fortress of Metz, where Bazaine's forces were invested. Macmahon's forces tried to come up to support Bazaine, but they were surrounded on September 1 at Sedan and surrendered.

10. See *Moltke's Projects for the Campaign of 1866 against Austria,* trans. and précis for the General Staff, War Office, by S. Wilkinson, from *Moltke's militarische Korrespondenz. Aus den Dienstschriften des Krieges 1866. Theil I. Kriegsvorbereitungen* (London: Harrison and Sons, 1907); and *Extracts from Moltke's Correspondence pertaining to the War 1870–1871,* trans. Harry Bell (Fort Leavenworth, Kans.: Army Service Schools Press, 1911). Both documents are conveniently reprinted in Helmuth Karl Bernhard Graf von Moltke, *Strategy: Its Theory and Application: The Wars for German Unification, 1866–1870* (Westport, Conn.: Greenwood, 1971).

11. The crown prince of Prussia, Frederick Wilhelm, the son of Wilhelm I (1831–1888), began his military career in the war against Denmark; in the War of 1866 he received the command of an army consisting of four army corps. He was already mortally ill when he became Kaiser of Germany, dying only ninety-nine days later on June 15, 1888.

12. Prince Frederick-Karl (1828–1885), Prussian general field marshal, was in command of the forces that blockaded Bazaine in the fortress of Metz on August 13, and is credited with the victory at Saint-Privat on August 18, 1870, both discussed by de Gaulle below. The prince was later victorious at Lemans on January 12, 1871.

13. Karl Friedrich von Steinmetz (1796–1877), Prussian general field marshal, whose skillful and resolute leadership was shown in three battles—Nachod, Skalitz, and Schweinschädel—won on three successive days in the War of 1866.

14. Ludwig Ritter von Benedek (1804–1881) was reluctant to be placed in command of the Austrian Army of the North against the Prussians in the War of 1866. Only the personal command of the Austrian emperor and the requests of the Archduke Albert prevailed upon Benedek to accept this command,

which he saw as a sacrifice of his honor. He knew that he was a stranger to the troops and to the country in which he was to fight; his despondency was increased by the passive obstruction he met with from his officers and by the unpreparedness of his troops.

15. La Point du Jour is a mile east of Mars-la-Tour on the road to Longeville and Metz, some eight kilometers south of Saint-Privat. The French held it on 17 August, when the battle began.

16. The French Army of the Rhine was under the command of Achille Francois Bazaine (1811–1888). He had been ordered by Napoleon III to evacuate the fortified city of Metz quickly, but a recent flood had destroyed many of the bridges this would have required. His command became "the Army of Metz" because Marshal Bazaine anticipated that his slow-moving troops would be headed off and brought to battle if they ventured out; by keeping them close to his stronghold, he hoped to inflict damaging repulses and heavy slaughter on the Germans. This hope was not unfounded, as on 14 August the Prussians lost over 5,000 officers and men in the Battle of Borny just east of Metz, whereas the French lost about 3,500.

17. The Germans stumbled into the battle of Borny, where they were met by strong French fire and were at a disadvantage. Both sides thought themselves victorious in this inconclusive engagement, the French because they had held and thus "broken the spell" of a string of Prussian victories.

18. Frederick-Karl believed that if the German Second Army turned north before the Meuse, Bazaine's army would already have departed the area safely, and would be able to complete its retreat across the Meuse just to the west of Verdun. By heading south and west, Frederick-Karl could get his Second Army to the Meuse just above Commercy (thus avoiding the steeper terrain to the east of the Meuse), and engage Bazaine's retreating army after it crossed the Meuse by Verdun.

19. Frederick-Karl had thus divided his army. His Tenth Corps, commanded by Voigts-Rhetz, was disposed toward Vionville, closest to the French in Metz. His Third Corps was commanded by the most forceful of all his officers, Constantin von Alvensleben, who rightly thought he could place the Third Corps between the retreating French army and Verdun at Mars-la-Tour, more than three kilometers to the west of Vionville. But he thought most of the French had already passed to the west. Because he greatly underestimated the real strength of Bazaine's army, which actually numbered 160,000, the maneuver was potentially suicidal, especially once Voigts-Rhetz's cavalry encountered the French outposts at Vionville, alerting them to the presence of German forces and thus depriving von Alvensleben of the advantage of surprise. See Figure 3b for Frederick-Karl's conception.

20. Had Frederick-Karl obeyed, his entire Second Army would have moved northward with Alvensleben's Third Corps. See Figure 3a.

21. Only by moving north and northwest immediately could the Second Army have placed itself in a position to attack the retreating Army of Metz in concert with the attacking Third and Tenth Corps at Mars-la-Tour and Vionville (see Figure 3a). By marching due west and only then turning north up the Meuse to Verdun, Prince Frederick-Karl removed the rest of his Second Army from the engagement (Figures 3a–d).

22. While the rest of Frederick-Karl's Second Army was marching southwestward toward the Meuse, the Third Corps (von Alvensleben) and the Tenth (Voigts-Rhetz), were moving east from Mars-la-Tour and Vionville toward Gravelotte and Metz (Figures 3c, 3d). Had Bazaine taken advantage of his overwhelmingly superior numbers to attack with his full strength, he could have destroyed both Corps and retreated to the Meuse behind and to the south of Frederick-Karl, who by then would be racing north toward Verdun. But Bazaine occupied himself entirely with protecting his communications with Metz to the east, instead of seizing the opportunity to break out with a relatively easy victory toward the west. He thus allowed his entire army to be entrapped near Metz.

23. Sadowa, a village of Bohemia, now in Czechoslovakia, is six kilometers northwest of Königgrätz; it was one of the principal and most hotly contested Prussian positions in the battle of July 3, 1866, now usually called Königgrätz. The Austrians—and their sometime allies, the French—preferred to call this the Battle of Sadowa, and so de Gaulle sometimes refers to it by this name.

24. Alfred, Count von Schlieffen, was chief of the General Staff of the German Army from 1891 until 1907, exercising an extraordinary influence on the development of the General Staff and indeed of the whole army. His strategic conception, famous as the Schlieffen Plan, was the basis of the German attack in 1914; but Moltke the younger diluted it and executed it without its original uncompromising commitment to turn the French left flank with overwhelming forces. Moltke hedged his bets by withholding substantial forces to prevent a French counterattack; the situation was also complicated by the early Russian attack in 1914. Schlieffen's plan would not have assigned such substantial forces as were required to hold the Russians back in East Prussia.

25. Luxemburg, in Luxembourg, was more than 200 kilometers across contested terrain, away from Kluck's First Army, which was near Paris.

26. The Battle at Guise (August 29–31, 1914) was the last of the "battles of the Frontiers." The action of Lanrezac in attacking during this battle, without relying upon assistance from his left, confirmed Kluck in his view that Lanrezac's army, on the right of the British, was in consequence the extreme left of the French line. He was wrong; new French forces were assembling to the east of Paris on his flank.

27. Decorated for valor in the disastrous campaign of 1870, Michel Joseph Maunoury had risen to the rank of general before he retired into the reserve cadre in 1912. In 1914, at age 67, he volunteered for duty. General Joffre, retreating from defeat in the Battle of the Frontiers, decided to resume the offensive with a mobile force consisting of the Fifth French Army (under Franchet d'Esperey), the British Expeditionary Force (under Sir John French), and the new Sixth French Army (see Figures 4b–d). On 25 August, he put Maunoury in command of the Sixth Army, which was being constituted in the Amiens region, for the defense of Paris against Kluck's First German Army (Figure 4d). On March 11, 1915, Maunoury was blinded by a German shell and so saw no further action. His funeral, on Easter Sunday of 1923, became a memorial for the Battle of the Marne. He was made a Marshal of France after his death. See Général Brécard, *Le Maréchal Maunoury (1847–1923)*, lettre-préface par M. le Maréchal Franchet d'Esperey (Paris: Editions Berger-Lavrault, 1937).

CHAPTER TWO

1. Born in Prussia in 1849 to parents who were not Junkers, Tirpitz was made a noble only in 1900. Thus he was not one of the "old Prussians" by birth, as de Gaulle evidently believed, but only by adoption.
2. Grand Admiral Alfred von Tirpitz, *My Memoirs* 2 vols. (1919; reprint, New York: AMS, 1970),1:281–95.
3. Ibid., 1:371.
4. Ibid., 1:372; see also Tirpitz's letters on Hintze, in *Memoirs,* 2:234–36, 247.
5. Tirpitz, *Memoirs,* 2:229.
6. Reichsfinanzminister Matthias Erzberger, *Erlebnisse im Weltkrieg* (Stuttgart: Deutsche Verlags-Anstalt, 1920), 208–11.
7. After the defeat at the Marne, Falkenhayn hoped to win the "race to the sea" and to turn the Allied left flank. Defeat in the Battle of the Yser in Belgium spelled the failure of this project, checking the German advance toward Calais and the English coast. The fighting commenced on 16 October 1914 and ended on 31 October.
8. Tirpitz, *Memoirs,* 2:146–47.
9. Ibid., 2:149.
10. Ibid., 2:150. Cf. Erzberger, *Erlebnisse im Weltkrieg,* 212–13.
11. On 2 May 1915, at Gorlice, the Central Powers launched a successful attack under the command of Mackensen, in the Dunajec sector of the Eastern Front, and by 14 May, Mackensen had reached the San River, eighty miles (128 kilometers) from the initial lines. On 3 June, Przemysl was retaken, less than three months after it fell to the Russians; by 22 June, Mackensen had captured Lemberg, cutting the Russian front into two separated portions. In the West, the French under Foch launched an offensive be-

tween Lens and Arras in Artois on 9 May, which was not abandoned until June 18.

12. The Vimy Ridge is located in Artois between Lens and Arras. On 9 May 1915, French troops under Foch launched an attack on the German positions there; some of the troops advanced a full three miles (almost five kilometers) behind the German lines to the villages of Vimy and Givenchy. Thus at this moment, Falkenhayn seemed to have his hands full just containing the Allied forces on the Western Front.

13. Tirpitz, *Memoirs,* 2:162.

14. Ibid.

15. Ibid., 2:164.

16. Ibid.

17. Ibid.

18. Ibid., 2:165–66.

19. Ibid.

20. Erzberger, *Erlebnisse im Weltkrieg,* 213.

21. Ibid., 210.

22. Ibid., 214.

23. Tirpitz, *Memoirs,* 2:172.

24. Ibid., 2:172.

25. Ibid., 2:173.

26. Ibid., 2:174.

27. Ibid., 2:175.

28. Ibid.

29. Erzberger, *Erlebnisse im Weltkrieg,* 216.

30. Ibid.

31. Tirpitz, *Memoirs,* 2:178–79.

32. The Serbian and French assault on the Salonika Front, launched on 10 November 1916, pushed the Bulgarians back across the Serb border; on 19 November, Serbian, French, and Russian cavalry units entered Monastir in Serbia. Elated, the French general Sarrail called it the first French victory since the Battle of the Marne.

33. Erzberger, *Erlebnisse im Weltkrieg,* 211.

34. Ibid., 217–18.

35. Ibid., 218.

36. Ibid.

37. The passage appears in Hindenburg, *Aus meinem Leben* (1920; reprint, Leipzig: S. Hirzel Verlag, 1927), 233–34. In English, see Marshal von Hindenburg, *Out of My Life,* 2 vols., trans. F. A. Holt (New York and London: Harper & Brothers, 1921), 2:46–47.

38. For de Gaulle's statement of the principle in question, see the opening paragraph of this chapter.

CHAPTER THREE

1. Grand Admiral von Tirpitz, letter of 2 April 1915, Charleville, *My War Letters,* included in Tirpitz, *Memoirs,* 2:330.

2. In this assessment of the Emperor Franz Joseph, de Gaulle concurs with Karl Friedrich Nowak, *Der Weg zur Katastrophe, mit Briefen, Gesprachen, Dokumenten und Karten* (Berlin: Verlag fur Kulturpolitik, 1926), 185–88.

3. Nowak, *Der Weg zur Katastrophe,* 70.

4. On the Battle of Sadowa, see this edition, Chapter I, section I.

5. See Nowak, *Der Weg zur Katastrophe,* 60.

6. Ibid., 62.

7. Ibid., 79–80.

8. A. von Cramon, *Unser Österreich-Ungarischer Bundesgenosse im Weltkriege* (Berlin: Ernst S. Mittler und Sohn, 1920), 12. See also General Hoffman's critique of Falkenhayn's pettiness in this matter, in Max Hoffmann, *The War of Lost Opportunities* (London: A. E. Chamot/Kegan Paul, 1924), 100.

9. Nowak, *Der Weg zur Katastrophe,* 90–91.

10. Cramon, *Österreich-Ungarischer Bundesgenosse,* 22–23.

11. Ibid., 23.

12. Ibid., 104.

13. On the surrender at Sedan, see this edition, Chapter I, note 9.

14. The passage appears in Hindenburg, *Aus meinem Leben* (1920; reprint, Leipzig: S. Hirzel Verlag, 1927), 129–30. In English, see Marshal von Hindenburg, *Out of My Life,* 2 vols., trans. F. A. Holt (New York and London: Harper & Brothers, 1921), Vol. I, Chap. 7, 176–77.

15. King Constantine of Greece, though adopting an official policy of neutrality, had strong ties to Germany; at this time Greece was under great pressure from the Allies, who demanded the complete demobilization of the Greek army, which threatened their operations in Macedonia. In June 1917, the Allies insisted on the king's departure; he returned in December 1920, but was never recognized by Great Britain or France.

16. De Gaulle refers here to General A. von Cramon, the German delegate to Conrad's headquarters, who is mentioned several times earlier in this chapter. Cramon's book is cited in note 8 above.

17. Nowak, *Der Weg zur Katastrophe,* 166–67.

18. In July, Brusilov's successful surprise offensive on the southern section of the Eastern Front had driven the German and Austrian forces back, as far as the Stochod River to the north and, by August 1916, to the Carpathian Mountains to the south. Had Conrad's proposals been accepted, von Linsingen would have received the divisions from Falkenhayn to reinforce his positions to the east of the Stochod before Brusilov could drive them back.

19. De Gaulle does not correct this unfounded belief; Conrad's second wife was not Jewish.

20. Cramon, *Österreich-Ungarischer Bundesgenosse,* 65–66.

21. The Verdun offensive began on 21 February 1916. The first phase of the attack ground to a halt eight days later. The last German attack of their stalled offensive began on 3 September and marked the end of the months-long battle. In late July 1916, Brusilov began the new Russian offensive on the Eastern Front that de Gaulle discussed earlier in this chapter.

22. Nowak, *Der Weg zur Katastrophe,* 195–96.

CHAPTER FOUR

1. See Reichsfinanzminister Matthias Erzberger, *Erlebnisse im Weltkrieg* (Stuttgart: Deutsche Verlags-Anstalt, 1920), 220.

2. Wilhelm II suffered several humiliations that he attributed to his chancellor, Prince von Bülow. The most severe and most public was the *Daily Telegraph* affair, in which Wilhelm's remarks in a reported interview were taken amiss, both in England and in Germany. There was an excited debate in the Reichstag on the Kaiser's personal conduct of foreign affairs. Bülow publicly admitted his oversight in not reading the article before publication. But the Kaiser always believed that Bülow had actually read the article and allowed it to be published, with the deliberate intention of exploiting the public excitement, which he foresaw, to put pressure on his master, whom he had attempted by this means to force into submission.

3. Parma had been formally incorporated into the new kingdom of Italy in 1860. Erzberger had interviews with several members of the House of Parma, whose influence in the Austrian court was strong because Zita, the wife of the heir-apparent Charles, was the daughter of the Duchess of Parma. At the death of Franz Joseph, Charles and Zita became emperor and empress of the Habsburg Empire. Erzberger won the duchess and her daughter over to the policy of further Austrian concessions to Italy.

4. By 1870 the secular Italian state begun by Cavour had annexed all the Italian territories held by the Vatican, including the Romagna and the city of Rome; the pope was in effect imprisoned in the Vatican itself. Erzberger was thus proposing a limited solution to "the Roman question" in Italy.

5. As the head of the Ottoman Empire, the sultan held authority over Jerusalem. The cenacle or coenaculum is the "upper room" in which the Last Supper was celebrated. A small Christian church had existed on the spot from the time of the Roman emperor Hadrian; the complex of buildings on this site included the Dormitian Church (1900) and the Dormitian Abbey (1906).

6. In 1883, Romania had entered into a secret treaty that bound her to the Habsburg and the German Empires. However, despite its terms, at the outbreak of war in 1914 she followed a policy of armed neutrality under the leadership of Ionel Bratianu (1864–1927), prime minister and leader of the

Liberal Party. King Ferdinand favored the Allies; and in the spring of 1916, Bratianu was negotiating with the Allies what became the treaty of 7 August 1916. Thus, had Erzberger's effort been successful, Romania would not have declared war on Austria-Hungary in August 1916. (De Gaulle had earlier described the impact of Romania's entry; see this edition, Chapter 2, section IV.)

7. Erzberger, *Erlebnisse im Weltkrieg,* 107–10.

8. Ibid., 252; see also 267.

9. Erich Ludendorff, *The General Staff and Its Problems,* 2 vols., trans. J. A. Holt (1920; reprint, Freeport, N.Y.: Books for Libraries Reprints, 1971), 2:447–48. For original, see Erich Ludendorff, ed., *Urkunden der obersten Heeresleitung Über ihre Tätigkeit, 1916–19181* (Berlin: E. S. Mittler und Sohn, 1920), 396.

10. Ludendorff, *General Staff and Its Problems,* 2:450; for original, see Ludendorff, *Urkunden,* 398.

11. This letter from Hindenburg to the Kaiser is not included in Ludendorff's edition of documents (*Urkunden/General Staff and Its Problems.*)

12. Erzberger, *Erlebnisse im Weltkrieg,* 253–54.

13. Ibid.

14. Ibid., 254.

15. Ibid., 254–55.

16. Ibid., 256–57.

17. Ibid., 257. Major-General Hans Joachim von Zieten (1699–1786) led the famous Zietenritt (Zieten's ride) around the enemy's lines to deliver Frederick the Great's order to a distant detachment. He later became general field marshal of Prussia.

18. Erzberger, *Erlebnisse im Weltkrieg,* 259–60.

19. Ibid., 260.

20. Ibid., 261. De Gaulle has deleted a clause from the resolution; in the original, the first sentence reads: "The Center Party of the Reichstag judges that Mr. Bethmann-Hollweg's remaining in the office of chancellor, in view of the circumstance, that he led the policy of the empire at the outbreak of the war, would aggravate the difficulties of eventual peace negotiations."

21. Erzberger, *Erlebnisse im Weltkrieg,* 262.

22. Wilhelm I's son, Crown Prince Frederick Wilhelm, had repudiated his father's Prussian traditions and had been kept wholly outside official business because of this rebellion. In turn, Wilhelm II, the son of Crown Prince Frederick Wilhelm, was greatly at variance with the spirit reigning in his parents' house. This is the "tradition within his family," of rebellion against one's father, to which de Gaulle refers.

23. Erzberger, *Erlebnisse im Weltkrieg,* 263.

24. Ibid.

25. Ibid., 53–54.

CHAPTER FIVE

1. *Crise morale* can be rendered equally well as "crisis of morale" or "moral crisis."

2. The October 1917 Revolution overthrew the Kerensky government and over-turned its policy of continuing the war with Germany. Although the Brest-Litovsk negotiations, which began in December 1917, did not result in a treaty until March 1918, it was clear that Russia would no longer be a factor in the war.

3. In the previous four chapters, de Gaulle kept the reader informed of the location of the German General Headquarters. Its omission here is another indication that Chapter 5 was written in 1919–20 and only slightly revised for inclusion in the book. Headquarters for the 1918 campaign was located at Bad Homburg.

4. Harry Count von Arnim (1824–1887) was a Prussian diplomat whose opposition to Bismarck led to his prosecution and condemnation; he went into exile and anonymously published a pamphlet entitled *Pro Nihilo,* attributing his prosecution to Bismarck's jealousy. For this, he was sentenced in absentia to five years of penal servitude. When de Gaulle says that Kühlmann was of Arnim's "school," he probably has in mind von Arnim's spiritedly independent defiance, his way of conducting himself toward Bismarck, rather than a doctrine of diplomacy. For a telling example of that spiritedness, see the account of Kühlmann's actions later in this chapter.

5. The French is *sans mesure.* Such absence of measure among the German political and military leaders—their disregard for the limits laid down by common sense, experience, and the law—has been de Gaulle's leitmotif since the author's foreword.

6. This uncorrected reference to a long-suppressed and obscure faction that most readers would not recognize in 1923 may be further evidence that Chapter 5 dates from the winter of 1919–20: by 1923, the reality of Bolshevik dominance over the October 1917 Revolution had been clear for some years. The Maximalists had been the most violent wing of the Social Revolutionary Party; between 1905 and 1907 their campaign of terror claimed hundreds of lives. Kerensky represented a different wing of the Social Revolutionary Party. When his government fell in the October Revolution in 1917, the Maximalists were part of the revolutionary coalition of extremist parties that assumed power. Fighting ceased in November but resumed briefly when a German offensive forced the coalition government led by Lenin's Bolsheviks to sign a treaty. Lenin's government accepted the German terms at Brest-Litovsk on 3 March 1918; the Maximalists disagreed with the terms of the treaty and resigned from the revolutionary coalition government.

7. De Gaulle may be judging impressionistically here. Friedrich Naumann had long been a friend, political associate, and student of Max Weber; he had

endorsed the Machtpolitik doctrine of Weber's Freiburg inaugural address in 1895 and was not guilty of abandoning his long-standing principles and policies in the manner that de Gaulle suggests. On the long-standing strain of realism in Naumann's thought, see Wolfgang J. Mommsen, *Max Weber and German Politics, 1890–1920* (Chicago: University of Chicago Press, 1984), 19–20, 69–71, 134–36, 217–19, 225–26, 275, 280.

8. Raymond Poincaré was president of France. Georges Clemenceau initiated his war administration, which came to power at the nadir of France's fortunes, in an address before the Chamber of Deputies on 17 November 1917. This is probably the address de Gaulle has in mind. It was a statement of intransigence, of France's unconquerable determination to fight through to victory. For Churchill's account of this famous address, see the essay on Clemenceau in Winston S. Churchill, *Great Contemporaries* (1937; reprint, Chicago: University of Chicago Press, 1973), 301–15. As Gilbert observes, Churchill "was to echo those very sentiments twenty-two years later when Britain had lost its main ally, France, and London seemed as much in danger as Paris had been with Russia's withdrawal from the war in 1917." Martin Gilbert, *The First World War* (New York: Henry Holt, 1994), 378.

9. *Vorwärts* (*Forward*) was the newspaper of the German Social Democratic Party. As de Gaulle makes clear ten pages later, when Scheidemann announced on 2 July 1918 that the Socialists would vote against the trimester war credits, it meant the end, since the government would no longer have funds to continue the war.

10. Ludendorff's objective was to drive the British from the Somme and the French from the Aisne and, again, as in 1914, to threaten Paris.

11. On 26 March after an emergency conference of Allied politicians and generals at Doullens, Foch was given overall charge of the Allied armies.

12. Extraordinary long-range artillery, made especially by Krupp, began to bombard Paris on 23 March from a gunsite seventy-four miles (118 kilometers) away, at Crepy-en-Laonnaise. The shells fired from these guns took four minutes to reach Paris.

13. The Bulgarians had expected greater rewards for their role in eliminating the Romanians from the war. On the Doubroudja, see note 21 below.

14. The river Piava runs from the Dolomites to the Gulf of Venice. The Austrian offensive was launched on 15 June 1918; by 24 June the last Austrian troops had withdrawn north of the Piava.

15. On 18 July, Foch launched the Allied counterattack with a 2,000-gun artillery bombardment along a 27-mile (43-kilometer) front; more than 200 tanks took part. The Germans were driven back a full four-and-a-half miles (7.2 kilometers); 20,000 German prisoners and 400 heavy guns were captured that day. The threat to Paris was over.

16. *Dans l'histoire de la guerre* can mean both "the history of the war" or "the

history of war in general." No English equivalent has been found to capture this dual meaning of the phrase.

17. On the novelty in the history of war of an entire people—rather than merely an isolated fighting unit—experiencing such a moral crisis, see the section entitled "De Gaulle's Practiced Reserve" in the Introduction above and its accompanying note 36 on Catroux.

18. *Avait faussé le jeu logique et nécessaire des pouvoirs dan l'Etat* might mean "had skewed the logical and necessary interplay of the powers of the State." I choose the connotation of untuning an instrument or putting its strings out of harmony because de Gaulle has stressed images of measure and harmony since the end of his Foreword.

19. The French expression *gage du poing,* translated here as "proof of strength," is difficult. *Gage* might be translated "pledge," "pawn," "security," or "forfeit." *Poing* is "fist" and, by extension, "will" or "strength."

20. Courland is a coastal district of what is now Latvia. Anciently it was inhabited by the Cours or Kurs, a Lettish tribe, who were subdued and converted to Christianity in the first quarter of the thirteenth century by a German military order. In 1237 Courland passed under the rule of the Teutonic Knights, whose head governed it as Duke of Courland until Courland came into close relation with Russia in 1710. In 1795 the assembly of nobles placed it under the Russian sceptre.

21. The Ottoman Empire's expansion into the Balkans began in 1362 with the conquest of Adrinople, advancing up the Maritsa Valley as far as Plovdi (Phillippopolis), taking Sofia in 1385 and decisively defeating the Serbs at Kosovo in 1389. The line of the River Maritsa or Meri was the line of the most long-lasting claims of the Ottomans in the Balkans. Until 1878, all of Bulgaria had been in their empire, which had extended to the Maritsa line as late as 1885; much of the territory south of the river was Ottoman until 1913. In the summer of 1912, Serbia, Bulgaria, Greece, and Montenegro came together, remarkably, in a Balkan League and were victorious. By the terms of the treaty, the Ottomans lost Crete, Macedonia, and Thrace, which they had held for more than 500 years. The Bulgarians claimed the Doubroudja, on the southern border of Romania, as the ancient homeland of their nation.

22. The French is *le Haut Commandement avait trouvé son maître chez l'ennemi,* echoing the title, *La Discorde chez l'ennemi.*

23. The Sobranie is the Bulgarian National Assembly.

24. Romania began the war in 1914 by violating her secret treaty of alliance with Germany; was neutral until joining the Allies in 1916; was then conquered by the Central Powers; and now reentered the war on the Allied side.

25. Karl Liebknecht was arrested on 16 April 1917 for organizing an antiwar rally at the Potsdamer Platz in Berlin; 50,000 machine workers turned up to sup-

port him at the trial. He was freed by the government of Max von Baden, as part of a general amnesty.

26. Ludendorff was already informed of Wilson's address at the Metropolitan Opera House on 27 September 1918; there, Wilson had said: "They observe no covenants, accept no principle but force and their own interest. We cannot 'come to terms' with them. They have made it impossible. The German people must by this time be fully aware that we cannot accept the word of those who forced this war upon us. We do not think the same thoughts or speak the same language of agreement." This effectively made the abdication of the Kaiser a condition of armistice and of U.S. participation in peace negotiations. The speech precipitated a meeting of Hindenburg, Ludendorff, the crown prince, and the Kaiser on 28–30 September, in which they pressured Wilhelm into making Prince Max von Baden chancellor, and set in motion his abdication. On these meetings, see extract from de Gaulle's notebook, in note 40 of my Introduction, above.

27. The communication to President Wilson from Prince Max von Baden, Imperial Chancellor, was sent on 8 November 1918.

28. The Spahis were native Algerian horsemen serving in the French Army; they normally served in Africa. The idea presumably is that German Christians would expect nothing but ferocity and rapine from Arab Muslim cavalrymen.

29. The Siegesallee (Victory Avenue), completed in 1901, was arguably the most outlandish monument of the era, but it was a precise expression of Wilhelm II's imperious opinions. Designed to commemorate the empire-building achievements of the Hohenzollern dynasty, it was 700 meters long, stretching through the Tiergarten from the Königsplatz to the Roland fountain in the Kemperplatz, and featured thirty-two "stations of national pride," of opulent white marble statuary, each glorifying a Hohenzollern prince and his closest advisers. A grandiose attempt to outdo Paris and indeed the Renaissance, it quickly became the symbol of Wilhelm's pomp, arrogance, and imperial ambition; and made Berlin a laughingstock among Europeans of good taste.

30. The rumor was true. Admiral Scheer, who was in command of the German fleet mothballed in the port of Kiel, wished to save the honor of his navy by mounting a "death ride" straight into the heart of the British fleet. This did not appeal to the men. The uprising at Kiel began on 3 November 1918, when 3,000 sailors and workers raised the red banner; on 4 November, they were joined by 20,000 factory workers and garrison troops.

Index of Minor Characters

This supplementary index is meant to spare readers the considerable research that would be required to identify all the characters who play minor parts in de Gaulle's narrative. Many of these people do not appear either in current encyclopedias or in commonly available reference works on World War I. Teaching editions of foreign-language texts often include a glossary that serves the student in place of a bilingual dictionary. This list serves a similar purpose, making *The Enemy's House Divided* more useful as a teaching text.

Capelle, Eduard von (1855–1931): admiral, secretary of state of German naval office (1916–18), xlviii, 49, 52, 98, 99, 100

Cuno, Wilhelm (1876–1933): German statesman, in charge of imperial grain office (1914–July 1916), Batocki's chief assistant in food department (July 1916–Nov. 1917), director of Hamburg-Amerika steamship line until end of war, 44

Czernin, Ottokar, Count (1872–1932): Austro-Hungarian statesman, 91

Dandl, Otto von (1868–1942): Bavarian minister-president, follower of Hertling, 134

Danev, Stoyan: Bulgarian politician, 122

Dankl, Viktor, Freiherr von (1854–?): Austro-Hungarian general, 61

David, Eduard (1863–1930): Social Democratic Reichstag representative, minister (1919–20), 87, 105, 107

Ebert, Friedrich (1870–1925): chairman of German Social Democratic Party from 1913, leader of Majority Socialists from 1916, chairman of Reichstag budget commission (1918), 87, 96, 101, 118, 139–40

Eitel, Frederick (1856–1929): prince of Prussia, second son of Wilhelm II, 113

Enver Pasha (1881–1922): Turkish minister of war (1914–18), leader of Young Turks, 71, 83

François, Hermann K.: German general, 155 (n. 68)

French, Sir John (1825–1925): general, 22–28

Gantscheff, Peter: Bulgarian soldier, trusted advisor to Czar Ferdinand of Bulgaria, 71, 74, 83

Goltz, Colmar, Freiherr von der (1843–1916): Prussian general and military writer, 71

Gothein, Georg (1857–1940): Reichstag deputy, leader in Progressive People's Party, 90, 105

Groeber, Adolf (1854–1919): Reichstag deputy, leader in Catholic Center Party (1917–19), 97, 130, 134

Groener, Wilhelm (1867–1939): German general, 137

Haase, Hugo (1863–1919): leader of Social Democratic Party in Reichstag (1914), head of Independent Socialists (1917), 87, 97

Hutier, Oskar von: German general, 137

Ledebour, Georg (1850–1947): leading Independent socialist, sharp critic of Majority socialists, 87, 97

Linsingen, Alexander von (1850–1935): Prussian general, 68, 81

Louvois, François, Marquis de (1641–91): French statesman, war minister of Louis XIV, xlvii

Luxemburg, Rosa (1870–1919): cofounder of Spartacus League, editor (with Liebknecht) of communist newspaper *Rote Fahne*, 97

Macdonald, James Ramsay (1866–1937): creator of British Labour Party (1899–1906), leading oppo-

General Index

Moltke, Helmuth Carl Bernhard, Count von, xxxix–xli, 4–22, 124, 157

Moltke, Helmuth Johannes Ludwig von, 16–22, 34, 59–62, 65, 85, 157 (n. 6)

Mommsen, Wolfgang J., 149 (n. 29), 166 (n. 7)

Morrisey, Will, 150 (n. 30), 153 (n. 54)

Nicholas Nicholajevitch, 64, 67, 69, 72, 73

Nietzsche, Friedrich, xvi, xxiii, xxxv–xlix passim, 2–3, 16, 148 (n. 21), 153 (n. 57), 154 (nn. 60–63)

Orlando, Vittorio, 91

Pascal, Blaise, xvii, 147 (n. 4)

Pétain, Philipe, xviii, xxvi, 47, 126

Peyrefitte, Alain, 148 (n. 16)

Poincaré, Raymond, 119

Porch, Douglas, 149 (n. 17)

Pouget, Jean, xviii, xix, xx, xxv, xix

Radoslovov, Vasil, 74, 122

Radziwill, Prince Janus, of Poland, 128

Rey-Herme, Yves, xxxv–xxxvii, xlii, xliv

Richthofen, Hartmann von, 101, 102, 105, 107, 134

Ritter, Gerhard, 151 (n. 42), 154 (n. 66)

Rivarol, Antoine de, 154 (n. 58)

Roosevelt, Franklin D., 148 (n. 13)

Ruprecht (crown prince of Bavaria), 120, 131

Salandra, Antonio, 91

Scott, Paul, 156 (n. 87)

Steinmetz, Karl Friedrich von, 5, 14, 158 (n. 13)

Stern, Fritz, xxviii

Strauss, Leo, xxviii, 150 (n. 35)

Tappen, Gerhard (general), 6, 141, 144

Tirpitz, Alfred von, xlii, xlvi, xlviii, 1, 34–55 passim, 56, 57, 89–90, 90, 102, 121, 124, 161 (n. 1)

Tisza, István, Count, 71, 80, 122

Valéry, Paul, 154 (n. 64)

Vendroux, Jacques, xxix

Vigny, Alfred de, 148 (n. 21)

Weber, Max, xxvi, xxxiv, 149 (n. 26)

Wilhelm (crown prince of German Empire and Prussia), 82, 109–11, 120, 151 (n. 40)

Wilhelm I, 157 (n. 2)

Wilhelm II, xxv, xliii, 2, 4, 33, 34, 38, 42–44, 46, 47, 54, 56–59, 62, 64, 68–69, 82–85, 90, 94, 104–11, 115, 120, 123, 126–27, 129, 135–36, 157 (n. 5), 164 (n. 2,) 169 (n. 26)

Wilhelm Frederick (crown prince of Prussia), 5, 8–13, 158 (n. 11), 165 (n. 22)

Wilson, Woodrow, 37, 40, 49, 54, 88, 94, 116, 117, 119, 128, 135, 169 (n. 26)

Wolf, Theodor, 49

Zieten, Hans Joachim von, 102, 165 (n. 17)

Zita of Bourbon-Parma (empress of Austria-Hungary), 119, 164 (n. 3)